Comparative and International Criminal Justice Systems: Policing, Judiciary and Corrections

Comparative and International Criminal Justice Systems: Policing, Judiciary and Corrections

edited by

Obi N. Ignatius Ebbe

Butterworth–Heinemann

Boston   Oxford   Melbourne   Singapore
Toronto   Munich   New Delhi   Tokyo

Library of Congress Cataloging-in-Publication Data

Comparative and international criminal justice systems : policing,
  judiciary and corrections / edited by Obi N. Ignatius Ebbe.
        p.   cm.
    Includes bibliographical references (p.   ) and index.
    ISBN 0-7506-9688-5 (alk. paper)
      1. Criminal justice, Administration of.   I. Ebbe, Obi N.
    Ignatius.
    HV7419.C65   1996
    364—dc20   95-39398
                                                       CIP

British Library Cataloguing-in-Publication Data
A catalogue record for this book is available from the British Library.

The publisher offers discounts on bulk orders of this book.
For information, please write:

Manager of Special Sales
Butterworth–Heinemann
313 Washington Street
Newton, MA 02158–1626

10 9 8 7 6 5 4 3 2 1

Printed in the United States of America

Dedicated to my daughter:

Nneka Ebbe

Contents

Contributors

Obi N. I. Ebbe, Ph.D.
Department of Criminal Justice
State University of New York,
    College at Brockport
Brockport, NY 14420

Mary Clifford, Ph.D.
Department of Political Science
    and Criminology
Appalachian State University
Boone, NC 28608

Ian K. McKenzie, Ph.D.
University of Portsmouth-Institute
    of Police and Criminological Studies
2 Kings Terrace
Southsea
Portsmouth, ENGLAND, UK

Michael Bullock
Gloucestershire Constabulary
6 Wessex Drive Cheltenham
Gloucestershire GL 5 25 AU
ENGLAND, UK

Zelma W. Henriques, Ph.D.
Law, Police Science & Criminal Justice
John Jay College of Criminal Justice
899 Tenth Avenue
New York, NY 10019

John A. Arthur, Ph.D.
Department of Sociology & Anthropology
University of Minnesota
Duluth, MN 55811

Bankole Thompson, Ph.D.
Criminal Justice Studies
Kent State University
Kent, OH 44242

Yingyi Situ, Ph.D.
Criminal Justice Program
Richard Stockton College of New Jersey
Pomona, NJ 08240

Weizheng Liu, Ph.D.
Criminal Justice Department
Monmouth College
West Long Branch, NJ 07764

Robert Davidson, Ph. D.
Northern Michigan University-Criminal
    Justice Department
Greis Hall
Marquette, MI 49855

Zheng Wang, Ph.D.
Texas Southern University
Administration of Justice and Public Affairs
3100 Cleburne Avenue
Houston, TX 77004

Elmer H. Johnson, Ph.D.
Distinguished Professor Emeritus
Southern Illinois University at Carbondale
Carbondale, IL 62901

Preface

Comparisons, an adage has it, are odious; but this is not the case in Comparative Criminal Justice Systems. Reading this book, you will find that in the criminal justice system of some nations, normative standards and punitive measures emanate from traditional religions. However, in the process of time, industrialized and non-industrialized nations in their march to civilization learned various aspects of criminal justice from each other. The following scholarly essays describe diverse justice systems that provoke tears of pain and smiles of joy.

Socio-cultural philosophies of a society set the tone for its reaction to the deviant. Whether you approve or disapprove of a justice system of a country, do not forget the cultural significance of the system to the people involved. The American social philosophy says, "Do your own thing and go your own way." The intolerance for social control in this individualistic philosophy has weakened the reintegration model of corrections in the American Criminal Justice System. One might weigh the American social philosophy against the Japanese, which says: "Find your own group and belong to it. You and your group will rise or sink together. Without belonging you will be lost in the wilderness. Apart from dependence there is no human happiness" (Ozaki, 1978:183 cited in Elmer H. Johnson, Chapter 12: "Guided Change in Japan: Correctional Association Prison Industrial Cooperative (CAPIC) and Prison Industry"). The humane Japanese approach to policing and correction reflects Japanese social philosophy. Certainly, such philosophy influences a society's attitudes toward offenders; this is evident in all of the eight countries and regions studied in this text.

Every topical study presented in this book is in its original form. The scholarly analyses and the comparative structure of the text will be particularly useful for courses in comparative and international criminal justice and criminology. Only in this book are criminal justice systems of all major continents (Africa, Asia, Europe, and the Americas) represented. Policing, judiciary, and corrections in industrialized and non-industrialized countries are presented side by side, giving faculty, students, and practitioners diverse perspectives from which to compare and contrast the characteristics and changes in criminal justice systems today.

This text can be useful to undergraduate and graduate students in criminal justice and criminology, enabling them to compare and contrast their own systems of justice with those of other countries. It will also help clarify why some countries copied the policing and correctional methods of others. It can be used as the major text in comparative criminal justice courses, or as a supplement to other texts.

There are four sections in this book. Section I deals with the nature of comparative and international criminal justice. Section II treats America and Europe, Section III Africa, and Section IV Asia. Countries studied include Brazil, China, Denmark, Japan, Nigeria, Sierra Leone, the United Kingdom, and the United States. There is a regional chapter on West Africa. The first section includes an essay on "The Purpose of Comparative and International Criminal Justice Systems," provided in order to answer an important question:

given differences in customs, traditions, standards, values, and criminal law across cultures, why should we study comparative criminal justice systems? It is hoped that this essay will provide a convincing answer, and also arm the student and the instructor with knowledge to comprehend the diverse systems presented in subsequent sections.

After justifying the need for the study of comparative and international criminal justice systems in Section I, American and European criminal justice are analyzed in Section II, thus forming grounds for comparing them to the criminal justice systems of African and Asian countries, described in Sections III and IV respectively. The criminal justice system of the United States is the first presented in this section and in this book, because most of the students and instructors using this book will be in the United States. Starting from the known and proceeding to the unknown will make comparisons and contrasts flow more smoothly.

Europe and America are presented in the same section because of the profound affinity between European laws and American laws; indeed, English law formed the basis of American law.

Section III, on Africa, is presented just after America and Europe, because the laws of the African countries studied are also based on English law, as the countries are former British colonies. The United States, Great Britain, and the African countries studied belong to the English common law tradition.

The last Section, on Asia, is presented after Africa because African and Asian countries have many common cultural beliefs and standards. Both the African and the Asian countries presented in this book use village councils and lay judges in their criminal justice systems; both also hold entire communities or villages responsible for the crimes committed within a community or by village members; and both have dual systems of criminal justice—formal and informal.

The chapters have been arranged in a logical order, with those dealing with a complete criminal justice system preceding those dealing with an agency of the system at issue.

Chapters dealing with policing, therefore, come before chapters on courts, and chapters on courts before chapters on correction.

I have developed discussion and revision questions at the end of each chapter to help both student and instructor in their readings. Also, at the end of the text, I have developed a glossary of terms used in various chapters, including foreign terms. Teachers have additional recourse to the accompanying instructor's manual and test bank, which I developed based on my thorough study of the chapters.

This is the first book of readings ever published in comparative and international criminal justice systems. My profound regards to the late Harold Smith, of the OICJ at the University of Illinois at Chicago, who encouraged me, in 1988 during the Academy of Criminal Justice Sciences (ACJS) annual meeting in San Francisco, California, to compose a book of this nature. Also, my thanks to all the international contributors who submitted articles (both those whose papers fit and those whose papers did not fit the focus of this book), for without their interest, getting a book of this nature together would have been a wild goose chase. I am also highly indebted to the following reviewers whose suggestions helped enormously: Robert McCormack, Trenton State College, Gregg Barak, Eastern Michigan University, and Liqun Cao, Eastern Michigan University.

I am also very much obliged to Laurel DeWolf and her associates at Butterworth-Heinemann Publishers for their interest in this topic. Finally, I say gracia to the Director of Document Preparation at the State University of New York at Brockport, Jeanne Saraceni and her team of Keyboard Specialists.

While every contributor is responsible for the facts and figures presented in each chapter, I am entirely responsible for any editorial inadequacies.

Obi N. I. Ebbe, Ph.D.
State University of New York,
College at Brockport
May 1995

SECTION I

The Nature of Comparative and International Criminal Justice

Obi N. I. Ebbe

To understand criminal justice one must study the criminal law and constitutional law of a country or state, the agencies of the justice system, and what happens to the accused from the time of his/her arrest to disposal of the case. Comparative criminal justice studies build on such knowledge, investigating similarities and dissimilarities in the structure and operation of the criminal justice agencies of various nations or states. The factors which make two different countries have similar or dissimilar methods of handling offenders are religious belief; custom and tradition; historical experiences such as civil war, international war, ethnic or racial conflicts; economic structure; and political organization.

Studies of international criminal justice, on the other hand, focus on one country's criminal law, criminal procedure, and penology when the accused is a foreigner, and when the criminal law and penology of the home country of the accused differs from the criminal law and penology of the country in which the crime was committed. For example, the United States and Singapore do not agree on the appropriate punishment for vandalism. When Michael Fay vandalized a car in Singapore with graffiti in 1994, Singapore prescribed ninety days in jail and 24 lashes, while the United States would have disposed of such an offense with probation, warning, or reparation.

International criminal justice also addresses the attempts of two countries to resolve a crime incident where citizens of one country victimize those of another—as when Singapore and the United States debated over Michael Fay. Such situations may be resolved by deporting the offender and allowing the trial to take place in the offender's country, or by getting the victim's country to reduce the severity of the crime's penalty.

International criminal justice also includes the administration of extradition agreements between nations, and criminal laws and court procedures in communities of nations who have agreed that legal violations by citizens will all be treated in a certain way.

This section descriptively analyzes systems of comparative and international criminal justice, highlighting important features of comparative criminal justice. It is intended to arm the student and the instructor with the ability to understand and consider various ways of handling offenders in different countries, and assumes the perspective of one who has basic knowledge of the American system of criminal justices.

1

The Purpose of Comparative and International Criminal Justice Systems

Obi N. I. Ebbe

Introduction

This chapter answers the question, "Why do we study comparative and international criminal justice systems?" Some scholars have wondered why some countries have very low crime rates, while others have very high rates. Some studies have shown that procedures and mechanisms for handling offenders may contribute to high crime and delinquency rates (Ebbe, 1988 and 1989). While some mechanisms for handling offenders in a given culture are very effective, others are criminogenic.

It is expedient that there be a text that provides students and scholars an opportunity to know how criminal justice systems vary across cultures, and the good reasons for engaging in comparative studies of criminal justice systems. Study of comparative and international criminal justice systems goes beyond controversy, sharpening our awareness of the ubiquitous operational dynamics in criminal law and of the variety of cultural concepts which brought different criminal justice systems into being.

In the process of studying the ways social order is achieved and maintained across nations, we learn how to modify our own society, bearing in mind that what works for one country may not work for another. Cultural values define behavior as good or bad and also determine the mech-

anisms for offender disposal. However, cultural values can change through international or inter-ethnic relations. For example, persons found guilty of crimes of "abomination" (such as incest or murder of a kinsman) in pre-colonial Southern Nigeria were dedicated to the gods as outcasts or untouchables.[1] This mechanism of offender disposal, however, became obsolete when English laws and cultural values overtook most of Nigerian society and condemned the outcast disposal mechanism. Presently the Holy Shrines to which the outcasts were dedicated are still in existence, but they are no longer used as offender disposal mechanisms.

Furthermore, the use of halfway houses in the United States to reintegrate an offender who has spent some years in prison and has one year or less before final release was borrowed from European correctional methods, particularly from Scandinavia (Sweden, Norway, Denmark) and the Netherlands. The interdependency of countries today enables them to learn from each other's way of life, and this includes their social control methods.

I postulate here seven motivating approaches to studies in comparative and international criminal justice systems: the varied political history of nations; the international character of the modern crime scene; the usefulness of "varied social control mechanisms and learning from others' experiences" (Fairchild, 1993); the philosophical and utilitarian ideals that propel the criminal justice goals of various nations; the provision of bases for research and comparisons; acquaintance with the nature and dynamics of the criminal law of nations; and the provision of a source of governmental policy modifications in criminal procedures, law enforcement, and corrections.

Varied Political History of Nations

Criminal justice systems reflect a nation's government (unitary, federal or confederate) and its politics (democratic, socialist, or communist), and therefore reflect a nation's political history. Consequently, criminal justice systems vary, both within continents and between continents.

Given the changes which have occurred in governments in Africa, Asia, the Middle East, and South America, the criminal justice systems of countries in those parts of the world clearly will reflect their political evolution. The dynamics in the various criminal justice systems of African and Asian countries may issue in developments useful to both industrialized and non-industrialized countries' systems of criminal justice. The historical backgrounds of various criminal justice systems enable us to pose and answer two important questions: Do countries with similar historical experiences have similar systems of justice? If not, why not?

In the historical dimension, we must note that political system, economic system, religious belief, tradition, and custom determine the criminal justice system of a country and its unique position in international criminal justice.

International Character of the Modern Crime Scene

Criminal victimization has taken on an international character. We have seen this especially in the areas of terrorism, money-laundering, and narcotics trafficking (Stewart, 1989; Bossard, 1990). The existence of the International Police (INTERPOL) for many decades now shows the international nature of some crimes since the "Age of Discovery" (A.D. 1400–1700), when people began to trespass into others' territories.

Because crime has become a world-wide social problem, the need for research in comparative and international criminal justice systems is more pressing today than ever before. There are crimes perpetrated today in both Western and non-Western countries which have foreign origins, including acts of terrorism, industrial burglary to steal manufacturing secrets, industrial sabotage, organized crime, counterfeit currency trafficking, narcotics drug trafficking, money-laundering, and computer fraud (Stewart, 1989; Grassi, 1989; David and Brierly, 1989; Kube, 1989; Bossard, 1990; Martin and Romano, 1992). Criminals have found international crime to be a very lucrative enterprise (Chang, 1976). The rewarding nature of international crimes has even attracted officials of numerous governments leading to wholesale official corruption such as the Iran Contra affair in the United States, the Noriega drug hysteria in Panama, the illegal money-laundering in Great Britain by Umaru Diko of Nigeria, and the looting of the Ugandan and Philippine treasuries by Idi Amin and Ferdinand Marcos, respectively. The fabulous amount of money involved in narcotic drug trafficking and illegal arms trafficking has caused them to develop into "multinational systemic crimes" (Martin and Romano, 1992): even if the United Nations imposes economic sanctions against an offending country, there are multinational syndicated criminals who are ready to provide that country with the needed goods. These multinational syndicated criminals have formed a transnational criminal cartel (Rodriquez, 1989) to provide necessary information and other needs to their members in various continents.

Unless comparative and international criminal justice systems are studied, effective control of national and international crimes will continue to be insignificant: presently, very few attempts are being made to study international crimes. Comparative and international criminal justice studies will help identify the various crimes in each country, determine those that are international in execution, and suggest solutions for their control through international cooperation. The high human toll taken by international crimes and transnational crimes thoroughly justifies comparative criminal justice studies, which can be applied to shore up legitimate governments, and fend off threats to the lives of innocent citizens.

Varied Social Control Mechanisms and Learning From Others' Experiences

Industrialized and non-industrialized nations around the world use various mechanisms of social control. While industrialized nations have very formalized social control systems, the non-industrialized nations often depend on informal control mechanisms.

Non-industrialized countries generally have lower crime rates than industrialized nations (Adler, 1983; Archer and Gartner, 1984). These lower crime rates may result from the non-industrialized countries' frequent use of informal criminal justice. If this is true, one should ask in what ways the industrialized nations can apply both formal and informal methods of criminal justice, as in civil cases in the State of New York and other parts of the United States. In New York, a state court is allowed to submit a civil case such as a divorce to a third party mediator, who meets with the parties in an informal setting. Most divorce cases in the State of New York are settled in this manner; and in most of the non-industrialized world, this is how most criminal cases are settled. The third party could be an individual (an elder), a chief, a council of chiefs, or a council of elders. This is typical of African and Asian societies in both property and personal crimes. Third party mediation in criminal matters in the State of New York certainly would eliminate the use of incarceration for some minor property and personal crimes. One of the advantages of using informal control mechanisms in the criminal justice systems of industrialized countries would be the reduction of prison overcrowding.

Philosophical and Utilitarian Ideals That Propel the Criminal Justice Goals of Various Nations

Whenever there is a unique system of social control, there must be some philosophical and functional thrust behind it. If such a unique social control mechanism is effective, such as the "Maxi Trials" or "Bunker Courts" in Italy (Grassi, 1989), other nations may learn from those philosophies and ideals.

I strongly agree with Pope Clement VI, that any punishment which makes the offender not commit a crime again is worth administering; and that a punishment which does not correct should not be given (Schafer, 1976).

Comparative and international criminal justice studies therefore should evaluate various cultures' offender disposal mechanisms for their effectiveness and for worthwhile philosophies which may lie behind their use.

Provision of Bases for Research and Comparisons

Studies of the criminal justice systems of other nations have the potential for stimulating similar studies in other countries. In the process of accumulation of criminal justice data, interest in international comparison is aroused. For example, a study of "the crime rate in Tokyo, Japan and the number of police officers per 100,000 population" can trigger similar studies in large cities of other industrialized countries. When "special tribunals" are used in Nigeria for the trials of persons accused of armed robbery, narcotics drug possession and trafficking, and counterfeit currency trafficking, a foreigner may ask how these tribunals work, how they differ from the regular criminal courts, and why the government uses special tribunals. Such questions are grounds for empirical research. Non-participant observation of a Maxi Trial or a special tribunal trial of an armed robber can be very beneficial to comparative criminal justice.

Acquaintance with the Nature and Dynamics of the Criminal Law of Nations

By studying the criminal justice systems of various countries we come to know the nature of their laws. Also we may come to know why certain forms of behavior are criminal in one country but not in another.

Criminal law, belonging as it does to the social sciences, is dynamic rather than static. As a nation grows and becomes more complex through urbanization and industrialization, new laws are created to meet the exigencies of that difficult period. Also under the heterogeneous social conditions of urban areas, values may change as time passes, rendering old laws obsolete. Comparative criminal justice therefore amounts, in many cases, to studying how criminal laws of nations change.

Part of the study of comparative criminal justice includes the study of criminal codes and penal codes of countries (Stewart, 1989; Bossard, 1990). Such studies emphasize the diverse features of those codes and the similarities and dissimilarities between Western and non-Western criminal codes: the distinctive features of codes in countries where common law, Roman law, or Islamic law prevail.

The development of nations' criminal law has always paralleled their political history and development; therefore, such developments vary from society to society (Gutteridge, 1949). Among the factors that influence the development of criminal law are war, coup d'etat, technological innovations, migration and immigration, urbanization, industrialization, religious conflict, national economic disaster (e.g., depression), colonization, international trade and transportation, inter-ethnic conflict, multi-ethnicity, and increase or decrease in political power. Among these factors we can trace the ones that played a part in the enactment of various laws in a country. Generally, countries with similar political experiences have come under the same groups of laws, as we see in the similar historical backgrounds of the common law countries, Roman law countries, and Islamic law countries.

Study of the criminal codes or penal codes of nations is very much essential, because different codes often mandate different penalties for the same offenses. The criminal code is very much determined by substantive criminal law—the law of crimes and penalties (Day, 1964). For instance, the Netherlands' permissive policies toward use of cannabis "contributed to the emergence of Amsterdam as an important transit place for narcotic drugs in the 1970s" (Bossard, 1990). Furthermore, one must keep in mind that a criminal code does not contain all of the criminal laws of a country. Students of comparative and international criminal justice must also study statutory law, applicable "judge-made laws" (*stare decisis*), and law reports and arguments of university legal scholars which are accepted by courts in some countries such as France and Nigeria as sources of law (Day, 1964). To understand criminal justice, one must comprehend and compare systems of criminal law in all their complexity. Transnational crimes influence legislation, and very often contemporary criminal court judges are confronted with situations neither covered by the criminal code nor by statutory law. In these cases, judges effectively create new laws through their own discretionary power, basing their decisions on the circumstances of the case, and on other exigencies of the situation.

Provision of a Source for Governmental Policy Modifications in Criminal Procedures, Law Enforcement, and Corrections

There is no aspect of the criminal justice system of any country more volatile than criminal procedure, law enforcement, and correctional mechanisms. Almost all of the industrialized and non-industrialized nations are uncomfortable with these three aspects of the criminal justice system. Global increase in crime rates, resulting from global increase in population and urbanization, has rendered inadequate some old methods of offender disposal. Consequently, many countries are initiating as experiments new methods of handling offenders.

The United States, for instance, is one of the non-European countries that has copied the practices of halfway houses, day fines, and prison structures from Sweden and the Netherlands. Governments are eager to copy what works in other countries for social control.

Of course, there are some pitfalls in comparative studies that should be guarded against, such as ethnocentrism in gathering and interpretation of foreign-based data, and the effects of governmental corruption on the reliability of official data from developing countries.

Also, comparing arrest, prosecution, conviction, and incarceration rates across cultures may yield little or no reliable evidence, because many developing countries such as India, Nigeria, Ghana, and Kenya have resorted to static law enforcement systems in which the police do not routinely patrol the neighborhoods watching for law breakers, but rely instead on victims and concerned citizens reporting crimes to their nearest po-

lice station. Not every victim and not every concerned citizen will report crime to the police; and, even if reporting were dependable, many developing countries have not adopted systematic record keeping of criminal justice data. In short, countries with a static law enforcement system may have lower arrest rates than countries routinely patrolling neighborhoods, but the comparison is not sound. Similarly, comparing prosecution, conviction, and incarceration rates is not wise, for perception of seriousness of criminal offenses varies from culture to culture (Ebbe, 1977).

Summary

Comparative and international criminal justice studies provide nations with an opportunity to know and learn from offender disposal mechanisms that are effective in other countries. By studying comparative and international criminal justice, we learn the varied political history of nations, the international character of the modern crime scene, the varied social control mechanisms of nations and the possibilities of learning from the experiences of others, and the philosophical and utilitarian ideals that propel the criminal justice goals of various countries; we are also able to provide bases for research and comparison of results, to get acquainted with the nature and dynamics in the criminal law of nations, and finally to provide a source for governmental policy modifications in all aspects of the criminal justice system.

Our study of the justice system of selected countries will start with the United States in the next section followed by treatments of the United Kingdom and a contrast between Denmark and Brazil.

Notes

1. The Outcast or Untouchable institution was a status created in pre-colonial Southern Nigeria, prevalent among the

Igbos, for disposing of offenders who committed an abomination such as incest, murder of a kinsman, or a son having sexual relations with one of his father's wives when his father was still alive. The individual was ostracized, dedicated to a god, and he became an untouchable. The Holy Shrine grove, the home of his god, was his abode. His only companions were a few other untouchables. He was proscribed from shaving his hair or taking a bath (Achebe, 1959). He was dehumanized.

Worst of all, the status was inherited. In 1955, however, the Eastern Region Government of Dr. Nnamdi Azikiwe abolished the untouchable institution by a law. But the abolition did not stop discriminative attitudes towards the descendants of untouchables; and throughout Igboland, the descendants of untouchables are still not allowed to take the ozo title. (The ozo title is a cultural initiation taken only by the sons of nobles or aborigines of a town. Women do not take the title. Only when a man takes the title does his wife become an adjunct—a lolo-ozo—to the title.)

Now, why should anybody suffer the consequences of a crime committed by another, especially when the person who committed the crime died centuries ago? Yet the Nigerian government is doing nothing to remedy the situation, mainly because the descendants of untouchables do not want to go through the trouble of identifying themselves in order to solve the problems imposed on them by society.

Discussion and Revision Questions

1. What factors determine the nature of the criminal justice system of a country?

2. What are the seven motivating approaches to the study of comparative and international criminal justice systems?

3. Give at least eight examples of international crimes.

4. What is a "multinational systemic crime?" Give two examples of such crimes.

5. What are the merits and demerits of the use of a third party mediation or arbitration in a criminal case?

6. What did Pope Clement VI recommend regarding punishment?

7. Name at least three different classes of law in the Western world.

8. What factors lead to the development of criminal law?

9. What is substantive criminal law?

10. Can criminal court judges create crimes? If yes, how?

11. What are some of the pitfalls in comparative criminal justice studies?

12. What is a static law enforcement system?

SECTION II

America and Europe

Obi N. I. Ebbe

Introduction

The criminal justice system of the United States has observable affinities with the criminal justice systems of European countries. American criminal law, for instance, is rooted in English law, and its principle of *stare decisis* emanates from the English common law tradition. Additionally, the United States is a member of the North Atlantic Treaty Organization (NATO) which provides for extradition among member nations. Therefore, it is expedient to analyze and discuss the American system of criminal justice in company with European countries' justice systems.

We begin in Chapter 2 with the criminal justice system of the United States, presented here as a standpoint from which to evaluate other justice systems presented in subsequent chapters.

Chapter 3 (Separate But Equal: Non-Discriminatory Policy and Practice in British and American Policing) analyzes the organization of the British police, the problem of policing in the United Kingdom and the United States, and problems with implementing equal opportunity legislation in law enforcement agencies in the United Kingdom and the United States.

McKenzie concludes that equal opportunity (EO) legislation is more effective in the United States than in Britain because the written nature of the U.S. Constitution, and its interpretation by the U.S. Supreme Court gives leverage to the equal opportunity debate not available in the unwritten constitution of the United Kingdom.

In Chapter 4, Michael Bullock compares community policing in the United Kingdom with community policing in the United States, and suggests consultations with members of the community and maintaining a high quality of service will reduce community disorder and mistrust of the police.

Chapter 5, the last in this section, is an interesting contrast of penology and corrections in Denmark and Brazil. Here we find demonstrated our earlier observation that what works for one country may not work for another. The Danes are very humane in their treatment of offenders, while the Brazilians are ruthless; this difference will be shown to have emerged from the history of the two nations.

Criminal justice in selected African countries whose legal systems also originate in English law will be presented in Section III.

2

Criminal Justice System in the United States[1]: General Overview

Mary Clifford

Brief History

The contemporary American system of criminal justice is a result of centuries of evolution and social change. American colonists settling in the new world brought the criminal procedures, courts, and crime definitions of the English common law tradition along with them (Henderson, 1985). This tradition originally did not define crimes or their remedies as public matters, but rather considered them private matters between the individual who was wronged and the wrongdoer (Siegel, 1992). Later, the concept of public crime developed, but it was confined to acts committed against the king, with individuals and their families left to resolve their own disputes. Church representatives handled those acts considered to be sinful, and local courts dealt with most secular violations. Because royal administrators were not constantly present in each community, a system developed for holding court sessions in each county several times a year. The royal administrator, or judge, used local customs and rules of conduct as a guide for determining an appropriate sentence for an offender (Siegel, 1992). The structure and content of this English system was modified to meet different community needs and geographic circumstances in the new world (Chapin, 1983).

Early in the development of the American system of justice, the framers of the United States Constitution (1787) gave Congress considerable latitude to "establish inferior courts, to define crimes and stipulate punishments, and to provide for modes of process and procedures to be used in the courts" (Henderson, 1985). According to the Constitution, Congress must "set up all tribunals (federal courts) inferior (lower in rank) to the Supreme Court . . ." and legislate "to decide which acts that take place at sea are piracies (thefts) or felonies (serious crimes such as murder), to make laws to punish these crimes, and crimes against international law . . ." (Cullop, 1984:4). Response to the original draft of the Constitution resulted in the passage of several amendments known as the Bill of Rights, adopted in 1791. The Bill of Rights includes ten amendments identifying personal liberties (individual rights) not listed in the Constitution, but which people had come to believe were their rights as citizens of the United States (Cullop, 1984).

Several provisions within the Bill of Rights are of particular importance in the United States system of justice. The Fourth Amendment prohibits unreasonable search and seizures. The Fifth Amendment requires an indictment to be held on a capital offense; no double jeopardy (i.e., only one trial per offense); no compulsion to be a witness against one's self; and no deprivation of life, liberty or property without due process. The Sixth Amendment assures that one accused of a crime will have a speedy trial, the right to confront adverse witnesses, and the assistance of counsel. The Seventh Amendment guarantees the right to a trial by jury. The Eighth Amendment prohibits both excessive bail and cruel and unusual punishment.

The Constitutional provisions, the adoption of the Bill of Rights, and the Crimes Act of 1790 formed the initial structure of the federal criminal justice system (Henderson, 1985). The Crimes Act of 1790 defined 17 crimes ranging from obstruction of process to treason. Death by hanging was the penalty for six crimes: treason, murder, piracy, accessory to piracy, forgery, and rescue of a person found guilty of any capital crime. Henderson (1985) argues that the crimes listed in the Act of 1790 were consistent with the constitutional authority of Congress, and reviews several additions which followed the initial provisions, including the Judiciary Act, the Neutrality Act, Sedition Act, and the Logan Act.

Legal System

The American legal system, reminiscent of the legal system the Puritans left behind in England, mandated courts similar to English courts (Stucky, 1986), which employed the "trial by adversary" process (Weston and Wells, 1987). In this process, legal counsel represents both parties involved in a case. It is believed that such partisan advocacy develops the best possible arguments for the guilt or innocence of the parties involved.

Also significant in the American legal system is the concept of "due process." Due process assures the accused of basic individual rights and freedoms in the United States. The tenets of due process are outlined in the Fifth Amendment and more thoroughly described in the Fourteenth Amendment (Kolasa and Meyer, 1987). Due process of law assures the accused that

he/she will receive a fair hearing, and that the provisions in the Constitution and Amendments four through eight will be followed. At all levels of justice proceedings, however, implementation of due process can be difficult. Social, economic, and political factors often influence outcomes of legal actions in this and other areas of the justice system (Kolasa and Meyer, 1987).

American law has developed along two lines: 1) a civil law system, and 2) a common law system. The operation of the judicial process is the primary difference between the two systems (Kolasa and Meyer, 1987). Adjudication under civil law is made by the judge, who follows an existing or an established set of laws. Common law, on the other hand, develops through the decisions of judges applying prior court decisions to the current case (Kolasa and Meyer, 1987).

Since the passage of the Constitution, Congress has made several changes to the structure and organization of various courts. The number of Supreme Court Justices has been changed, as have the number and forms of the lower courts (Vito and Holmes, 1994). Most states have created their own systems of specialized lower courts. Usually these courts hear civil cases, divorces, cases of property, and wills. Criminal courts address felonies and misdemeanors.

System of Government

The three branches of government outlined in the United States Constitution (the legislative, executive, and judicial powers) divide governing power into three segments capable of functioning together effectively (Weston and Wells, 1987). Article I of the Constitution establishes the legislative powers (Cullop, 1984), Article II establishes the executive powers, and Article III establishes the judicial branch of government. This structure provided a system of checks and balances, with each branch of government being allowed to operate independently but in relation to the other branches. While federal laws usually take precedence over state laws, states and local communities establish their own priorities in their own legislation, design the structure of their court system, and may identify specific acts as priorities at local community levels.

Crime

Classification of Crime

In the United States system of justice, before a crime is said to have been committed, there must be 1) a law that defines the crime, 2) an act or an omission by the accused, called *actus reus*, 3) a guilty state of mind, also called intent (*mens rea*), 4) a joining of the act and the intent to act, 5) harm that affects society or a person, 6) a causal relationship between the act or omission and the harm caused, and 7) a punishment as stated in the criminal code (Cole, 1981). English law classified crimes into three categories: treason, felonies, and misdemeanors, with emphasis on felonies and misdemeanors (Lindquist, 1988). Felonies were "common-law" crimes; that is, crimes that the people defined through traditional ways of living rather than through statute. Reid (1992) argues that there were very few common-law felonies: murder, manslaughter, sodomy, larceny, robbery, arson, and burglary. The misdemeanor classification developed much later than that of felony, emerging in the sixteenth century. Prior to that time individuals were fined, but their offenses were not considered crimes (Walsh, 1932). The misdemeanor category emerged from the notion of trespass (Lindquist, 1988), and was regarded primarily as a means of raising money for the Crown.

Felonies have been distinguished from misdemeanors using two traditional terms, *mala in se* (acts that are inherently wrong, i.e., felonies) and *mala prohibita* (acts that are wrong because they are prohibited by law, i.e., misdemeanors); this description, however, has been called into question by several scholars. Inciardi (1984) argues that "the felony-misdemeanor classification goes beyond the *mala in se–mala prohibita* distinction since a number of felonies fail to reflect moral turpitude." All such dispute is actually irrelevant in the United States, where all crimes are defined arbitrarily and conventionally by political apparatus (Michael and Adler, 1971).

Because state laws define felony and misdemeanor crimes, both vary from state to state (Lindquist, 1988). As a consequence, it is important to look at the statute in each state, not only to determine which acts are classified as misdemeanors or felonies, but also to understand how local law defines the terms. Length of sentence and where the sentence is served generally distinguish misdemeanors from felonious offenses. Generally, misdemeanors are defined as offenses punishable by no more than a year in a local jail, and/or a fine.

Sheley (1995) identifies four factors which can be used successfully to avoid being classified a criminal in the legal system: self-defense, action under duress, insanity, and age. In self-defense, the amount of force used must not exceed the amount of threatened harm. Furthermore, if one could have avoided the danger by flight, the defense cannot be used. Self-defense can be used only when no other avenue existed to protect one's self from deadly and imminent bodily harm. Another way to avoid criminal classification is the insanity defense. In the U.S. court system, "insanity" is a legal, not a medical, concept. One who uses the insanity defense argues that he/she could not avoid committing the crime in question because of a mental defect. Definitions of insanity vary by court systems. About a third of states use a formula based on the *M'Naghten Rule*, a definition of insanity established in England in 1843, for determining whether the accused may use the insanity defense at trial.

The duress defense against criminal classification is available when the defendant is forced by means of a deadly force to break the law or to help another break the law. For example, a criminal gang might enter a bank manager's house at night and enjoin him or her under gunpoint to go to the bank and open the bank vault. If the bank manager were to obey and later was accused as an accomplice, he or she could claim to have acted under duress.

The final defense against criminal classification is age of criminal responsibility. Juveniles who commit specific acts are treated differently from adults in the United States system of justice. "The term 'juvenile delinquency' or a 'delinquent act' is a non-criminal classification for acts done by juveniles (usually under age 17 or 18 depending on the state) that would otherwise be a violation of federal or state criminal law, or local ordinances. In about half the states, it should be noted, this terminology of delinquency extends to non-criminal offenses (status offenses) to include: unruly children, truancy, incorrigibles, and youngsters beyond the control of parents" (Weston and Wells, 1987).

Classification of Illegal Possession of Narcotic Drugs

The classification of illegal possession of narcotic drugs changed from misdemeanor to felony during the twentieth century. (Jones, Shainberg, and Byer, 1979). Siegel (1992) reviews several of the laws introduced to regulate drug use in the United States. The Pure Food and Drug Act (1906) required manufacturers to list the amounts of habit forming drugs on the labels of products but did not restrict their use. In 1914, the Harrison Narcotics Act restricted the importation, manufacture, sale, and dispensing of narcotics. "Narcotics" were defined as any drug that produces sleep and relieves pain, such as heroin, morphine, and opium. In 1922 the

act was revised to allow the importation of opium and coca leaves (cocaine) for qualified medical practitioners. The Marijuana Tax Act of 1937 required registration and tax payment from all persons who imported, sold or manufactured marijuana. Because marijuana was classified as a narcotic, people who registered were subject to criminal penalty.

Many drug statutes include specific penalties for violating federal drug laws. The Boggs Act of 1951 provided mandatory sentences for violations of federal drug laws. The Durham-Humphrey Act of 1951 made it illegal to dispense barbiturates and amphetamines without a prescription. The Narcotics Control Act of 1956 increased penalties for drug offenders.

Drugs of Abuse (DEA, 1985), a Drug Enforcement Administration publication, references the Comprehensive Drug Abuse Prevention and Control Act of 1970, which regulates drugs at the federal level and classifies drugs into five schedules according to their abuse potential. Since 1970, a variety of federal laws have attempted to limit the manufacture and sale of new drugs. The Controlled Substances Act of 1984, the Anti–Drug Abuse Act of 1986, and the Anti–Drug Abuse Act of 1988, identify types of illegal drugs and penalties for violations of drug laws, and set up programs for addressing the drug problem. For the most part state laws mirror federal statutes (Siegel, 1992).

The classification of drugs as legal or illegal is at present a rather tricky business. Alcohol, tobacco and caffeine are currently legal drugs in the United States. These substances, however, have not always been legal (Brecher et al., 1972). At present, the legal status of marijuana varies by state. Between 1973 and 1978 eleven states decriminalized marijuana. One of these states, Alaska, has recriminalized marijuana, but the decision is under appeal and the law is not yet enforced (Sheley, 1995).

Crime Statistics

Two primary sources exist for the collection of statistics on crime in the United States: the Uniform Crime Reports (UCR) of the Federal Bureau of Investigation (FBI) and the National Crime Victimization Survey (NCVS) of the Bureau of Justice Statistics (BJS). More specific attention will be given to the NCVS below, in the section on victims. Because they differ in methodology and crime coverage, these two sources of data are not necessarily comparable; but they can be used as complementary sources which together expand our understanding of the crime problem. The UCR program, it should be noted, is expanding to become a more comprehensive and detailed reporting system called the National Incident-Based Reporting System (NIBRS) which will provide detailed information about each criminal incident and expanded category list of offenses (FBI, 1994:385).

Ever since 1929, the UCR has collected and reported information on all crimes reported to law enforcement agencies, whether or not there is further action on the case (Reid, 1994). The data are compiled from monthly law enforcement reports submitted directly to the FBI, and they reflect active law enforcement agencies from approximately 95% of the total U.S. population. Covered crimes include homicide, forcible rape, robbery, aggravated assault, burglary, larceny-theft, motor vehicle theft, and arson—eight crimes known as Index Crimes or Part I Crimes. A crime is classified as an Index Crime based on a combination of three factors: high degree of seriousness of the offense; high degree of reportability of the offense; and high degree of occurrence of the offense. Serious offenses such as white collar crime, organized crime, and narcotics drug smuggling lack one or more of the three factors, and therefore are not included.

Various factors affect the volumes and types of crime from place to place, and from year to year. Factors identified in the Uniform Crime Reports include population density; urbanization; variations in population (particularly youth); stability of population; available modes of transportation; economic conditions; cultural factors; educational, recreational, and religious characteristics; family conditions; climate; strength of law enforcement; administrative and investigative emphasis of law enforcement; policies of other components of the criminal justice system; citizens' attitudes toward crime; and crime reporting practices of the citizenry (FBI, 1994).

All of these factors must be taken into consideration as one reviews and analyzes the data reflected in the UCR. Here we will treat the UCR definitions and statistics for four crimes: murder, serious property offenses, forcible rape, and drug offenses.

For murder and non-negligent manslaughter, the definition is "the willful (non-negligent) killing of one human being by another" (FBI, 1994). The classification of this offense, and all other crimes in the UCR, is based solely on police investigation, not on the determination of a court, medical examiner, coroner, jury, or any other judicial body. The total number of murders in the United States during 1993 was estimated at 24,526, a 14% rise from murder counts in 1989. During the 10 years since 1984, the count rose by 31% (FBI, 1993:14).

The crime of robbery is a serious property offense defined by the UCR as "the taking or attempting to take anything of value from the care, custody, or control of a person or persons by force or threat of force of violence and/or by putting the victim in fear." The UCR estimated the volume of robberies in 1993 at 659,757 offenses. The national robbery rate in 1993 was 256 per 100,000 people, 3% lower than in 1992. (Again, this information reflects the number of reports to the police.)

Forcible rape is defined as "carnal knowledge of a female forcibly and against her will. Assaults or attempts to commit rape by force or threat of force are also included; however, statutory rape (without force) and other sex offenses are excluded." In 1993 an estimated 104,806 forcible rapes were reported to law enforcement agencies in the United States. This figure was down 4% from the 1992 volume, and showed the first decline in forcible rape since 1987.

Drug abuse violations are state and local offenses relating to "the unlawful possession, sale, use, growing, and manufacturing of narcotic drugs" (FBI, 1994). They can include any of the following categories of drugs: opium or cocaine and their derivatives (morphine, heroin, codeine), marijuana, synthetic narcotics, manufactured narcotics that can cause true addiction (demerol, methadone), and dangerous non-narcotic drugs (barbiturates, benzedrine). In 1993, drug abuse violation arrests were up 4% from the 1992 level; they were 14% lower than in 1989, but 56% higher than in 1984. Of total drug arrests in 1993, 29.7% were for sale/manufacture, and 70.3% were for possession (FBI, 1994:216).

In addition to drug abuse violations, drug abuse has often been associated with involvement in other serious crimes. The *Sourcebook* (BJS, 1991:457) reports that 67% of arrested men and 66% of arrested women tested positive for some type of drug abuse.

Crime Regions

For the purposes of FBI statistics, the United States is divided into regions, divisions, and states. Further breakdowns are based on population figures, and proximity to metropolitan areas—i.e., community type (FBI, 1994:382). There are four regions: Northeastern States, Midwestern States, Southern States, and Western States. These four state-based regions are further divided into nine divisions within each region.

The UCR data are presented in aggregations representing three types of communities: 1) Metropolitan Statistical Areas (MSAs), 2) Cities outside MSAs, and 3) Rural counties outside MSAs. Each MSA

includes a central city of at least 50,000, suburban cities, and suburban counties. Non–MSA areas include cities outside metropolitan areas, and rural communities. As a general rule, sheriffs, county police, and state police report crimes committed within the limits of the counties, excluding the city limits, while the local police report crimes committed within the city limits.

Victims

The second primary resource for reviewing crime statistics in the United States is the National Crime Victimization Survey (NCVS). Beginning in 1973, the NCVS has collected information from the victim's point of view on the frequency and nature of the crimes of rape, personal robbery, aggravated and simple assault, household burglary, personal and household theft, and motor vehicle theft. It does not measure murder, kidnapping, and "victimless" crimes (public drunkenness, prostitution, drug abuse) (BJS, 1994e). Because the NCVS gathers data directly from crime victims, it can provide information on both reported and unreported crimes. When an act of victimization is reported, the most severe act is classified; for example, if a victim is raped and robbed, the rape is recorded. The NCVS documents crime data according to four regions defined by the Census Bureau: Midwest, Northeast, South, and West.

According to the Department of Justice statistics, 20% of all of the crimes committed in 1992 were violent crimes (BJS, 1994e). These include rape, robbery, and assault, and are considered the most serious offenses by the NCVS. Personal/household larceny made up 60% of offenses in 1992. Household burglary and motor vehicle theft accounted for the last 20% of victimizations. The level of violent crime did not differ from 1981, which was a peak year for violent offenses. This breaks down into 6.6 million violent victimizations, 12.2

million personal thefts, and 14.8 million American households victimized (BJS, 1994e:10).

Blacks are more likely to be victims of violent crime than whites. People under the age of 25 have a higher victimization rate than older persons. Households with lower incomes are more likely to be violent crime victims than households with higher incomes. The statistically overrepresented victims of street crimes are male, young, poor and black (Sheley, 1995:122).

Historically, the victim of a criminal act was not represented in the adversarial process. Victims would sign the complaint, which set the justice process in motion, and were brought into courtrooms to serve as "evidence" and to testify for the prosecution (Sheley, 1995:161). In 1982, Congress enacted standards for the fair treatment of victims and witnesses, and throughout the 1980s states granted to victims greater opportunities to participate in decision-making within the criminal justice process. But there is no penalty against a state that fails to allow victim participation in decision-making in the criminal justice process (BJS, 1991).

The National Victim Center of the victim's rights movement has outlined a model amendment for state constitutions that reads, "The victim of crime or his or her representative shall have the right to be informed of, to be present at, and to be heard at all criminal justice proceedings at which the defendant has such rights, subject to the same rules which govern defendants rights." See Austern (1987:23–27) for a listing of Victim/Witness assistance units by state.

Police

Administration

The American system of policing was modeled after the London Metropolitan Police, formed in 1829 by Sir Robert Peel (Reid, 1994:505). According to the FBI, the public

law enforcement community services a population of over 224 million and employs 553,773 officers and 212,353 civilians (FBI, 1994:288). Unlike such countries as Kenya, Nigeria, and China, the system of policing in the United States is decentralized, having separate systems at the local, state, and federal levels of government. An additional police agency which is becoming more popular, but which does not have full police power, is called the private or special-purpose police (Langworthy and Travis, 1994:118).

Police agencies are organized bureaucratically (Reiss, 1992:69). Municipal police organizations are structured in several different ways, but the accepted model in the United States is the bureaucratic pyramid, with the chief of police at the top, management (reflecting specializations within the department) in the middle, and patrol officers at the bottom (Langworthy and Travis, 1994:143). Historically, police organization was borrowed from the military model as outlined initially by Peel in England (Skolnick and Fyfe, 1993:117). Using the military model helped to combat traditional British mistrust of official authority, and made it easier to convince the skeptical British public that a new sort of official was needed to address social disorder and crime.

Rural, county, and municipal police agencies are found at the municipal or local level (Reid, 1994). Local police agencies are relatively small organizations, and little is known about municipal operations (Langworthy and Travis, 1994). State and federal police agencies emerged as a response to a perceived lack of effectiveness in local police, with state-based policing developing as a hybrid between the federal and local experiences. All states except Hawaii have a statewide police or highway patrol. Policing at the state level is divided into state police and state patrol officers, with patrol officers responsible for traffic control, and state police enforcing certain regulations (Reid, 1994). Today, American police are predominantly associated with local government (Sheley, 1995). Most crimes committed in the United States are state crimes, but the FBI may, when requested, assist state and local enforcement agencies in solving a state crime, in addition to attending to federal crimes such as bank robbery, explosive trafficking, bombing of public buildings, and counterfeiting currency.

At least sixty-three distinct federal agencies exercise police powers or serve police functions (Langworthy and Travis, 1994:99). Four commonly known agencies are the Federal Bureau of Investigation; the U.S. Marshals; Alcohol, Tobacco and Firearms Bureau (ATF); and the Drug Enforcement Administration. Their primary functions as federal police agencies are specific and clearly defined, with detection and investigation being their primary responsibilities.

Resources

According to a 1993 Bureau of Justice Statistics study of State and Local Law Enforcement units, state and local governments funded 17,358 police and sheriff's departments, including 12,502 general purpose local police departments, 3,086 sheriff's departments, 49 primary state police departments, and 1,721 special police agencies. These agencies employed approximately 604,000 full time sworn officers with general arrest powers and 237,000 non-sworn civilian personnel (1993). The U.S. Department of Justice (BJS, 1991) reports that $60,980,334,000 was spent at all levels of government in the criminal justice system. At the federal level, the expenditures were $7,794,136,000. At the state levels of government, the total expenditures were $19,279,179,000. Local expenditures were $33,907,019,000, including municipal expenditures of $19,533,908,000 and county expenditures of $14,373,111,000.

For police, these expenditures included $27,955,660,000 for all levels of government.

This breaks down to $3,555,248,000 at the federal level for police, $4,513,297,000 at the state level, and for rural, county, and municipal police the expenditures for police protection are $10,332,148,000, $4,015,310,000, and $5,539,657,000 respectively (BJS, 1991:2).

Police jurisdictions differ across the country. In addition to the 49 primary State police departments, the 1993 study included 12,502 general purpose local police departments. County governments operated 59 of these local departments and municipalities. The study reflected 3,086 sheriff's departments operated by counties and independent cities, and 1,721 special police agencies. Included in the latter category were 751 county constable offices in Texas and 970 state and local agencies with special jurisdictions or specific enforcement responsibilities.

Sheley (1995) argues that policing has been dominated by white males who have modest amounts of formal education and training. In addition, certain ethnic and racial groups have not been well represented in policing, particularly African-Americans, Asians, and Hispanics. Women are clearly underrepresented in the American police forces. According to the 1993 UCR information, males made up 91% of all sworn employees both nationally and in cities, 93% of those in rural counties, and 88% of those in suburban counties.

Technology

Police have implemented innovative technology at various levels. Computer aided dispatch, computerized record keeping procedures and radio communication have become standard features in modern police departments; and, in some jurisdictions, video technology and computer terminals are used in patrol cars. Computers now allow information to be exchanged between dispatch and the police officer on patrol without tipping off the criminal (Newcombe, 1993). Technologies such as fingerprinting,

DNA testing, and voice identification technologies are being used and perfected (Jasanoff, 1989) to aid in investigations (Sessions, 1992) and convictions.

Although police and other criminal justice officials have found innovative technologies useful throughout the adjudication process, such innovations have also provoked significant public attention and intense debate. In New Hampshire, police have been criticized for using high-tech thermal imaging devices to find marijuana growing operations (West, 1992). Stephens (1990) argues that police surveillance (audio and video) technology devalues individual rights.

The capture on video of the brutal arrest of Rodney King in Los Angeles in 1991 resulted in a highly public denunciation of the police and the arrest process (Skolnick and Fyfe, 1993). This negative publicity has prompted police to employ "less than lethal force" (Edwards, 1995), subduing offenders with technologies such as foams and pepper sprays.

In order to better understand how technologies can be used by the police in enforcing the law, the National Institute of Justice is developing the National Law Enforcement Technology Center (NLETC) and regional law enforcement technology centers (NIJ, 1995). Some technologies explored at the Technology Center are geared toward insuring police officer protection; for example, the development and use of soft body armor, and videotaped interrogations (Geller, 1992). Standards for use and manufacture of soft body armor, vehicle tracking, security systems, pistols, and other innovative technologies continue to be examined at the Technology Center (NIJ, 1995).

Training and Qualifications

Few police departments require a college education to enter the force or to be advanced within the ranks, although college education can be important in promotion

decisions (Carter, Sapp, and Stephens, 1989). Since 1967, most states have mandated minimum entry-level training standards, and many departments require much higher levels (Ostrom, Parks, and Whitaker, 1978). This trend toward professionalism in policing has resulted in departments requiring more formal training and education from their personnel. Reid (1994) cites the President's Commission on Law Enforcement and Administration of Justice report (1967) which identified "intelligence, education, tact, sound judgment, physical courage, emotional stability, impartiality, and honesty" as important qualities in a police officer; she also finds psychological factors such as ability to handle racial tension an important factor. Because earlier research findings reported police to be emotionally maladjusted, extremely cynical and authoritarian, and impulsive risk takers, she argues that temperament and personality should be important in qualifying to be a police officer (Reid, 1994:514).

Discretion

Police are expected to detect crime, to investigate how a particular criminal act happened, and then to make arrests when necessary. But because circumstances can vary in the arrest process, no aspect of police function is entirely predictable. Ultimately, individual officers must decide whether to arrest or to release a suspect. Studies of officer training and officer action are focusing increasingly on these discretionary powers.

Sworn police officers have the authority to make an arrest. In most cases the arresting officer will have a warrant. Officers are required to give an individual being arrested "adequate notice," which includes outlining the intention to arrest, the cause of the arrest, and the authority to make the arrest (Weston and Wells, 1987:25). A law enforcement officer also has the right to stop and frisk a suspect "when she/he observes unusual conduct which leads the officer to reasonably conclude, in the light of . . . experience, that a criminal activity may be in progress, and that the person involved may be armed and presently dangerous; when, in the course of investigating this behavior, she/he is identified as a police officer and makes reasonable inquiries; and when nothing in the initial stages of the encounter serves to dispel reasonable fear for the officer's or others' safety" (Kolasa and Meyer, 1987).

Although police are trained to use no more force than necessary, encounters with alleged law violators can result in the most extreme use of force—deadly force. The use of deadly force is governed by the criminal laws of individual states, which authorize officers to resort to this level of coercion in the imminent defense of their own lives or the lives of others (Skolnick and Fyfe, 1993). Because language permitting the use of deadly force can be vague in criminal law, well-run police departments generally supplement these laws with administrative guidelines and policies.

Brown v. Mississippi was a landmark case concerning the actions of police in securing a confession from an accused offender (Skolnick and Fyfe, 1993). In *Brown v. Mississippi* (1936), the issue was whether convictions which rest solely upon confessions shown to have been extorted by officers of the State by brutality and violence are consistent with due process of law required by the Fourth Amendment of the Constitution of the United States. The Federal Court of Appeals reversed the Mississippi Court conviction (Perkins and Boyce, 1984). Many court cases have since considered what actions are appropriate or acceptable in police interrogations. In many cases, misrepresentation of information by the police in an interrogation has been considered acceptable.

Manning (1989) identifies several issues associated with police decision-making: uncertainty, mutual dependence, autonomy, and authority. Police are confronted with many issues which are not openly ex-

pressed. Further, they are constantly relying on other officers to help them fend off physical, emotional and career threats. Police officers treasure their ability to exercise judgment independently, and consider this privilege essential.

Although scholars have given little attention to how police officers exercise their discretion, several note that departments give substantial leeway when they determine whether certain police actions are required or unnecessary. This would imply that the issue of police discretion and accountability needs increased attention.

Accountability

Reiss (1992) identifies a number of institutions intended to influence police practice, and to limit the authority of the departmental hierarchy. These external bodies to which police are accountable include: mayors, city managers, civil service boards, civilian review boards, police unions, prosecutors, the judiciary, labor relations boards, and a variety of other federal and state regulatory agencies. Lobbyists or other community groups can also affect how police are held accountable for their actions on the job.

Because of concern about the rights of individuals arrested by police, the Supreme court ruled in *Miranda v. Arizona* (1966) that procedural safeguards should be in effect to inform an accused person of his/her right of silence. The Miranda warning states that the individual has the right to remain silent, and that any statement made can be used as evidence against him or her in a court of law. The accused is also informed of his or her right to an attorney, either retained by the accused or appointed by the court (Reid, 1994:473). This Supreme Court decision has proven to be extremely controversial and has resulted in extensive litigation.

Reid (1994) identified several methods to control police discretion. The exclusionary rule says that if police violate the rights of individuals accused of committing a crime by illegally seizing evidence, the evidence so obtained cannot be used at trial. This rule is not found in the systems of criminal justice of Nigeria, Sierra Leone, China, or Japan; particularly in Japan, society's rights take precedence over individual rights. Police officer misconduct can also be controlled by holding individuals accountable for their actions (traditionally, the police department has been held accountable for a police officer's action). Civil suits brought by individuals who argue that they have been harmed by a police officer's action are becoming more common, and have succeeded. In contrast, bringing a court action against a police officer in African and Asian countries is rare, and the few actions attempted have failed.

Prosecutorial and Judicial Process

Rights of the Accused

According to Nagel (1972), the specific rights of someone who has been accused of committing a crime can be divided into four segments: rights prior to the first court appearance, rights from first court appearance to trial, rights during the trial stage, and post-trial rights of the defendant. Prior to the first court appearance, a suspect can be arrested or searched only if there is a probable cause, and the suspect is protected against self-incrimination or giving involuntary confessions. Once the accused has made his or her first court appearance, he or she is assured release pending a speedy trial, the right to hire or be provided with counsel, and a formal notice of the charges against him or her. Once at trial, the defendant is guaranteed an impartial jury, and the right to cross-examine and subpoena witnesses. After the trial, the defendant can neither be subjected to excessive fines or punishment, nor be denied the right to appeal, and he or she can not be placed in double jeopardy—i.e., tried again for the same allegations.

Criminal Procedures

The standard processing of an accused offender through the system includes the officer making an investigation prior to an arrest, which includes (among other things) interviewing witnesses and checking for evidence. The arrest is followed by the "booking" of the accused, which includes logging the name of the suspect and the locations, time and purpose of the arrest. The accused may then have an initial appearance and preliminary hearing where all of the evidence against him or her is considered. The suspect will then be presented for "information" or before a grand jury to determine whether there is enough evidence to warrant a hearing. At the arraignment, the defendant is formally presented with the charges, and he/she may enter a plea. It is at this time that plea bargaining might be arranged. If there is no agreement, the defendant then appears at trial. If found guilty, he or she will be sentenced (Reid, 1994).

Being arrested and charged with a crime does not make it certain that one will appear in court. Because of the large number of initiated cases, certain informal measures have been taken which are not included in the formal court process. One of these efforts to reduce court overload is plea bargaining, where a prosecutor accepts a plea of guilty from the accused in exchange for a lesser sentence. Providing this "deal" to the accused, both the prosecution and the defense are saved the time and expense of a formal court proceeding (Kolasa and Meyer, 1987). In minor criminal cases, plea bargaining is the preferred outcome. In more serious cases, negotiations take much longer: the more serious the case, the fewer concessions will be offered by the prosecution; and the weaker the case, the more concessions will be offered (Sheley, 1995).

Another common practice to reduce the burden of the courts is to "funnel the offender away from the criminal justice system" (Reid, 1994:649) by placing the offender in a diversion program. This may include an acceptable program for rehabilitation such as supervised probation (Kolasa and Meyer, 1987). Much of the decision to pursue a specific case at this point depends on the prosecutor's determination of the likelihood of conviction at trial. In more recent years, the use of arbitration, mediation and other forms of alternative dispute resolution have been accepted as standard practice for first offenders or minor offenses (Fox and Stinchcomb, 1994).

Pre-trial Incarceration

Most people assume that all people in jails are convicted, but this is not necessarily true. Fox and Stinchcomb (1994) argue that only 49% of the total jail population have actually been convicted of wrongdoing. The other 51% are awaiting trials. While the primary justification for detaining the accused is to ensure his/her presence at trial (Weston and Wells, 1987), about 63% of all felony defendants were released (on bond or otherwise) before court disposition, and some did commit crimes while on pre-trial release. Among those defendants already on pre-trial release when arrested, 56% were released once again (BJS, 1994a). About 1 in 12 defendants released by state courts absconded before their trials and were still missing a year later (BJS, 1994a).

Efforts have been made to reduce the number of people being detained prior to trial by using diversion programs (Fox and Stinchcomb, 1994). In these, persons awaiting trial are kept apart from convicted and sentenced offenders; this helps the detainees to reconstruct events for use at their trial (Weston and Wells, 1987). The rights of pre-trial detainees are controversial because the individual being detained has yet to be convicted, and is presumed innocent until proven guilty. Most of the court decisions dealing with rights of detainees have ruled that any restrictions on individual rights are for jail security and

not intended to punish the detainee (Weston and Wells, 1987: 53).

Bail may be granted an accused offender for release prior to trial, except in the case of crimes punishable by death, where bail is at the discretion of the court. The institution of bail derives from the basic presumption of innocence upon which our system of criminal justice is founded. While release on bail is a right at the federal level, it is not delineated as a right at the state level (Weston and Wells, 1987).

Judicial System

Administration

Court proceedings for federal cases start at federal district courts. In larger states, there may be more than one federal district court in the state. Appeals from federal district court decisions go to the U.S. Court of Appeals, and appeals from decisions of the U.S. Court of Appeals go to the U.S. Supreme Court (Kolasa and Meyer, 1987). The United States is divided into eleven federal judicial circuits. Each has a Court of Appeals known as the U.S. Court of Appeals for that circuit. The U.S. Courts of Appeals are intermediate Appellate Courts created by Congress in 1891, and were known until 1948 as U.S. Circuit Courts of Appeals (Black, 1979).

At the state level, cases begin at the trial court of limited jurisdiction. This court handles less serious criminal cases and misdemeanors, such as traffic or prostitution law violations. The next level of state courts is the trial court of general jurisdiction where felony cases or major civil disputes (e.g. domestic violence, wills) are adjudicated. The next level of courts found in about half the states is the intermediate appellate court. The highest state court is the appellate court of last resort or the state supreme court. Cases appealed from the state appellate courts of last resort or the state supreme court may be heard by the U.S. Supreme Court.

Special Courts

The U.S. system of justice includes several specialized federal courts. Below the Supreme Court are the U.S. Courts of Federal Claims, U.S. Court of International Trade, Special Court Regional Rail Reorganization Act of 1973, a Judicial Panel on Multidistrict Litigation, the U.S. Court of Appeals for the Armed Forces, the U.S. Tax Court, and the U.S. Court of Veterans Appeals (Brownson, 1994).

Judges

The function of the judiciary in the judicial process is responsible supervision. They oversee the work of the police, prosecution, opposing counsel, and the jurors, and preserve due process of law throughout the procedures (Weston and Wells, 1987). At the federal level, judges are chosen by the President of the United States with the advice and consent of the Senate. At the state level, many systems choose judges through bipartisan nominations and special bar association advisory committees, while in some states they are elected. In 1989 the number of federal judges was 1,035 (BJS, 1991). At the state level, the number of judges varies, depending on the number of courts and the population of the state.

Penalties and Sentencing

Sentencing Process

For the purpose of sentencing, all crimes are classified into categories reflecting substantial differences in the gravity of the offense. Sentencing is a two-step decision process. The first decision is whether to release a convicted offender to a community correctional program, and the second is determining the length of probation or imprisonment to be imposed (Weston and Wells, 1987). The judge, in most situations, has wide discretionary power over the severity of sentence to be imposed (Kolasa and Meyer, 1987). In some jurisdictions, the judge will delay sentencing until he/she receives advice from a behavioral clinic or similar group of professional evaluators of behavior, if there is some doubt about the kind of sentence that will best achieve the goals of the criminal justice system.

Terms of sentence vary from state to state, and may be determinate or indeterminate. Determinate sentences send a convicted offender to prison for a specific number of years. In indeterminate sentences the offender receives minimum and maximum terms of imprisonment. At a later date, the case is reviewed to determine the convict's parole worthiness and a final release date. Mandatory sentences call for the sentencing judge to impose certain terms of imprisonment, as they have been outlined by the legislature (Weston and Wells, 1987).

Types of Penalties

Penalties for commission of a criminal offense vary dramatically depending on the type of crime committed. Sentencing alternatives include fines, probation with or without supervision—which reserves decision on a sentence until a time when (if) the offender is arrested and prosecuted again—commitment to a local jail for a short term, commitment to a state prison for a more lengthy term, and in some states, the death penalty (Weston and Wells, 1987).

This issue of capital punishment remains a constant controversy in the U.S. criminal justice systems. It is used in some states, but only for the most serious crimes. BJS Bulletin (1994d) states that ten states executed 38 prisoners in 1993, and a total of 2,716 prisoners are on death-row in various states. Only six prisoners in federal custody are on death-row (1994d). In 1991, 10,354 inmates in federal and state facilities were sentenced to life in prison (BJS, 1991:625).

Prison

Description

According to the 1990 BJS Census of State and Federal Correctional Facilities (1992b), of the 1,207 state and 80 federal correctional facilities, 234 were maximum security, 403 were medium security, and 650 were minimum security. Maximum and medium security facilities are the most secure prison structures, typically surrounded by high walls or fences, secured with razor wire, and watched by armed correctional officers in observations towers (Reid, 1994:610). Minimum security facilities are surrounded by fences with barbed wire, but may or may not have armed correctional officers present. The total number of prisoners under the jurisdiction of the federal or state correctional authorities at the end of 1993 reached a record high of 948,881, with the states holding 859,295, and the federal jurisdiction holding 89,586 (BJS, 1994a).

The most recent information out of the U.S. Department of Justice identifies males as 92% of the federal prisons population, with females comprising 8% of the population (BJS, 1994a). For federal prison inmates, the median age is 36, 38% are white, 30% black, 28% Hispanic, and 4% other races; 38% are married, 30% are divorced or separated, and 33% have never been married; 77% have at least a high school education, and 18% are foreign nationals.

At the state level, males comprise 95% and females 5% of the prison population. Median age for state inmates is 30, and 35% are white, 46% are black, 17% are Hispanic, and 2% are other races; 18% are married, 27% are widowed, divorced, or separated, and 55% have never been married; and only 4% are citizens of other countries.

The average daily population of jail inmates in 1990 was 408,075. This breaks down to 368,091 adult males, 37,844 adult females, and 2,140 juveniles (BJS, 1991). The ethnic breakdown of jail inmates in 1990 included 46% white males, 5% white females, 43% black males, 4% black females, and 2% male and 1% female others (Native Americans, Aleuts, Asians, and Pacific Islanders).

When considering the types of crimes committed which resulted in the individual's incarceration, BJS (1994a) reports 17% committed violent offenses, 10% property offenses, 58% drug offenses, 12% public order offenses, and 2% other offenses. BJS studies show that 47% of state inmates are incarcerated for violent offenses, 25% for property offenses, 21% for drug offenses, 7% for public order offenses, and .4% for other offenses.

Administration

Each correctional institution within a state is headed by an administrator, whose title is typically a chief warden or a superintendent. Their responsibilities are: coordination of administrative divisions; establishment of institutional policies and procedures; personnel decision-making; preparation of the facility's budget; and development of external relationships with civic groups, professional associations and the like (Fox and Stinchcomb, 1994).

Expenditures for a correctional facility depend on such factors as where the prison is located, the number of inmates, the number of personnel needed to staff the facility, the level of security, and the number of programs and treatment. Because the state level of government is responsible for the majority of prison operations in the United States, the states bear the primary financial responsibility. Fox and Stinchcomb (1994) state that about 28.6 cents of every "justice dollar is spent on corrections," and break this total down: the federal government spends 1.5 cents or 5%, the state government spends 17.7 cents or 62%, and local governments spend 9.4 cents or 33% of overall corrections funding.

Using Bureau of Justice Statistics, Fox and Stinchcomb (1994) reviewed construction costs for new facilities ranging from: over $70,000 per bed for maximum security state prisons, to just under $30,000 per bed for minimum security facilities, to approximately $26,000 per bed for juvenile institutions. Operating costs vary from almost $6,000 to over $23,000 per inmate. Fox and Stinchcomb observed in their review that the cost of keeping someone in prison has increased to $14,000, but other studies placed the range much higher at $30,000 to $60,000.

Correction officer training has come a long way, and it had a very dubious beginning. Lombardo (1989) suggests that early prison training programs were run by the inmates. Because experienced officers were reluctant to instruct new correctional officers, new officers had to turn to the inmates they were supervising for advice. At present, the American Correctional Association's training standards for officers call for a minimum of 40 hours of orientation prior to job assignment, followed by 120 hours within the first year of employment (along with an additional 40 hours each year thereafter).

According to the *BJS Sourcebook* (1991), state correctional personnel in adult systems includes 160,115 white men and 58,814 white women; 36,117 black men and 19,526 black women; 10,953 Hispanic men and 3,720 Hispanic women; and all other races comprise 7,302 men and 3,131 women. At the federal level, correctional personnel includes 10,128 white men and 3,136 white women; 2,270 black men and 1,125 black women; 1,030 Hispanic men and 247 Hispanic women; with all other races including 272 men and 76 women.

Conditions

The "crisis in corrections" has been synonymous with conditions of overcrowding. Gottfredson and McConville (1987) suggest that in addition to overcrowding, many prisons and jails are old and rotting; they are often inadequately staffed, lacking

in medical care, and can not adequately protect inmates from physical abuse. Although not as bad as Brazilian and Sierra Leonion prisons (see chapters 5 and 7), conditions in prisons in the United States have been controversial. As indicated above, overcrowding has remained a constant problem. In 1993, according to the BJS report, 13 states reported they were operating at 99% of their highest capacity. Federal prisons were estimated to be operating at 36% above their capacity. At the state level, 22 jurisdictions reported a total of 50,966 state prisoners were held in local jails or other facilities because of overcrowding in state facilities.

Overcrowded conditions have caused some prisons to resort to early release programs. Some argue that early release programs are related to the rehabilitative functions of the prison systems. Prisoners can "earn" reduced sentences for "good time" (Thomas, 1987). However, many argue that the inmate should serve the time sentenced. This ongoing debate among criminal justice officials is commonly referred to as "truth in sentencing."

Inmates are often allowed to work within the prison system. Institutional programs for inmates include basic education, computer instruction, college education courses, vocational training, library services, and recreation. Unfortunately, the prison industry of the Danish, Chinese, and Japanese corrections (see chapters 5, 9, and 12) are not used currently in America.

The seven areas of inmate complaints which have been most frequently litigated by the courts in recent years are the use of force, mail and visitation rights, isolated confinement (keep-locked), disciplinary proceedings, religious rights, legal services, and parole issues (Palmer, 1973). Three additional issues which have caused controversy are the right to treatment (see *Holt v. Sarver, Jones v. Wittenberg,* and *Rouse v. Cameron*), the right to medical aid, and the right to life (see *Furman v. Georgia*) (Palmer, 1973:126–131).

In recent years, the Texas prison system has been regarded as an example of how bad prison conditions have become in the United States. Martin and Ekland-Olson (1985) submitted that the Texas system had allowed "an agency with conglomerate business, agricultural, medical, and educational activities to escape accountability for its fiscal mismanagement, illegal operations, and the dehumanization of persons under its control." In what became the largest prisoner's rights lawsuit in the history of American jurisprudence, David Ruiz in June 1972 filed a prisoner petition claiming that the Texas prison system was oppressive, brutal, and in violation of the Eighth Amendment (prohibition against cruel and unusual punishments). An agreement was reached in 1985 by a court order, but the Texas Department of Corrections (TDC) failed to comply. Consequently, on December 31, 1985, the Texas Department of Corrections was held in contempt of court order and threatened with fines as high as $24 million per month if it did not comply with the 1985 settlement agreement.

While the actions of the Texas prison system are not representative of all state and federal prison systems, many express concern over the deterioration of prisons and jails in the United States. Recent years have witnessed unprecedented prison population growth, and acute violence among inmates (Sheley, 1995). Prison populations are soaring, while budgets are being reduced (Reid, 1994). Reid argues that some difficult decisions need to be made by the public and by legislators to determine what we want our prisons to do for inmates.

Discussion

The U.S. Criminal Justice System has been organized around the notion of protecting the rights of the accused, while preserving the welfare of the public. This can often prove to be a difficult and delicate balance.

Because this system fundamentally presumes that the accused is "innocent until proven guilty," it has been argued that the adjudication process should consider the rights of the accused before the rights of the victim(s). More and more provisions, therefore, protect the rights of criminals, yet the public is confronted with rising crime rates, drug abuse, and violence. Sometimes it can seem that this system of justice benefits criminals rather than the non-criminal public.

The system of justice in the United States can at times be a long, drawn out, tedious process. China allows a maximum of three days for an appeal, and Nigeria, Ghana, and Sierra Leone require that an appeal be filed within 30 days. In the United States, however, filing an appeal can take 6 months or longer. This aspect of the criminal justice system in the United States places an unacceptable burden on the overall working of the system. Efforts to protect individual rights, one might argue, have resulted in a system of justice that is at best inefficient, and at worst ineffective.

The American system of criminal justice has also been targeted by a debate over the role that wealth and positions of power can play in securing one's defense or innocence. Sometimes the rich and famous prove to be beyond incrimination. Critics argue that large sums of money can buy enough "reasonable doubt" to result in an acquittal. If one has the funds to secure the most powerful legal minds or the best team of investigators, it may be practically impossible to convict you. On the other hand, if you lack sufficient funds and are accused of a crime that you did not commit, you may be found guilty despite your court appointed defense attorney because of inadequate legal support.

Some have also said that the present criminal justice system was designed to combat "street criminals" and does not adequately address other types of crime. The public fears street crime, and the criminal justice system has attempted to respond to this increasing concern. It has not, however, responded effectively to several new and possibly more destructive criminal enterprises of the privileged class, such as white collar crimes, corporate crimes, computer crimes, and environmental crimes. While some legal scholars identify such actions as criminal, "legal loop holes" presently allow individuals (when and if arrested) to escape conviction. Furthermore, when one of the privileged class is actually convicted, punishment is usually quite lenient when compared to that meted out to "street criminals."

The American people are concerned about protecting themselves from criminals. They are disturbed by early release programs and other actions taken to address prison overcrowding problems, and have grown skeptical of the system's ability to protect the public. This concern, in conjunction with the prevalence of drug abuse and misuse, and the availability of guns to every sort of person in the society, poses a significant problem for the entire criminal justice system and the American public.

Innovative programs have been established in an effort to address these and other concerns about the criminal justice system in the United States. The revised data collection process of the Federal Bureau of Investigation provides one good example of such efforts. Better information on criminal acts, victimization, the role of drugs, and other related factors will aid the attempts at all levels of the criminal justice system to determine how to address criminal actions effectively. Focusing public attention on problems caused by crimes of all types—both those committed on and those committed off the street—will provide a context for public reexamination of "victim's rights," and increase popular awareness of how one can avoid being a victim of crime and of how to prevent crime in high places.

Finally, it must be admitted that defense lawyers and the U.S. criminal justice system have focused their attention on preserving the rights of the offender to the detriment of the safety and interests of the masses. Until our social control agencies make the safety and interests of the public central in their adjudication and disposal of offenders, our criminal justice system will continue to be a toothless bulldog.

Notes

1. This chapter follows an outline for writing criminal justice systems developed by Professor Graeme Newman of the State University of New York at Albany.

Discussion and Revision Questions

1. What are the provisions of the following in the U.S. Constitution?

   a. The Fourth Amendment.
   b. The Fifth Amendment.
   c. The Sixth Amendment.
   d. The Seventh Amendment.
   e. The Eighth Amendment.

2. What were the provisions of the Crime Act of 1790?

3. What is meant by the English common law tradition?

4. What is "due process of law?"

5. What is the adversarial system of criminal justice?

6. What do you understand by *mala in se* offenses and *mala prohibita* offenses?

7. How did misdemeanor crimes come about?

8. Briefly explain the following:

   i. *mens rea*
   ii. *actus reus*
   iii. offense committed under duress
   iv. M'Naghten Rule
   v. UCR and NCVS (NCS)

   vi. Miranda Rule

  vii. Exclusionary Rule

 viii. Double Jeopardy

   ix. Determinate and Indeterminate
       Sentences

    x. Death-Row

9. What is a mandatory sentence?

10. Which are the two states in the United States where the Court of Appeal is the highest appellate court for criminal matters?

3

Separate But Equal:

Non-Discriminatory Policy and Practice in British and American Policing

Ian K. McKenzie

Introduction

In the American capital lies the nation's conscience. The National Archives in Washington D.C. contains the paperwork of nationhood: the original documentation of the American Constitution, the Declaration of Independence, and the Bill of Rights. Alongside these historic records stands an exhibition of oppression: the persecution of the Native Americans, the injustice of the "peculiar institution" of slavery, and the oppression of religious minorities. There is a link in this historical collection between two nations which share a "special relationship": the United States of America and the United Kingdom.

Ignore the fiscal incompetence of King George III; dismiss the outcome of the Revolutionary War; set aside the Churchillian notion of "Two nations divided by a common language": the link is far more fundamental. In the Archives, close to the American documentation lies a 1297 version of Magna Charta, presented by Ross Perot, its presence intended to show to the nation the source of the idea of codification.

The shared heritage of these two nations also includes direct involvement in slavery, active participation in genocide, and

religious oppression of such an order that many of the American colonies were founded in order to escape it.

That darker link remains a shared concern. Although there has been improvement in equality and equal opportunity for minorities and special needs groups, continued improvement remains critically important. This paper will address equal opportunities issues in law enforcement, particularly police activities in relation to three specific groups: women, members of ethnic minorities, and homosexuals.

The Structure of Policing

Before considering hiring and employment practices for these three groups, we shall briefly discuss the nature of policing in the two nations. The land mass of Britain (England and Wales, Scotland and Northern Ireland) is about the same size as Georgia, but Georgia has a population of about four million while Britain's is close to 55 million. Britain has three separately administered units of police activity which differ significantly: England and Wales, Scotland and Northern Ireland. Northern Ireland has one single, national police force—the Royal Ulster Constabulary (RUC). Policing in

Scotland and in England and Wales, which was once centered in villages, towns, boroughs, cities and counties, is now administered and controlled in Scotland through eight regional forces, and in England and Wales through 43 constabularies.

There are a number of commonalities between these three elements of British policing. Every force is supervised by a chief constable (called a commissioner in the two London forces), and each constable has independent authority. Only one police force in England and Wales has less than 1000 officers, and the average establishment has approximately 3500 sworn staff. Some of the resources for British policing are centralized, and slightly more than half of the necessary funding comes from the central government, but each chief constable is autonomous and is theoretically able to interpret British constitutional law free from political interference, especially in "operational matters" (McKenzie and Gallagher, 1989). Currently, chief officers have considerable security of tenure, with some serving for 10 years or more. Supervision of police activity is undertaken by officials of the Home Office and through the Home Secretary of the British Cabinet. Also, the public has a limited involvement in policing through "police authorities," a partly elected body of people loosely analogous to public safety committees in the United States.

The law and the administration of law, however, do differ in each of Britain's three major geographical areas. The RUC, the regional police forces in Scotland, and the 43 forces in England and Wales are considered, for all practical purposes, separate entities. Much of what follows is, to some extent, applicable to all these entities, but hereafter we will concentrate on Equal Opportunity (EO) issues as they apply to England and Wales with no reference to other parts of the United Kingdom.

The constitutional autonomy of the chief constable means, in practice, that the Home Office does not seek to impose direction of either policy or practice on individual chief constables. The Home Office, rather, issues "memoranda" which each chief can accept, adapt, or (in theory) ignore. In many areas, this procedure has produced disparate policy and practice, in some cases making comparisons difficult.

In the America, the 17,613 police departments (McKenzie and Gallagher, 1989) are a complex and multifaceted, multi-tiered arrangement, defying taxonomy. Jurisdictional conflicts and direct political involvement, including involvement in operational matters are (by British standards) commonplace. Departments can range in size from less than ten officers to thousands, but 98.1% of departments have less than 200 sworn staff (McKenzie and Gallagher, 1989). Chiefs cannot depend on security of tenure, particularly where their post requires popular election.

Access to Work: Legislation and Background

England and Wales

In Britain, access to work is controlled theoretically by the provisions of the Race Relations Act (1975), the Sex Discrimination Act (1975), and the Equal Pay Act (1970). This legislation encouraged employers to exercise fairness in hiring and retention practices and was intended to prevent overt discrimination. At the same time, the legislation attempts to ensure that the ethnic majority does not suffer unfair disadvantages. Two government funded bodies support this national and legalistic approach to equality: the Commission for Racial Equality (CRE) and the Equal Opportunities Commission (EOC). Both seek to mediate complaints of discrimination, but neither often prosecutes.

The existence of two supervisory bodies, each charged with the oversight of grievance procedures and with necessary mediation, is an anomaly. The separation implies that race is a different problem from equality, a view supported by

Fairmanner (1992) who cites the claim of the vice-chairman of the EOC that there remains "a clear delineation . . . between the duties of the CRE and those of the EOC." Recently, the Home Office (Home Office, 1989a) suggested that minority ethnic recruitment in policing should not be considered under the category of "discrimination," but rather under the more general category of "equal opportunities." Nevertheless, the Race Relations Board has continued to exist, and the notional separation in other social and work-areas will continue.

United States

In America, equal opportunity to work is controlled by the Equal Opportunity Act of 1964 (42 USC, 2000e et seq.), the Equal Pay Act of 1963 (29 USC, 206(d)), and the Age Discrimination Employment Act of 1967 (29 USC, 261 et seq.). The Equal Opportunity Employment Act, otherwise referred to as Title VII of the Civil Rights Act of 1964, prohibits preferential treatment of minorities, and has "created more litigation than the other two acts combined" (Yett, 1989).

The Department of Justice has declared its intention to use vigorously "litigation and the threat of litigation to achieve the hiring rights of minorities and women" (Raphey, 1979). However, this has effectively limited the potentials of the legislation. Fortunately, the litigation itself has nullified these limitations. The possibility of some employers not obeying the Equal Opportunity Acts, and of women and minorities suffering discrimination without government intervention, is eliminated in the United States through litigation, as the Acts did not provide for a stringent enforcement mechanism. Case law and the interpretation of the statutes have produced a system that seeks to ensure that selection and retention criteria are "job related," and thus, in theory, not discriminatory in *any* direction.

Practices Prohibited Under American Equal Opportunity Legislation

Disparate treatment cases (Subsection (a)(1)) are those in which a claimant alleges that an employer has treated him or her less favorably than others because of his or her race, color, religion, sex or national origin (*International Brotherhood of Teamsters v. United States*, 431, US 324 (1977)). Burden of proof rests on the plaintiff; and because one form of disparate treatment is failure to hire or promote based on unjustifiable and discriminatory grounds, this provision has been interpreted as meaning that, "everyone is part of a protected class. Black males are part of a protected class, but so are white females, black females, Hispanic males, Hispanic females, Italian males and white males" (Yett, 1989 and *McDonald v. Santa Fe Trail Company*, 427 US 273 (1976)).

A *disparate impact* case (subsection (a)(2)) is a form of class action case. The attack is on a specific employment practice. Written tests, specific objective requirements, or height/weight requirements might be included in such cases. Burden of proof shifts in such cases from the plaintiff to the defendant and back again (*Albermarle Paper Company v. Moody*, 422 US 405 (1975)). Proceedings are complex because each side attempts to establish that the criterion under discussion either is or is not job-related. In addition to federal law, there are state laws of similar nature: examples would include the Municipal Civil Service System set out in Chapter 143 of the Texas Local Government Code, the Texas Commission on Human Rights Act of 1983, and similar legislation in other states.

Comparisons

What happens in the United States today, they say, will happen in the United Kingdom in the next 10 years. Nowhere is this clearer than in the legislation produced in each country to deal with discrimination in the workplace. But whatever one might say of equal opportunity legislation and its trends, discriminatory behavior in hiring and retention has been combated more successfully by American reliance on litigation, and through associated developments such as the Civil Service Reform Act of 1978 and the Equal Opportunity Commission's requirements that one avoid unfairness in hiring and maintain equality and job relatedness in on-the-job evaluations. The multi-million dollar awards made to successful litigants in some cases have encouraged employers to search for positive discrimination programs, affirmative action initiatives, and other avoidance behaviors. In Britain these are so few as to be almost nonexistent.

Approaches in the United Kingdom have been very different. Resorting to litigation has been the exception rather than the rule. According to research, many police officers believe that "positive discrimination is degrading and insulting" to serving minority officers (Taylor, Ainsworth, and Gallan, 1990). This perception is used as a lever to ensure that both positive discrimination *and* quotas are avoided (Scarman, 1981).

There is no legislation in the United Kingdom which allows the central government to restrict funding to constabularies which fail to comply with equal opportunity requirements. In North America there is the Canadian Employment Equity Act and the American law for "Contract Compliance" (i.e., denial of federal funding to public and private organizations which fail to meet "formal hiring quota" objectives set as part of the funding contract). The "mediate, mollify and minimize policy" of the British approach, by contrast, fails to address the critical need for minority ethnic representation in policing.

Litigation in Britain is confined to hearings before tribunals; criminal or civil hearings like those in America which assess financial liability through jury deliberations are not available. Although many Americans and non-Americans are critical of American litigation, substantial financial liability (or the threat of it) is a powerful force toward compliance. In Britain awards are generally "capped,"[1] and no such fiscal levers operate.

Access to Policing

Minority Ethnic Groups

In 1981, street riots occurred in Brixton, South London. The Brixton Street Disorders were precipitated by the intervention of police officers after a black youth had been stabbed in a street incident. A large crowd of people that gathered around the scene of the incident claimed that the police had caused the injury. When the police officers decided to take the youth to a hospital in a police vehicle, the angry mob began to throw stones, starting a general street disorder that continued for three days.

The underlying causes were later determined in the "Lord Scarman Inquiry" to have emanated from the neighborhood's distrust and suspicion of the police practice of "stop and search" procedures, and as a consequence of a special operation (called Swamp 81) designed to control thefts and robberies in the area. This special operation entailed large numbers of police officers patrolling the Brixton area (both on foot and in cars). Lord Scarman considered the strain of such patrols on police–community relations to be excessive (Scarman, 1981).

Lord Scarman's report suggested that steps should be taken to eliminate or control overt racist behavior by police officers against minority-group citizens, and to increase the number of ethnic minority police officers. In later reports, it was argued that efforts toward recruiting ethnic minorities were needed to ensure that "all officers understand that . . . the effect of months of hard work by officers at all levels can be destroyed by an isolated act of rudeness or insensitivity" (Home Office, 1982). The report also indicated a need to "make it clear that black and Asian[2] officers are treated the same as white officers by their colleagues and supervisors."

The Brixton Street disorder also prompted an offense of "racially discriminatory behavior" to be added to the national discipline regulations of the Police and Criminal Evidence Act (1984). Although this disciplinary offense apparently addresses police–citizen encounters, it could also be used as a sanction in police versus police encounters. So far, it has not been so used.

Pettigrew (1989) proposed that the single best predictor of a riot is the number of minority police officers in a police department: a conclusion that must be deeply insulting to law abiding minority group members who feel underrepresented in the policing of their community. The Home Office committed itself to resolving underrepresentation in British policing in 1986. This commitment, however, turned out to be a fudging exercise of the first order. Although the Office declared that it intended to achieve clear policy objectives and to demonstrate a viable and effective race relations policy by chief police officers, it refused to undertake direct intervention, choosing instead to adopt a supportive role.

This supportive role allows each chief officer to develop his or her own program of recruiting, monitoring, and retention—as it must do under British Constitutional Law. Many critics of this approach (Holdaway, 1990; Luthra, 1986) believed that attempts at reform without a clear, centrally directed strategy would be beyond the abilities of individual police organizations, especially in cases of promotion, appraisal, and the management of organizational change. At a national police seminar on equal opportunities, Skitt (1991) tried to introduce and explain such a centrally directed

strategy by pointing out that true equal opportunity would require both individual and organizational change. He added that the hierarchical and militaristic structure of policing led officers to believe that any group which did not conform to required behaviors could be labelled and dealt with as troublemakers; therefore, complaints of discrimination by both ethnic minority officers and women had been crushed and/or dismissed as mendacious. The view that litigation produces change rather than mediation was supported in *Nottinghamshire Constabulary v. Constable S. Singh* (1990)[3], where the finding was in favor of the plaintiff. The court also noted that the Home Office, Her Majesty's Inspector of Constabulary, and the Association of Chief Police Officers, had admitted that the problem did not solely relate to the force named in the case, nor solely to the specific difficulty of selecting detectives.

In the United States, as in Britain, many of the attempts to improve minority representation in policing resulted from street disorder. Holdaway (1990) points out that,

> Civil disturbances acted as a catalyst to a public consciousness of civil rights and a protest movement among black Americans. Legal change followed, first within a framework of equal opportunities. Affirmative action then developed as a prelude to the acceptance of positive discrimination and the setting of formal hiring quotas.

There are a plethora of cases in the United States which relate specifically to law enforcement (e.g., *Afro American Patrolman's League v. Duck*, 503 F, 2d 294 (6th Cir. 1974); *Hervey v. City of Little Rock*, 787 F. 2d 1223 (8th Circuit; 1986)).

Sex

Equal opportunity combats not only racism, but sexism as well. The lot of women in policing, despite an earlier entry than ethnic minority group members, has been and continues to be difficult. A review of literature, however, shows no cases of riots over underrepresentation of women in policing. Many women believe, however, that access to various positions will not guarantee promotion and unbiased appraisal.

The recently abandoned minimum height requirement for British police forces was effectively a form of institutional racism. Such implicit forms of discrimination against ethnic minority group members differ from the overtly discriminatory grounds on which women are rejected. Rejection on racial grounds has often been based on intellectual capacity, motivation to work, and acceptability to the public. Rejection on grounds of gender has been, in the main, based on negative assessments of physical competency, leadership ability, motivation to become a police officer, reasons for continuing to serve, and stress proneness (Coffee, Brown, and Savage, 1992). Of these, policemen's perceptions about women's physical competency have been most damaging. The stereotype of the "little woman" who is "only fit for two things and the other one's making coffee" has minimal justification, but tremendous power.

Studies in both the United Kingdom and the United States have repeatedly shown, despite beliefs to the contrary, that there is little difference between females and males on the measures of physical competency, leadership ability, motivation to become a police officer, reasons for continuing to serve, and stress proneness. In any case, the first of these factors may well be based on overvaluing of the importance of physical strength in patrol tasks. Furthermore, in an overview of a number of American studies, Balkin (1988) found that female officers performed as well as male officers in a wide range of assignments.

Nevertheless, it is the alleged physical danger of police work that predisposes male officers to use "protect the little woman" as a rationale to exclude women from policing: it is said that women should not be exposed to physical injury and death, and that in the event of life threatening duty a male officer should feel obliged to show "good breeding" by laying his life on the line. Such responses epitomize male attitudes toward female officers. According to research on both sides of the Atlantic, females can expect to achieve the full confidence neither of their supervising officers nor of their working colleagues; and they cannot expect to achieve the full range of duties attainable by male officers (Martin, 1979; Jones 1987). Past research did suggest that some women in policing lacked career ambition, avoided promotion and sought only to fulfill a feminine role in police work (Martin, 1979), but this trend seems to have changed.

Coffee, Brown, and Savage (1992), who asked women about their own experiences and compared their answers with the experiences of their male colleagues, demonstrated "that serving police women do aspire to specialist duties but are often inhibited from . . . applying in the first instance or believe that they are thwarted from being appointed because of perceived prejudice." Similar trends have been noted in Scotland (CPS, 1989).

Americans can cite Chiefs Elizabeth M. Watson (Austin PD, TX), Cathleen Manchester (Norway, Maine), Mary Ann Viverette (Gaithersburg, MA), Joan M. Henderson (Decatur, Michigan), Linda K. Wait (Union City, Michigan), and Linda K. Weaver (Johnstown, PA) as examples of women's freedom of access to head administrative positions in policing; Britain, however, cannot cite any examples, and this includes Scotland and Northern Ireland. McKenzie and Gallagher (1989) submitted that it was safe to refer to Chief Officers in the United Kingdom as "him" because in 1988 there were "no female chiefs yet." Since then, nothing has changed.

In the early months of 1992 there was more action in equality efforts than ever before, at least in policing circles. Alison

Halford, an assistant chief constable (ACC) in the Merseyside police, took action through the Equal Opportunities Commission against the Home Office, against her chief constable, against one of Her Majesty's Inspectors of Constabulary (HMI), and against the Northamptonshire police authority (roughly the equivalent to an American Public Safety Commission) to whom she had applied for a post as deputy chief constable. The case was brought on the grounds that she had been denied access to a higher rank (viz., Deputy Chief Constable) because of her sex. Halford was the first of three female officers to rise to the rank of Assistant Chief Constable. She claimed that she was denied nine applications made for higher posts, and that the posts were awarded to officers who were her inferiors in merit and experience. The respondents countered with allegations of homosexuality, excessive alcohol consumption and unprofessional conduct.

Halford's problems began, by her own admission, when she responded to a publication by Lock (1987). Lock posed a question about the likelihood of appointing a woman a chief officer by asking, "How long must she wait?" Halford (1987) cynically replied: "Until the twelfth of never." This response was used against her. In that article, Halford spoke of the "inability of some very senior men to cope with a woman of comparable rank," of "strong but covert resentment or mistrust of the competence of a woman," and of male perception of an "oddness" in a woman wanting to progress in her career at the expense of a male competitor, "who after all has a family to support."

The Halford case highlighted many embarrassing macho elements in policing, even at a high level. Following weeks of sensational allegations of repeated drunkenness, and gross and sexist behavior (*Independent*, 20 July 1992), all made and carefully reported in painful detail, the blinding glare of publicity proved too much for the plaintiff. An out of court settlement was the only viable alternative, and it was consummated.[4]

Because the case did not achieve a final conclusion within a judicial or even quasi-judicial process, the question of women's rights inside the British police has not been resolved. Women in British policing were poorly served, and some people have shown some concern about it (Bevins, 1992).

In 1992 about fifteen per cent of all officers in the United Kingdom were women. Home Office figures (July, 1992), however, showed that 14 of the 43 forces had no female officer at ranks higher than inspector (roughly equivalent to lieutenant or second level supervisor), and that two of those forces had no female officer higher than a sergeant. Of the remaining twenty-nine forces, three women held the rank of Assistant Chief Constable. There were 11 Chief Superintendents and 29 Superintendents (Bevins, 1992). Behind the scenes, the Home Office, Her Majesty's Inspectors of Constabulary, and the Association of Chief Police Officers probably have accepted that (as in the Singh litigation) the problems go beyond Halford's particular force, and beyond the particular issue of promotion of women to the highest levels of the organization. As Commander Sally Hubbard, an Assistant HMI, put it (*Independent*, July 26, 1992), "The Halford case has made police forces around the country realize that their policies and procedures are not as equitable as they thought." Data showing the most recent figures for ethnic minority and female recruiting in England and Wales are shown in Table 3–1.

British sex-discrimination cases, as in the case of racial discrimination directly related to law enforcement, are few. In U.S. law, on the other hand, multitudes of cases have taken place, with both the litigation itself and the attached financial awards having a positive effect. Two cases particularly stand out. In *Thorne v. City of El Sequenda*, 726, F2d 459 (9th Circuit, cert denied, 469 US 979 (1984), a female applicant for a position as a police officer proved that sex discrimination kept

Table 3–1. *Minority Ethnic and Female Members of All 43 Police Forces in England and Wales 1985 and 1991.*

Year	Minority Ethnic	Women Officers	National Strength
1985	761 (0.67%)	11,304 (9.38%)	120,707
1986	898 (0.74%)	11,707 (9.63%)	121,550
1987	1,108 (0.89%)	12,613 (10.16%)	124,102
1988	1,197 (0.96%)	13,192 (10.52%)	124,759
1989	1,306 (1.04%)	13,829 (10.97%)	126,110
1990	1,418 (1.12%)	14,513 (11.42%)	126,790
1991	1,592 (1.25%)	15,061 (11.85%)	127,127

Source: EO monitoring, F1 Division, Home Office and Home Office memorandum 104/91.

her from being hired. The defendant showed that responses in a polygraph examination relating to her sexual activities had affected her prospective employer's hiring decision, and these were seen by the court as being irrelevant. In *Curl v. Reavis*, 740 F.2d 1323 (4th Circuit 1984), a female deputy sheriff won her sex discrimination case upon showing that she had been denied promotion to a road patrol position by the sheriff. The latter contended before the court, "There is no way I would put a woman on the road in uniform."

However, an attempt to ensure female representation in higher ranks was overturned on arbitration in *City of Fort Worth, Tx. v. Police Lieutenant Thomas J. Brown* (American Dispute Resolution, Inc. Case No 206–122LA, Arlington, Tx.), where a female lieutenant had been promoted to the rank of captain over the heads of two male officers who had higher grades on a current promotion eligibility list. The arbitration court, relying on *Price, Waterhouse v. Hopkins*, 190 S. Ct 1775 (1989), held that the promotion was unlawful. All things being equal, promotion on the grounds of gender alone was prohibited.

Sexual Orientation

The lot of both male and female police officers who happen to be homosexuals and whose sexual orientations are known, resembles that of independent heterosexual women. The homosexual officer and the emancipated female officer are considered a threat to the family institution.

The emancipated woman and the homosexual may both be denigrated on the basis of religious dicta. According to Anthony (1992), in the context of police hiring, retention, and promotion practices, homophobia flourishes under cover of a lack of clear and unambiguous guidance from the top of the organization. This complex area beset with ethical, moral and legal difficulties, was even addressed in the U.S. presidential election of 1992, in which the two main candidates took different sides on the employment of homosexuals in the armed forces. President Clinton's decision to admit homosexuals was based on the fact that there were only four reported cases of sexual misconduct of a homosexual nature among nearly 200,000 American troops deployed in the Gulf war, while there were six courts-martial for rape and sixteen official complaints of sexual harassment. As President Clinton asserted, perhaps it is conduct rather than sexual orientation that is important. Homosexuality, he inferred, is less of a problem than heterosexual men harassing women.

Anthony's recent research (1992) demonstrated that those who denigrate the role of women in policing rely on unfounded assertions about "public opinion." The logic of the cited stereotypes is not, however, consistent. If heterosexual women are unsuited to policing because of innate tenderness, or some such thing, the supposed "butch" characteristics of homosexual women should make them more, not less, suitable for police work.

Jones (1987) and Whittacker (1979) have suggested that the real problem lies in male officers' resentments toward women who are capable of undertaking police work without resorting to stereotyped "masculine" behaviors. The same apprehensions arguably may also exist when, in the absence of fully stereotypic male behaviors, homosexual officers are found to be quite capable of doing the job. Darryl Gates, former Chief of the Los Angeles Police Department, showed the wisdom of this contention when he suggested that "female homosexual officers were to be admired because of their well developed upper body strength" (Interview 20/20 NBC TV, 1990).

Resistance to overt homosexual police officers is based on three separate but interlinked factors; ignorance, fear of corruption, and an alleged instability. There is a commonly held negative stereotype of the homosexual as a camp, limp-wristed, transvestite, would-be transsexual, and child abuser, with transvestism and transsexualism assumed to be chosen, deviant ways of life.

In addition to viewing homosexuals stereotypically, many believe that a person can be corrupted, that a heterosexual can become a homosexual merely by association, or through the teaching of homosexuality as an alternative lifestyle. The result of this is fear of homosexual assault. The

likelihood of such assault is low, but problems should be anticipated. Female officers fear harassment by male officers and the potential for sexist abuse, and supporters of equal opportunity seek to develop mechanisms of redress in such cases. If an officer of either sex were to use such mechanisms to deal with a homosexual harassment problem, one wonders how the authorities in question would respond. The heterosexual officer's fear of harassment by a homosexual colleague is made more acute by apprehension that the homosexual assailant might claim that his or her advances had been invited. Munyard (1988) contends, however, that, "Because of the social prejudice that exists, lesbians and gay men are, in fact, generally much more reticent than heterosexuals and would usually be very cautious about doing anything which could be misconstrued as a sexual advance." Smith (1988) suggests that it is personality integration, maturity, and the acceptance of societal homophobia that are the critical issues in achieving equal opportunity for homosexual officers. In other words, sexuality is not important. What is important is the extent to which the individual has come to terms with his or her own sexual identity. Here the American approach again wins hands down.

In Britain, beyond a certain patchy application of IQ testing, no psychological screening of applicants for the police service takes place (McKenzie and Gallagher, 1989). In the United States, applicants to police departments must be psychologically evaluated, and where an acknowledgement of homosexuality is made, the investigators must assess the extent to which psychological integration has taken place. Although homosexuality *per se* has been removed from the mental illness categories of DSM III–R, lack of integration can be assessed and classified on the basis of existent DSM III–R criteria (302.90 Sexual Disorder NOS). No such opportunity is provided in the British selection process.

Many patrol officers, supervisors, chiefs, and certainly many psychologists would deny employment on the basis of homosexuality. But hiring of homosexuals is just as important in exposing the majority to the minority as are quotas in the hiring of ethnic minority officers and females. In Britain, much has been left undone in the usual British manner; and it is covertly believed that keeping minorities invisible will solve the problem. Only thirteen of forty-three police forces have seen fit to include the words "sexual orientation" in their Equal Opportunities statements. Despite the existence of a very small support group of gay and lesbian officers (the Lesbian and Gay Police Association, LGPA), there is still considerable doubt about openly declaring sexual orientation at the time of application for a job as a police officer. To date, no case law in Britain reflects the court ruling in *Society for Individual Rights v. Hampton*, 63 FRD 399 (ND Cal. 1973), which held that an employer could not discharge a person merely because "he is a homosexual." Even if such a case were brought in the United Kingdom, no punishment more severe than a slap on the wrist would be given, and it is unlikely that it could bring any major and ongoing benefits.

Changing Behavior and Modifying Attitudes

Gender, racial or ethnic background, and sexual orientation are certainly complicated and divisive issues, and there could be little doubt that in both Great Britain and the United States of America, homophobia, racism, misogyny and misandry, will take a long time to die. One must settle, therefore, for two sorts of goals, long and short term. In the long term we must seek to eliminate unacceptable values and attitudes. In the short term, we must aim to keep these attitudes and values under control.

Some say it is impossible for legislation to alter attitudes. This may be true regarding the long term goal of eradicating unacceptable attitudes, but the short term aim of controlling attitudes may not be so difficult. An attitude of mind may be an inaccessible internal and personal collection of ideas, but a person's attitude can be inferred from a person's behavior, and psychologists have long argued that modification of attitudes is obtained through modification of behavior. Equal opportunity (EO) legislation has the power to modify behavior. According to psychologists, mere punishment is an inadequate method for changing behavior, but the opposite is true of reinforcement—both positive and negative.

Negative reinforcement is not punishment (with which it is often confused), but prompted avoidance behavior. Behavior which successfully avoids a noxious stimulus is likely to increase in frequency. In Social Learning Theory (Bandura, 1977), if a person sees another severely punished for an act, he or she will obviously avoid that behavior. Thus, where people are seen punished for espousing discriminatory practices, there will be an effect on others, provided that the punishment is seen as "sufficient." EO legislation supported by powerful sanctions is therefore of paramount importance because it serves as a negative reinforcer, increasing the likelihood of non-discriminatory behavior. However, EO legislation which offers mere mediation and minimal financial liability for non-compliance has only slight attitude changing ability. Where mediation is the norm, mendacity is the standard, but where financial liability and withdrawal of government approval are present, as in the United States, the likelihood of behavior change is increased.

Conclusion

One other reason should be mentioned to explain why the extent and effectiveness of EO legislation is greater in America than in Britain: the written U.S. Constitution.

William Gladstone, a British Prime Minister, described that document as "the most wonderful work ever struck off at a given time by the brain and purpose of man: The U.S. Constitution and the Bill of Rights the nation's conscience."

The written nature of the U.S. Constitution and its interpretation by the U.S. Supreme Court give a leverage to the EO debate not seen in the United Kingdom. Of course, Great Britain has a constitution, but it is a "hotchpotch of legal documents, gentlemen's agreements, and democratically agreed statute law" (McKenzie and Gallagher, 1989), which provides "implicit" rights in contrast to the "explicit" rights of the American documents.

To be sure, the interpretation of the Constitution by the U.S. Supreme Court has sometimes been divisive rather than inclusionary, as with "Separate but Equal" educational practices. But at least it gets interpreted openly. The implicit nature of British rights leads to two consequences. First, there is no open discussion of the ethical and moral nature of individual rights. Second, in the absence of judicial decisions about rights which lead to further litigation, each individual case is dealt with on its merits, and no "collective consciousness" develops.

By contrast, the dynamic American litigation approach has had a marked professionalizing effect on many aspects of law enforcement (McKenzie and Gallagher, 1989; Gallagher, 1992) and has led to specific avoidance activity. For example, when civil service promotion regulations are breached by Chiefs of Police, or when hiring practices are found to be discriminatory, substantial financial penalties may be imposed. In an effort to avoid future conflicts and financial outlay, litigants and others operating in the same arena change their behavior. In Britain, the approach is more "laid back," less confrontational (one might also call it the "play it down model" or the "if you ignore, it will go away" paradigm). It has brought far fewer significant results.

Although racism, sexism and homophobia continue to be seen in U.S. policing and in the entire society, powerful figures from the Supreme Court are seen to be actively involved. In the United Kingdom, by contrast, the control and limitation of unacceptable aspects of human nature is left in the hands of a faceless and tiny handful of CRE and EOC staffers. The penalties, furthermore, for non-compliance with EO legislation are laughable.

I strongly maintain that until British EO legislation and the attached sanctions echo those of the United States, Britain will remain far behind in its search for the Holy Grail of equality, in both law enforcement and broader social life. Women, ethnic minority group members, and those of minority sexual orientation will continue to be equal but separate, theoretically supported by the law but unable to obtain true and complete participation.

Notes

1. British law allows only an absolute maximum pay out of £10,000 plus costs. By American standards, this is a paltry sum.
2. In British vernacular, the expression "Asian" refers to those who come from the Indian sub-continent. Those from China, Vietnam, etc., are referred to as Oriental.
3. In which an Asian officer claimed that selection procedures for detective work were of an institutionally discriminatory nature.
4. At the maximum permitted level (see note 1) and with secured pension rights. Halford agreed to retire on an "ill-health" pension, a practice which she had denigrated whilst a serving officer.

Discussion and Revision Questions

1. In the United Kingdom the Chief Constable has constitutional autonomy. Discuss and comment.
2. What is a "disparate treatment case?"

3. In a disparate treatment case, who has the burden of proof?

4. What is a "disparate impact case?" Name one case of this nature that reached a United States court in 1975.

5. What were the consequences of the Brixton, South London street disorder of 1981?

6. What steps are being taken in both Britain and the United States to reduce street disorder?

7. In policing in the United States and Britain, what are the stereotypical images for discrimination against women and minorities?

8. What do you understand by Social Learning Theory?

9. In your own opinion, what is the essence of Equal Opportunity legislation?

10. What was British Prime Minister William Gladstone's opinion of the American Constitution?

11. What makes Equal Opportunity legislation more effective in the United States than in Great Britain?

12. What is the nature of the British Constitution?

13. What are the two consequences of the implicit nature of British rights?

4

Policing and Public Disorder in the United Kingdom

Michael Bullock

*Quality of Service! A Police Department puts out
a product to maintain peace and reduce crime
and violence so that people feel safe. Our goal
should be customer satisfaction, but rarely do we
bother to find out what the customer wants.*
Gates and Shah, 1992

Introduction

The above quote does not originate from England, where a considerable effort is being made to achieve high quality service to the community, but from the biography of Daryl F. Gates, retired Chief of Police of Los Angeles. The use of the terms "Quality of Service," "customer satisfaction," and "find out what the customer wants" illustrates the argument put forward in this chapter. Gates appears to have made the link between service and disorder, connecting action with community consultation and identification of customer desires, although he gives final primacy to agreement of expectation. Here, then are our central themes; namely, that consultation will affect the quality of service and standing of the police in the community, which will lead in turn to shared responsibility for policing the community and a reduction in the levels of disorder. The evidence for this hypothesis comes from research undertaken by the writer in 1992 and from data collected from American police departments and English police forces.

In this chapter we will consider what is meant by quality in police service in the United Kingdom, how such quality relates to the service function, and the need to consult with the community to achieve tranquillity. Communities have asked for a more caring police service, and police responded initially through service programs such as Metropolitan Police "Plus" and Thames Valley Police "Make Contact." These were undertaken by individual forces, and there was a need for a national approach; consequently, in October 1990, the British "Association of Chief Police Officers" (ACPO) met to launch "The ACPO Statement of Common Purpose and Values" (Hirst, 1990). Work undertaken to identify the police role in society in the 1990s had shown that such a statement would be helpful (Birch, 1990).

In 1975 the public considered the U.K. police poor performers, and subsequent surveys also recorded falling levels of public satisfaction with the police. The dis-

turbing number of incidents of public disorder during the late 1970s and early 1980s
were interpreted as symptoms of a loss of
confidence in the police (Smith, 1982;
Reiner, 1992), which was reflected in research. Studies carried out in those
decades showed a public loss of trust and
confidence in the police (Jones, Young and
MacClean, 1982). The Statement of
Common Purpose and Values sought to set
a standard which would counter claims of
poor service. It may be, however, that the
loss of confidence in the police was actually a response to the style of policing by
the police taking part in public disorders,
an issue only partly addressed by Scarman
(1981) in his seminal report on the Brixton
Disorders in London.

The community disorders of the 1980s
were also partly attributed to mistrust and
hostility toward the police (Benyon,
1987), with the Bristol City riots and the
Brixton Disorders in London seen as a wa-
tershed for British Policing. But they were
neither the first disorders (Geary, 1985)
nor the last, as was clear in 1985, 1990
(Metcalf, 1990), and 1991. Were these disorders primarily linked to a loss of confidence in the police, or was the policing
style of the 1980s a contributory factor?
If it was the latter, then changing the style
and improving the quality of police service may be one way forward. If the former, can we expect a mere improvement
in service quality to restore police standing in the community? In the United
States, several police initiatives have
been described varying from COP+
(Glensor, 1990) to problem solving
(Goldstein, 1990), and community policing (Skolnick and Bayley, 1986). But it is
not clear that these initiatives deliver the
quality of service that the British Police
Forces seek or that they were ever intended to do so. Some work in quality service has been done in America since the
early 1980s; Goldstein (1977) argued that
problem oriented policing would answer
many of the community concerns being
raised by the changes in society, and

would overcome the insular culture of the
police.

The Dilemma of Police Service

All police services face the dilemma of how
to deliver quality service acceptable to the
community, while simultaneously exerting a coercive force over that community
to maintain order. One commentator suggests that quality service is determined by
the discretion of individual officers, and
concludes that emphasis on quality service
is a mere cloak for the coercive function of
the police and does not eliminate it
(Brown, 1988). This criticism could be
evaded if quality service consistently were
linked to consent and accountability, and
not to response time and image, as is often
the case in the United Kingdom at present.
Current initiatives will be unlikely to succeed if they are arrived at without community consent, consultation or internal
support. But can this be achieved when
trust and confidence in the police have
fallen and civil rights issues have grown,
when the media increasingly question the
police role and court convictions are overturned on appeal? Objections are also made
to any assumption that the community is
one homogenous group; there are many
communities or "customers of the police,"
each with its own profile, hopes, expectations, and needs.

If policing in the United Kingdom is
now primarily measured by provision of
quality service, one must define both quality and service. Quality means an excel-
lence of disposition, a mental or moral
attribute, trait or characteristic, an accomplishment or attainment. It relates to professionalism, and varies from best to
acceptable, unacceptable, and worst. In
management terms, quality is the result of
a carefully constructed cultural environment. It must include the whole fabric of
an organization, not just a part of it.
Services of good quality often are assumed
to be customer driven, meeting customers'

agreed requirements at lowest cost, first time and every time (Crosby, 1990), but it might be said that goals should go beyond even this. Quality should be an ongoing process, always aiming to improve. Achieving this requires cultural change through training, planning, identifying and understanding customer needs and expectations, and developing a process for their accomplishment. From such analyses can be deduced a logistical formula for quality: the frequency of deficiencies (defects, errors, failures) divided by the opportunity for deficiencies (hours, beats, manpower levels) (Juran, 1989). Quality in policing might be defined as the totality of features or characteristics of a police service that bear on its ability to satisfy a given need; in other words, the provision of the right service at the right time, and at a reasonable price.

A "service" is a branch of public employment or body of public servants concerned with some particular work or supplying particular needs. The British Police serve the sovereign, the state, and the community. They also serve to enforce laws and maintain order as representatives of the community. It should be noted that this last point is not universally agreed on. Some insist that the police role is law enforcement and order maintenance only, that "such a role (service) does not belong to police work" (Kinsey, Lea, and Young, 1986). This point of view gains support from a number of police officers who do not regard service jobs as "real" policing. Some may think that the main police service is coercive action, but one must also take account of how the British police themselves view their role. The ACPO statement has been devised to support the following key service areas, all of which have been recognized by the central government in advice on monitoring police performance: (1) public contact management; (2) crime management; (3) traffic management; (4) public tranquillity; and (5) community partnership and reassurance.

Demands for community services from police, however, must be balanced against demands for police coercion and readiness to meet conflict: successful police forces will combine these two. Only once this balance has been attained will quality considerations enhance the service provision. Goldstein argues that the ultimate objective for all efforts to improve the police is to increase capacity to deliver high quality service and to equip police to do so in ways which are consistent with, and support, democratic values. Weaknesses in police response came from their belief that the best possible service was being provided already, from autocratic styles of management, and from lack of shared or devolved responsibility; in short, there was a general failure to appreciate severe shortcomings in the police's management of their service role.

Police and the Community

Goldstein advocated quality service as early as 1977, when police clearly were becoming isolated from the community. Low police visibility and lack of regular contact with the community had caused citizens to feel that there was no one to define and enforce social norms, and that the police neither knew nor cared about them (Brown and Wycoff, 1986). The police responded that they did care, but their response was not communicated adequately.

Obviously, there is only tenuous evidence of police consulting with the community to identify needs and expectations. Such procedures have their problems, and police occasionally believe that members of the community may not know what is good for them. Members of the community, however, know very well when they are not getting what they believe they deserve from the police. In the present writer's own experience of working through inter-agency approaches to crime with victim care schemes, crime prevention panels, and several other liaison groups, there has been a noticeable rise in demands throughout the community for more police time to be spent on service. The main qualities demanded today are concern, care and competency (not necessarily efficiency), effectiveness—and economy. Can such care be achieved in the face of constant demands for decreasing spending and increasing control from the central government? Recent government involvement in policing major industrial disputes which led to public disorder have continued a process which started as a response to the disorders of the late 1970s and early 1980s.

Under Conservative government, the U.K. Home Office has pursued national police policy demands for Value for Money (VFM). Police were notified of this policy through the Home Office Guidance Circular 114 of 1983, which introduced the three essential components of VFM: efficiency, effectiveness, and economy, supported by performance indicators designed to facilitate their measurement. The use of performance indicators can be regarded properly as a valuable tool for management, but the policy runs the risk of excluding the customer from decisions. It is unlikely that the police will ever give "value," whatever the cost, if the needs of the public are not addressed. The pursuit of efficiency probably would lead to a style of policing which leans more towards law enforcement than service provision, because the former can be more easily measured on a quantitative basis. Efficiency is easy to measure, but it leads to preoccupation with means rather than ends, and the goals of strategies based on efficiency tend to be short-term rather than long-term. Would this not create problems by failing to address the causes of community disorders? The police problem is not a Value For Money problem, but a crisis in policing itself and public confidence in the police. Quality is unlikely to be achieved through financial initiatives, and the present writer would suggest that the three "Cs"—competence, caring, and competition—will lead to greater public confidence in the po-

lice than the three "Es" of efficiency, effectiveness, and economy.

Confidence in the police will clearly be impacted if the public observes police injustice, improper conduct, repressive measures, or coercion. Injustice especially can lead to disturbances, and hostility to the police can be a primary cause of disorder (Scarman, 1981). This view was supported by a survey of Londoners, which suggested that between one-third and one-half of resident West Indians completely lack confidence in the police force, and that two-thirds have considerable doubts about police standards of conduct (Smith, 1982). In an independent enquiry into the disturbances at Broadwater Farm, Tottenham, London, conclusions confirmed the findings of the earlier survey of Londoners, but the evidence that was presented tended to be anecdotal and not subject to vigorous cross-examination. A report from the enquiry (largely critical of the police role) called for a strategy by which the police should cooperate at all levels with various agencies that represent the community in order to detect and deter crime (Gifford, 1986). But this argument generalized from London to the rest of the country, just as false a deduction as saying that the causes of the Los Angeles riot of April 1992 must have reflected the conditions in the rest of the United States. Policing must meet different needs in different communities and will require different strategies of crime and order control. A much wider British Crime Survey suggested that four distinct groups expressed most dissatisfaction in the police: young men, the unemployed, motorists, and ethnic minorities. In effecting any improvement in public confidence, there must be a drive for quality at both national and local levels, and it must be targeted at groups such as these which least trust the police.

Once one recognizes that police service provision has satisfied all of the community, one must ask questions about the gap between service provision and public expectation. Policing has always concentrated on crime, traffic and order mainte- nance when not specifically responding to demands for family intervention, care of lost property, or issuing a variety of cer- tificates. Little effort is, or can be, ex- pended on public nuisance offenses such as litter, dogs fouling the footway, or noisy motorcycles. Yet, presence of public nui- sances tends to dictate the public percep- tion of the police. There are constant calls for more officers on the beat, pressures for greater victim care, and the need to address the fears of crime felt by non-victims in the community. As a senior police officer said: "In neglecting to respond to the very real needs of those elements of the community we may appear to have lost the caring di- mension in the quality of our service and in consequence undermined public confi- dence in the police" (Hirst, 1990). In fact, police tend to be apprehensive about so- cial agency sorts of involvement, and about raising community expectations through such consultation and involve- ment. Due to conflicting requirements, whether national or local, they frequently have had to admit failure to respond or meet those demands. This conflict may be addressed by changing the culture of the police service. But in order to achieve that change, one must overcome any notion that the workforce alone is responsible for quality. Unless top management demands service oriented quality, the workforce will lack motivation. To change behavior, one must change attitudes: individual of- ficers must accept service as their role rather than perceiving service oriented quality as being imposed upon them. Only then will real quality of service, in addi- tion to law enforcement and order main- tenance, be achievable. A parallel process must be followed in educating the public in the external consultative process. The police ought to make it clear that they seek partnership with their customers in the community.

The police must gain both public sup- port and public consent to perform their role. However, in a society where conflict rather than consensus dominates political life, is that achievable? Some hold that society became deeply divided in the 1980s, and that this division precludes policing by consent of all of the commu- nity's members. In the United Kingdom, inner city problems, poverty, a weakened trade union movement, institutionalized groups, and racism all confront the police, and they will continue to do so. Police can- not work for the greater good merely in terms of some utilitarian calculation; rather, they need to pursue quality service for all in the community. If the traditional model of consensual policing is aban- doned for one based upon coercive force, the police will continue to lose the confi- dence of the public. They will become fur- ther isolated in performing their role, looking inward and merely reacting to events around them. To improve police role in the community and achieve qual- ity service, one must consult and gain con- sensus in order to succeed. A study of a 1990 survey showed that the public would prefer a service which worked with the community to solve crime matters, and that police discretion and crime preven- tion were the best means of dealing with crime (Birch, 1990). This has long been advocated through the problem oriented approach.

While accepting the importance of ex- perienced police judgment in deciding priorities, such judgment may be verified and strengthened through consultation. The question is, do police consult effec- tively? It might be said that the U.K. police do consult through the formal committees set up under Section 106 of the Police and Criminal Evidence Act (1984), but a Home Office review of these arrangements found that genuine community represen- tation was difficult, if not impossible, to achieve; that ethnic members of the com- munity were not attracted to the commit- tee groups; and that some sections of the community deliberately distanced them- selves from the consultation process (Home Office, 1989b). If quality service is a matter of meeting community expectations or needs, how are the police addressing their identification of those needs? Is informal consultation going on outside the parameters of the Section 106 committees where policing priorities are determined and policing operations agreed upon? It would seem that none are truly effective, and that the police in fact still decide their own priorities.

The present writer has undertaken research showing that quality oriented U.K. police have failed to adopt the central requirement for effective consultation in the United States; for, in Britain, consultations which occur in problem and community oriented policing are not usually driven by an identified need to provide quality service. In both countries, there has been a series of innovations which have attempted to overcome the alleged crisis which has arisen in policing during the past 30 years. Most of the innovations which aimed for quality service (such as consultation, contact, consent, meeting of agreed needs, reduction in the use of coercive force) have been carried out in the United States (Skolnick and Bayley, 1986; Brown, 1988; Sparrow, Moore, and Kennedy, 1990). Examples of particular team policing, contact programs, problem oriented policing, and community oriented policing abound in the United States, but can lessons learnt in that country be brought back to the United Kingdom?

U.S. and U.K. Innovations in Quality of Service

In comparing the United States and the United Kingdom, we will look at differing types of police departments in the United States which might be categorized as State Capital, Mid State, Tourist City, and Big City. These groups represent communities of up to 2 million whose police officer establishments of up to 4,000 compare favorably with the U.K. police forces, where the average police population and officer establishment per unit area tends to be much higher than in the United States. The State Capital has a population of just under half a million and an officer establishment of over 700. While the crime rate is comparatively low, the management style fosters community policing. As part of the city structure and its overall requirements of management with accountability, the department has adopted the city mission statement for quality of service which states: "We want City X to be the best managed and most liveable city in the country. We will accomplish this through people who genuinely care and provide responsive quality service." The city mission has always centered on a high standard of service, but recently even more attention has been focused on the police as public servants. Between 1990 and 1992, the city management plan gave "focus on customer service" top billing with a common theme of quality service permeating value statements. The city emphasizes quality customer service and regards the concept of community policing as a priority, actively supporting the Chief of Police in its achievement. To meet this prority, the City Police Department has decided that the key element in policing style is police presence. He or she fulfills an integral part of community policing strategy by redeploying resources to ensure that every police officer has a well defined area of the city to serve. As in China, each community will have one or more identifiable officers responsible for it.

Another key element in the State Capital's police service goals has been the full adoption of the Stephens/Goldstein model of problem solving, whose entire process is underpinned by qualitative rather than quantitative performance measures. The force recognizes the practical difficulties here, and has considered the findings of one unpublished report that *quality of police service is absent from most of the evaluative measures that are now in use. Response time is easy to meas-*

ure, but it is the quality delivered during the initial call until the customer's request for service has been met that is subjective and difficult to evaluate. To negotiate this difficulty, the department has appointed a full-time officer responsible for total quality management and quality of service within the State Capital Police Department. Having pursued reactive policing and having failed to deliver a good service, the department has changed its philosophy: it now can be proactive, but seeks to be coactive through collaboration and consultation. Quality of police service will emerge from the latter.

The Mid State, Tourist, and Big Cities Departments

The Mid State City is a relatively small department by English standards, with an establishment of 350 officers for a city population of 130,000. The city has an ethnic mix of white, African-American, and Hispanic reflecting the national average of 70%, 15%, and 10%. Its main source of income is tourism. Policing is community oriented, seeking to achieve three benefits: (a) improved delivery of police services; (b) improved community relations; and (c) mutual resolution of identifiable problems.

For some years this quality service approach to policing has been shown to be effective, and it closely resembles quality developments in the United Kingdom. Public attitude and satisfaction surveys are carried out bi-annually, and findings are now supported with internal staff surveys. The department uses three agencies to apply this data to its policing service objectives: (a) the Quality Assurance Bureau; (b) the Neighborhood Advisory Group (NAG); and (c) the Crime Analysis Unit.

The NAGs were much more effective at identifying community problems and expectations than the formal consultative groups in the United Kingdom. A plan for operational policing was agreed on which devolved community relations responsi-bilities, making the local officer accountable to the community.

The Quality Assurance Bureau coordinates departmental efforts to improve the service level to the community through consultation, external surveys, and internal surveys; and it is now recognized by the Police Executive Research Forum as a model American program. Its strength lies in public consultation, and its success in such programs as community storefronts. Over the past four years, these successes have led to an increased level of public satisfaction, and also to a reduction in community tensions and disorder.

Tourist City attracts visitors from around the world. Such cities are located over a wide area with a mixed population of about 1,000,000. The community tensions between African-Americans and Hispanics were also apparent between officers of both groups. The police department has over 1,500 officers and practices traditional community policing. However, innovations have met public concerns which primarily relate to tourism and to the increasing number of immigrants to the city from the Latin countries. One innovation, "crisis intervention," mandates a unit of individually selected and trained officers to work directly with area commanders, and to design responses to community problems identified through analysis of calls, citizen complaints or crime figures. The department also attends to the need for long-term solutions to community problems by encouraging joint inter-agency approaches. Projects have included derelict property cleaning and the establishing of City Regulation to control behavior. The crisis intervention officers have increased the ability of the department to respond to the public through community oriented initiatives addressed during the day across the City.

Big City Department is large and multicultural by any standards, with more than 4,000 officers serving a city of two million people. African-Americans and Hispanics are overrepresented within the community when compared to the national average. Relations between the two groups can be tense, as seen in very large cities of the United Kingdom. Several major policing programs have been developed; one, for example, encourages exchange of information between beat officers and neighborhood residents at community exchange meetings (often held in storefront premises). Police hope that this program will build community links through the consultative process, provide a forum for the exchange of information, and demonstrate care for the quality of life within neighborhoods. In practice, monthly meetings are held which bring together members of the police department and community representatives (including various civic groups). Each representative is responsible for reporting back to his or her group, and the meetings often achieve a change in police response to community or in identification of problems. The program resembles the Mid State Neighborhood Action Group concept, and it requires that beat officers encourage civic groups to discuss policing at the patrol officer rather than the management level. This will make it clear that it is local consultation that will make the project succeed.

Although the definition of quality has been far from clear in many cases, the concept of quality has been accepted generally by all U.S. departments and U.K. forces. Lack of a clear definition is not a problem, if all understand the philosophy under which a definition is being pursued; but all do not understand. State Capital's management centered approach, which seeks to achieve quality through the adoption of the City Management Mission Statement, differs considerably from that advocated by Mid State. Mid State adopted a personnel model addressing community needs, combining public feedback on expectations with internal analysis of staff needs and expectations. The management model approach, although coactive with the community, allows management to retain control of direction: the management staff determine priorities and employ their own professional judgments in their focus on customer service. The personnel model allows directional control to devolve to the community working with the lowest police ranks, with responsibility usually placed on a group which tends to be part of the Management Services, Force Inspectorate, or Audit Division. Of forces and departments surveyed, only 13 forces (31% of total) and three departments (10% of total) clearly identified a group with full-time responsibility. Since respondents often reported these as problem solving groups, Table 4–1 includes that category.

The actual use of problem solving techniques to address either quality or style is limited, partially because the English approach quality neither through the personnel model nor through the manage-

Table 4–1. *Frequency of Problem Solving Groups, Quality Circles and Quality Groups*

9	Problem Solv.	Level		Q. C.	Level	Q. G.	Level
U.S.	60 %	Policy	28%	24 %	24%	40 %	16%
		Management	12%		8%		12%
		Other	36%		26%		20%
U.K.	38 %	Policy	3%	24 %	0%	50 %	6%
		Management	6%		3%		6%
		Other	29%		21%		39%

Policy is represented by Chief Officer groups.

ment model, but through a combination of elements of both. The term "customer" is often used but not often clarified: although opinions on the issue are divided, it can be deduced that the customer is the community and not the internal members of the organization. Unfortunately, many police officers, both in America and in England, believe that the lower ranks and civilian staff are customers of the Chief Officer and the senior management team. The U.K. central government, however, takes the view that the term customer does not include internal employees of the police organization. If the police accept that the customer is the victim, service user or participative user, and offenders, whom should the police consult to identify customer needs? The current state of affairs is summarized in Table 4–2, which indicates the percentage of forces and departments that consult informally, the percentage that formally consult on matters of quality of service, and the percentage that formally consult on policing style.

The groups listed in Table 4–2 are the ones most frequently cited for police consultation on behalf of the community.

No such list, however, can be complete, and one might say that by selecting only certain customers for liaison, police still set the rules by which they will succeed. The survey data in Table 4–3 answers to this difficulty by being customer generated, indicating the most common demands by the community for police action; that is, the community needs.

The category "other" features strongly in English surveys, and most often contains demands for more information from victims about the crimes committed against them, along with demands for more action against burglars and car thieves, including "joy riders." This presents a further dilemma for the police particularly in England. If they enforce this area of the law, some communities may react violently, as was the case in Oxford, Newcastle, and other large city housing estates in the United Kingdom in 1991. However, if the police do nothing, public satisfaction decreases. It seems that police need to rely on more data gathering mechanisms than mere public surveys, ones allowing a better understanding of the police role and an airing of public views through effective consultation.

Table 4–2. Customer Groups—Consultation

	U. S.			U. K.		
	Informal	Quality	Style	Informal	Quality	Style
Statutory Agencies	44	12	20	85	15	30
Non Statutory Agencies	32	4	12	32	9	12
Victim Support	60	8	20	88	6	30
Political Groups	36	8	20	17	6	15
Neighborhood Watch	80	8	20	88	3	27
Chamber of Trade	76	8	16	65	3	27
Schools	76	4	16	82	3	21
Churches	60	0	20	82	3	6
Race Relations	24	0	12	35	0	7
Tenants Association	40	0	0	70	0	0
Property Owners	32	20	0	18	3	0

Table 4–3. Comparisons of Demands From Public For Police Action

Demand for Action	U.S.	England
More Foot Patrol	12 %	53 %
More Community Involvement	12	29
Enforcement of Nuisance Offenses	16	26
Greater Victim Care	8	23
Control of Domestic Violence	20	6
Enforcement of Drugs Law	20	15
Juvenile Crime	8	18
Other (includes demand for action against Burglary and Car theft.)	8	47

The Differences Between the U.S. and the U.K. in Community Policing

In America, problem solving is accepted and practised by many departments at the lower rank level, but in England the involvement of lower ranks is often poor. However, problem solving is now being addressed internally, particularly in community consultation and problem identification. Such consultation will allow a redefinition of the police role and function. It is not sufficient merely to pursue order maintenance or crime control; rather, police and community must define what local problems exist and the appropriate response. Consultation can occur through a multi-agency group, a community group, or through local teams of police officers providing contact and reassurance, as observed in Mid State and Big City. If consultation is the seeking of consent, how effective is that process and with whom do the police consult? Table 4–1 indicates levels of problem solving consultation within police forces and departments, while Table 4–2 indicates the groups most commonly consulted in the community on issues of quality and style. But are all these consultations true two-

way pursuits of consensus, or are they mere instances of contact such as a school visit or Neighborhood Watch talk? Consultation most often appears to be contact rather than agreement, used by the police as part of an information process in which they set their own priorities. This is highlighted by differences between English and American attendance of formal consultative meetings, as shown in Table 4–4.

Many informal meetings are regularly attended by lower ranking officers, but such meetings tend to be talks on offense prevention or safety; and no informal meetings about policing style in England have become evident to this writer. Not only are there rank differences between officers who attend formal consultative meetings in the United States and those who attend in the United Kingdom, but the frequency of such meetings also varies. One weakness in consultation programs is the limited opportunities they provide to discuss a response to problems as they arise. This is particularly noticeable in the United Kingdom, where formal meetings are held, on the average, once every 15 weeks. Another weakness is their tendency to represent a very large section of the area's population. Specific problems affecting only a

Table 4–4. Rank Attendance at Consultative Meetings

U.S.	C O P	CAPTS	LIEUTENANT	SERGEANTS	PATROL OFF
	32%	20	12	20	36
U.K.	A C P O	SUPTS	INSPECTORS	SERGEANTS	CONSTABLES
	9%	70	50	23	9

local community would be less likely to be known and raised at large group meetings. The average U.K. Police and Community Consultative Committee represent just under 100,000 of the population compared to less than 30,000 represented in similar committees in the United States. However, this comparison is not altogether just, because participation in such groups is not a statutory duty in America. This makes the precise defining of formal consultation groups difficult.

One cannot easily gauge whether representation by such a large group is effective, but one can deduce from the infrequency of meetings that they are not a suitable vehicle for attempting to meet community expectations and needs. Formal community consultation, then, has great weaknesses in addition to its underrepresentation of the young, males, ethnically marginal groups, and offenders, whose unwillingness to attend such a fomal forum compromises any hope that this style of consultation could achieve the goal of quality service. As a result, police will continue to choose their own policing style, subject to government pressures, and little effort will be made to address the causes behind lack of consultation.

In England, only 20% of forces surveyed felt that policing style had been changed to meet public demand: most interviewees felt that no real change had occurred. If changes in policing style and action do arise from community demand, police must evaluate the effectiveness of those changes by setting performance standards or targets (see Table 4–6).

If standards or targets in quality and style are not set, and feedback does not specifically address these aspects, how can the police know whether they are meeting community expectations and needs for quality? One alternative is to use an internal audit process by inspection departments. There are some 76% of forces and 40% of departments which allocate some responsibility to a specialist department or division, whether full-time (40% England, 14% America) or part-time (36% England, 26% America). This process was established for different reasons in each country—in the United States to meet accreditation requirements; and in the United Kingdom as a part of the "value for money" initiative. Quality, style, and communication may enable police to succeed, but if the young, the marginal groups, or the offenders are not consulted on these issues, it is no surprise when protest against authority and the police occurs. The disorders which affect society in the 1990s can be separated into three categories: those relating to issues, those relating to events, and those relating to communities. While there will always be some overlap between the groups, the general patterns observed are: a concern over a need to meet community demands; community consultation; unacceptable crime rate; evolution of style; changes in management style; style of the chief officer; need for success (Table 4–7).

Issues

Over 25% of forces experienced demonstrations in relation to political causes such

Table 4–5. *Frequency of Formal Consultation*

	No. of Formal Consult. Groups	Frequency of Meetings	Average Population	Population Per Con. Grp.
U.S.	131 (8 Dept.)	8 wks	0.47m	28k
U.K.	345 (28 Force)	15 wks	1.1m	98k

Table 4–6. *Setting of Standards of Performance*

	U.S.	U.K.
Are Standards Set	52 %	41 %
Quality Standards	40	29
Style Standards	80	12

as the Gulf War, animal rights, and anti-community taxation. Most passed with only a minimum of disorder. Others, such as the events at Trafalgar Square in March 1991, cannot be regarded so lightly; but they do not cause any real long-term problems. In the United States, abortion issues have led to disorder similar to those seen in parts of the United Kingdom.

Events

In the past two years in England, illegal dance parties and the re-emergence of the itinerant New Age Travelers have lead to confrontations with the police and sporadic outbreaks of violence. Sports events also have caused disorders. Again, these present no long-term problem for the police.

Community

Community oriented disorders are the sort which have, in the past years, been most frequent and crime related; usually they occur on large local authority housing estates and in areas of severe poverty. A solution to the problems encountered in such areas will only be found in long-term policing strategy. Developing an effective policing style will lead to an acceptable response from the community. Housing estate disorder affects nearly half of all forces in England, causes high levels of damage to community infrastructure, and reduces the general public satisfaction in the level of local policing. The frequency of U.S. housing project disorder is not as high as in England despite similar poverty, unemployment, and feelings of hopelessness observed among the disadvantaged. This is surprising given the added factor of racial tension between Hispanic, Asian, and African-American groups in the community. In Big City, the disorders relate to issues and rarely to the community, but this is not the case in other parts of the country.

The U.S. police do campaign against drug abuse, street crime, burglary, and vehicle related offenses, but there is no protest against policing style, law enforcement, or police presence. Why isn't there as much hostility toward the police as in the United Kingdom? In short, American police consultation programs have strengthened their communities' abilities to address identified problems.

Community disorder in State Capital is comparatively rare and relates to issues that attract demonstrations rather than to community unrest. It might be argued that the managerial approach to quality helps in the maintenance of public tran-

Table 4–7. *Changes in Police Style Arose From*

	U.S.	U.K.
A Need to Meet Demand	64 %	20 %
Community Consultation	36 %	9 %
Crime Level Unacceptable	20	3
Evolvement of Style	8	21
Management Style Change		3
Style of Chief Officer	16	12
Need For Success	4	3
Other		3

quillity. But other factors such as low crime rate, low number of police officers leading to selective law enforcement, and the imposition of a curfew on young people in certain districts, all play some part in community quality of life. In Tourist Town, the police respond to community disorder incidents through specialized units, supported by up to 200 officers trained in tactics, which very much reflects the U.K. approach. As noted earlier, there is an awareness of the problems with the Hispanic community and of public demand for police change. Since the West Coast riot of April 1992, greater "cultural sensitivity training" has been attempted to overcome the gap between the major Hispanic community and the predominantly white police department.

In England, the police appear confused about their role. On the one hand, they seek to provide quality service, which could be achieved through community contacts; on the other hand, they continue to place emphasis not on consultation but on instant response and being available to exert a coercive force. Such constant response, often to repeat calls, does little to address causes—causes which might be identified if the police were to depend on responsible low-level consultation. Current management oriented models for police quality

will be unlikely to attain the prime objective of community policing, that is, enhancing relationships between the police and the community. It seems necessary to consider a new model for English policing which not only meets community expectations on crime control and order maintenance but also meets the need for quality of life and feeling of safety, neither of which exists now. Let us assume that police ought to provide the latter in the context of crime prevention, using the standard model of problem solving.

The ACPO statement is a starting point, but it is general, and poses public tranquillity as an overriding need. Such tranquillity can be achieved through innovation and a readjustment in the means of determining policing. There are many examples of this happening in both countries, all of which include community police teams assigned to a clearly defined area with a specific responsibility for that area, with authority to consult and respond and be coactive with the community. Such teams, while accountable to the local community, should be part of a much shorter management structure within the police. They should form part of a basic command unit that has gained greater autonomy, an autonomy attained by lowering the rank level of formal community consultation in order to achieve three objectives. First, the formal group will represent a much smaller, more clearly defined section of the population; second, the community will take part in decision-making; and finally, a multi-agency approach will be adopted within the community in order to consider both crime and its causes and to give some level of public ownership to the statutory agencies' response.

No more than a handful of forces and departments have changed their basic policing style, preferring instead to examine performance, improve response, and seek a more visible caring image. Police officers are, by and large, caring and concerned, yet they are blamed for many of the shortcomings in society. Focusing on quality alone is unlikely to curb disorder, because it is the police law enforcement culture itself which provides resistance. Senior management does not devolve responsibility beyond the ranks of superintendent or captain, and forces consistently fail to consult effectively. The police need to be more competent and caring than they are now in order to be effective, but the drive for efficiency and economy through use of a management style for quality rather than a personnel style may preclude any service centered approach. The State Capital management approach to quality is not likely to have so good an effect in England as the community or personal approach practiced in Mid State City, but current English trends are toward the former rather than the latter. If possible, this should be changed. English policing needs to adapt to that philosophy of community policing which most empowers the local officer, and which links that officer with the community through effective consultation.

Can quality of service and community consultation reduce the number of disorders—particularly community disorders—which has been seen in the United Kingdom during the last ten years? On their own, probably not. But if taken as part of a style of policing which effectively delivers quality based upon consultation and de-

volved responsibility, one can be much more hopeful. Consultation and quality service within the community will reduce community disorder, and "community policing provides a powerful strategy for the police to employ in reducing the likelihood of collective violence in cities, and, arguably the most substantial short run program for meeting urban social needs" (Bayley, 1992).

Discussion and Revision Questions

1. What does Bullock mean by the "insular culture of the police?"

2. The British police serve three categories of people. Who are they?

3. "Police service job is not real policing." Discuss and comment.

4. The conservative government of Britain introduced a policy of "Value For Money." What is meant by value for money?

5. What are the three essential components of value for money?

6. According to Bullock, what are the three factors that could lead to greater public confidence in the police?

7. What are the major problems facing the British police in law enforcement?

8. Policing based on coercive force versus policing based on consultation and consensus: discuss and comment.

9. What are the principles needed to achieve quality of police services?

10. The key element in policing is police presence. Discuss and comment.

11. What are the three major benefits which "Mid State" policing is designed to achieve?

12. What are the differences between the United States and the United Kingdom in community policing?

13. There are three types of disorder which affect society in the 1990s. What are they?

14. According to Bullock, consultation and quality of service within the community will reduce community disorder. Discuss.

5

Treatment of Offenders in Denmark and Brazil

Zelma W. Henriques

Certain forces shape the posture of a given society, influencing the philosophy and policies which that society embraces. This paper identifies and examines the forces which have shaped two very different societies, those of Denmark and Brazil. Further, it provides a descriptive analysis of the organization of the prisons and treatment of offenders in each of these societies. Because of the significant differences between these societies, we will focus on contrasts rather than comparisons.

Among the benefits of a contrasting approach are the following:

1. It enables us to learn about other systems, and in so doing, we broaden our perspective;
2. We gain a greater understanding of the approaches used in other societies to address our own problems; and
3. It helps us to deal with international crime problems (Fairchild, 1993).

Denmark: An Overview

The Kingdom of Denmark is situated in Northern Europe between the North Sea on the west, the Baltic sea on the east, Norway on the north, and Germany on the south. Denmark's only land frontier is with the Federal Republic of Germany. The Faroe Islands (18 islands, 16 of which are inhabited) are Danish external territories.

Denmark is ethnically a Scandinavian, and occupies an area of 16,638 square miles. Its capital is Copenhagen, and its population is 5,129,778 (1990), making it the most densely populated of the Scandinavian countries (Hoffman, 1991).

Denmark is a constitutional monarchy. Under its 1953 constitutional charter, the hereditary monarch and the unicameral parliament (called folketing) jointly hold legislative power. For several decades, Denmark has ranked among those countries of the world that enjoy the highest standard of living.

The small size of Denmark and its excellent system of identifying and tracking citizens make it an ideal setting for sociological and criminological research. A personal code number is assigned to every individual domiciled in Denmark (Hornum, 1986:3).

During World War II, Denmark was under German occupation. This fact is significant, because the events of the war have helped to shape policies in Denmark, and have influenced the philosophy of the country in the important area of citizens' rights.

During the period of German occupation, many innocent Danish citizens were imprisoned, their only crime being resistance and opposition to the German presence. The civil rights of these confined citizens were extremely restricted. Danish citizens found the experience intolerable, and have not forgotten it. As a result, when they later addressed the issue of restricting the rights of their own citizens, they carefully designed and implemented a system in which individual rights were emphasized.

Today, Denmark stresses protection of civil rights and humane treatment. Although the Danes imprison their convicted offenders, they are careful to ensure that the rights of all citizens are protected. Parliament appoints an ombudsman who is assigned the responsibility of monitoring Danish law and ensuring that any defects in the law are corrected. The ombudsman also has the power to take action against public officials on behalf of the citizens. In criminal justice matters, the ombudsman may lodge complaints with the Department of Corrections or with the Ministry of Justice, regarding procedures or conditions in prison (Jepsen, 1991:132).

Philosophy of the Social Welfare State

A most important feature of Danish society is the idea of collective responsibility: all citizens are considered responsible for each other in all areas of life. For those experiencing hardship, there are social welfare programs that cover family allowance, rent subsidies, health care, unemployment benefits, accident, maternity benefits, institutional care, and retirement pensions. This ideology is particularly suited to countries with little structural or cultural diversity, and Denmark is racially, ethnically, and religiously homogeneous. Danish is the official language and English is taught in schools as a second language. There is almost no illiteracy in Denmark due to its free and compulsory education from age seven to sixteen. A large majority of the Danish population lives in cities and towns.

Criminal Justice Policy in Denmark

Criminal justice policy in Denmark must be viewed in the context of social and cultural homogeneity. The Danish penal sys-

tem results from a process of reform which began under the First Danish Criminal Code of 1866. The present criminal code was introduced in 1930 and has been revised several times. Important changes include the abolition of capital punishment and corporal punishment, the abolition of imprisonment with hard labor, the introduction of youth prisons in a form that reflects the English Borstal system, and the introduction of special forms of detention for professional and habitual offenders.

These changes led to a need for open institutions and overall changes in the penal system. The criminal justice system of Denmark reflects a high degree of centralization, cohesion and consistency. The country has low rates of interpersonal victimizations and crimes of violence, with most crimes being property crimes. The prison system policies supported by parliament and the government are very liberal: capital punishment was abolished over 100 years ago. However, pre-trial detention continues to be very restrictive. For example, Denmark currently uses lengthy pretrial detention, with total isolation of the defendant to keep evidence "pure" (Umbreit, 1980: 27).

Organization of Prisons and Penal Sanctions

The Danish Prison and Probation Service (Direktoratet for Kriminalforsorgen) is organized in a directorate under the Ministry of Justice with the director responsible to the Minister of Justice. The directorate has a hierarchical structure including two departments: an administrative department, and a department concerned with the treatment of inmates, probationers, and parolees (Greve et al., 1984:3).

The department responsible for the treatment of inmates deals with use of prison and probation service, treatment programs, research, statistics and international cooperation in the field of criminal policy. Within this department, there are the following six special sections:

i. a section in charge of cases concerning inmate release on parole, complaints, and furloughs;

ii. a section for the formulation of general rules governing the treatment of inmates;

iii. a social service and welfare unit;

iv. an inmate education unit;

v. a prison factories unit which handles orders for their factory products from other government agencies, and organizes work for inmates; and

vi. a section for total economic management of the institution (directorate).

The Department of Prison and Probation is the agency responsible for the enforcement of all criminal sanctions in Denmark. Consequently, it is responsible for probation and after-care as well as for prisons and local jails. As of July 1993, the total staff of prisons and probation offices was 3,800.

There are 14 prisons and 36 local jails. Of the 14 prisons, five are closed prisons, equivalent to maximum security prisons in the United States, and nine (mostly older structures) are open prisons, that is, minimum-security. Most of the prisons in Denmark are small, with the largest accommodating 230 inmates. A population of 90 inmates in a prison is considered normal in size. Small prisons are maintained in order for staff to get to know inmates and to work with them toward a better understanding of their problems.

The total prison capacity is approximately 3,597 spaces, allocated as follows:

8 -	Open State prisons	1,299
5 -	Closed State prisons	1,305
	Local jails	993
	Total Prison Capacity	3,597

The prison at Copenhagen (a closed institution for remand prisoners) has a capacity for 570 inmates. Total present prison population in 1993 was 3,516. There are 68 inmates per 100,000 population. The average length of sentence is 6.2 months of imprisonment; 4.9 months for ordinary imprisonment; and 18 days for lenient imprisonment. The staff-inmate ratio is 83.4 per 100 inmates, and the total prisons staff and probation officers are 3,800.

Ordinary imprisonment and lenient imprisonment are the most common incarcerative sanctions used in Denmark. To the Danes, the penal feature of a sentence of imprisonment is the deprivation of liberty to move about in society. Therefore, when the Danes imprison, their major concern is with humane treatment (Umbreit, 1980: 25). According to Erik Andersen (former Danish prisons administrator), "prisons are used in Denmark because we do not have a better solution. The goal is to abolish prisons." The Danes view imprisonment as a brutally negative experience, because it separates the individual from family and community, and leads to disintegration of social ties. Hence, in every case, incarceration is used only when inevitable, and in such cases, every attempt is made to keep the offender in or near his or her local community.

Furthermore, the policy is to impose the shortest sentence possible. Most of the inmates are sentenced to open prisons, but are transferred to closed prisons if they violate the rules. Convicted offenders can receive sentences from one month to life. Lenient imprisonment is the most common of all incarcerative sanctions used in Denmark. Eighty-five percent of persons sentenced to lenient imprisonment are drunken drivers. Violations of the penal code, especially various offenses against property, are the most common crimes leading to sentences of imprisonment.

Two percent of all sentences are for two years or longer. Most sanctions are fines and suspended sentences, sometimes combined with probation, lenient imprisonment, ordinary imprisonment, day fines (related to the individual's income and assets), and restitution.

Rather than emphasizing punishment for offenders, the Danes believe that it is in the interest of society to provide for inmate education and rehabilitative treatment. Standard officers, the equivalent of correction officers in the United States, are assigned to duty in each wing of the prison and work closely with each inmate. They are assisted by professional officers such as welfare officers who act as consultants to provide special services. This staff enables a single group of officers with professional skills in a variety of areas to perform all duties related to prison services. These include security work, instructing of inmates at work, and service as guards and as welfare officers.

During her numerous visits to prisons in Denmark, this researcher observed inmates engaging in a range of activities, many of which related to their interests and/or abilities. The prison industries include furniture making, boat building and repair, and construction of a solar power system.

Treatment of Inmates

The rights of Danish inmates while incarcerated are determined by rehabilitative goals. Inmates have the right to vote, to own private property, to be accommodated, to have free time activities, and to have contact with the outside world. They wear their own personal clothes, have personal possessions, plan their free time, receive money, make unlimited telephone calls, and have the keys to their own rooms. These privileges provide the inmates with a sense of responsibility and allow them considerable personal influence in their daily routine.

At Ringe, a closed prison, male and female inmates live next to each other and are free to interact. Here inmates cook their daily meals in a kitchen where they live, using their meal payment to buy the food items in a shop in the prison complex operated by a local store owner. Once a week, inmates receive cash as wages for work and to pay for meals. They are responsible for budgeting their funds, and a local bank op-

erates a prison "bank room" where payments are made.

Leave policies for prisoners are quite liberal; however, prisoners cannot go on leave whenever they want and for any reason whatsoever. Instead, certain time conditions must be fulfilled, and there must be special reasons for each inmate's wish to go on leave of absence (Greve et al., 1984:115). One can go on leave after serving four weeks of one's sentence. There are also "day leaves" which are granted for employment or vocational training whenever such a job or training is not available in the institution. All inmates are required to work and be productive in prison, as established in Section 35 of the Danish Penal Code (Jepsen, 1991:132). Prisoners may fulfill their work requirement by participating in basic and advanced vocational training courses which are designed to help the inmate even after release.

It is not difficult to understand why Danish prisons are highly esteemed internationally and represent the fond dreams of prison reformers everywhere (Serrill, 1977).

Brazil: An Overview

The Federal Republic of Brazil is in South America, and is bounded by Venezuela, Guyana, Suriname, French Guiana, and the Atlantic Ocean on the north; by the Atlantic Ocean on the east; by Uruguay on the south; and by Argentina, Paraguay, Bolivia, Peru and Colombia on the west. The capital is Brasilia. Brazil occupies a total area of 3,286,488 square miles, and its population is approximately 150 million (The World Almanac, 1991). Sixty percent of the population are of European descent, 25 percent are mulattoes and mestizos, 10 percent are of African descent, three percent are Asians, and two percent are native Indians (Info Please Almanac, 1981).

Brazil operated under a military dictatorship for 21 years (1964–1985). A new constitution was prepared in 1988 which provided for the election of a president every five years. In 1989, Fernando Collor De Mello became the first democratically elected president in 30 years. He resigned in 1992 following his conviction on charges of corruption (Heikers, 1993). Brazil's National Congress maintains a bicameral structure, and the country is moving slowly toward civilian democracy.

Portuguese is the official Brazilian language, but many speak German and Italian, especially in the southern cities. For years, Brazil glossed over its racial divisions with the concept of a "racial democracy," which is based on the idea that the black Brazilian man or woman knows his or her "place" (Santos Rodrigues, 1993), i.e., that black people know their role in Brazil is not leadership in government and business but a concentration in service and non-intellectual employment. They know that they are not supposed to aspire beyond blue-collar and janitorial careers.

A Legacy of Authoritarianism and Violence

Many believe that violence became a way of life in Brazil during its period of military dictatorship. Some, however, question this explanation, contending that violence was present even before military rule, and that the popular classes, including petty criminals, were victimized in order to enforce social hierarchies. The recently installed democratic government was not able to modify the situation coercively lest it risk its popularity in future elections: as one critic has noted, the democratization of government does not lead, automatically, to victory of the principles over repressive apparatus (Pinheiro, 1992). In the case of Brazil, illegal practices strengthened during the move toward democracy.

In Brazil the law has never served the interest of the poor, the miserable, the indigent, the black, or the mulatto, and in practice there is little difference between arbitrary extra-legal power and the rule of law. Brazilian values include violence as a legitimate, imperative, and effective behavior in many sectors of social life (Pinheiro, 1992). The middle and ruling classes have established uses of force as a means to subordinate the poor.

Violent death is common. A substantial proportion of these deaths continued even after the end of the military regime, and were attributed to death squads, to vigilante groups, and to "justiceiros" (gunmen). On the peripheries of big cities, there are approximately two hundred extermination groups. In most cases, they are financed by local communities and business owners (Brooke, 1992b).

In Brazil, the fight against crime follows the illegal lines of the period before democracy, although there are some innovative practices such as the militarization of the police patrol approved by the democratic constitution of 1988. Brazil currently leads the democratic countries of the world in number of deaths in police conflicts with the masses (Brooke, 1992a). Clearly, the legacy of authoritarianism continues to influence Brazilian society, and this includes the functioning of its prisons.

Criminal Justice Policy in Brazil

The penal system of Brazil is based on the Penal Code of 1940, which has two sections, the first of which addresses general principles, distinctions among various types of crimes, and specification of various kinds of punishments.

Capital punishment (in the form of execution by firing squad) was revoked by the constitutions of 1946, 1964 and 1967, but was reintroduced by a constitutional amendment in 1969. At the present time, the Constitution of Brazil prohibits capital punishment; however, there has been talk of reintroducing the death penalty because of increasing rates of violence (Kowalski, 1993).

Decree number 898 stipulates a maximum of thirty years in prison as equivalent to life imprisonment for serious felonious offenses. First offenders may be paroled after serving half of their sentences. The prison population in Brazil is 110,000 inmates (Luiz, 1993), with the overall prisoner-to-population ratio being 82 per 100,000 (Weschler, 1993:132).

There are approximately 5,000 penal institutions in Brazil, including 51 correctional institutions, 27 penitentiaries, six houses of custody and treatment, 12 agricultural colonies, and six houses of correction. There are 12 military prisons, 1,580 regular adult prisons (cadeias), 2,803 jails (xadrezes), and five institutions for minors. Fourteen of these institutions have a capacity of over 500.

A shortage of prison space has caused extensive overcrowding, with prisons in Brazil holding more than twice the number of prisoners they were designed to accommodate (Weschler, 1993:132). The states of São Paulo and Minas Gerias have begun a major building program to construct medium and maximum security regional prisons. First-time offenders are often housed with those convicted of the most serious crimes, resulting in homosexual rape of younger prisoners. Young people are sold by guards who then place them in the same cells as the buyers (Americas Watch, 1989). Brazil has been cited frequently for human rights violation in its treatment of inmates (Pinheiro, 1992).

A system of murder by lottery is operated by inmates in some prisons as a means of relieving overcrowding. In Belo Horizonte, 17 inmates were ritually murdered over a two month period by fellow inmates in a so-called "death lottery" designed to protest prison conditions. Prison riots in Brazil claim lives of many inmates. The São Paulo prison riot of October 1992 ended with the deaths of 111 inmates at the hands of the police. Human rights workers said the prison killings manifested a "shoot to kill" policy (Brooke, 1992b). Among the 111 known fatalities of the 1992 São Paulo prison riot, 84 were pre-trial detainees, while the rest were serving sentences ranging from two to thirty years. All were housed together (Americas Watch, 1989:15–16).

Penal institutions for women are somewhat different. They are operated by religious orders, and are not called prisons. Conjugal visitation is allowed, and children are accommodated with their mothers. Clothing for both inmate and family member(s) and a family allowance are provided by the state.

Penal Conditions

Due to overcrowding, prison conditions are poor. Sanitation is primitive: the toilet is a pan on the floor, and water for drinking and washing runs through a pipe that drips. Cells are poorly ventilated, and most of them have bare concrete floors with no bed or mattress; others have beds without mattresses. Inmates are fed one meal a day and are often beaten. Many spend their time in semi-darkness, never being allowed outside their cells to exercise or to breathe fresh air. Inmates complain that cells are hot and stuffy in summer, and cold and damp in winter (Americas Watch, 1989:7). Medical care is poor or non-existent, and AIDS-infected inmates are mixed with the non-infected inmate population. Traditional prison industries include manufacture of clothing and straw mattresses, carpentry shops, and machine and welding shops; but because the system is overcrowded, it is not unusual for inmates to be idle.

Treatment of Inmates

Inmates are controlled by violent beatings brutally meted out by prison guards. Such beatings are an "extra-official punishment for disciplinary infractions—ranging from arguing with a guard to attempted escape— as well as a means of intimidating and controlling prisoners" (Weschler, 1993:133). Inmates have no rights and may expect to serve longer sentences than determined by the court or the penal code, especially those in police lock-ups. Bureaucratic chaos reigns throughout the system.

São Paulo's House of Detention (DEIC) is designed to hold prisoners for a few days, but many of its 214 inmates serve out their entire lengthy sentences in this facility. Since such facilities are meant for short-term stay, the needs of inmates are poorly addressed. The DEIC also happens to have a reputation as a torture center. Police routinely extract confessions from criminal suspects with beatings, electric shock, water torture, and the infamous "parrot's perch," on which a tied person is suspended on a cross-bar by the knees and then abused. The screams of those so abused are unbearable. Generally, inmates are treated in brutal fashion and have no legal recourse to address these human rights violations.

Brazilian Penal Policy in Contrast with Danish Penal Methods

We will now contrast Brazil's system with Denmark's. With its high standard of living and its social welfare philosophy and programs, Denmark operates on a model based on inclusion and responsibility for all citizens. This model functions effectively because the population is both small and homogeneous. Brazil, on the other hand, with a distinctly different population both in terms of composition and of size, is faced with the problems of inequality, poverty, and inhumane treatment. In reaction to the restriction of its citizens' rights during World War II, Denmark designed a humane and liberal system for the treatment of all citizens including inmates. These policies have the support of both the Danish government and its populace. Brazil, on the other hand, having experienced strict militarism and harsh controls for a period of 30 years, has become accustomed to the use of force and violence, resulting in disregard for the rights of a significant portion of its citizens, particularly the rights of political

offenders and members of the lower socioeconomic classes.

There is support in Brazil for the killing of criminal suspects, especially in São Paulo's impoverished working-class periphery. Very often, it appears that the police have been given a license to kill poor people, or those considered marginal in Brazilian society. The level of force used by police in the São Paulo prison riot was extremely high: 5,000 bullets were fired in a space of one hour, resulting in the death of one hundred and eleven inmates (Brooke, 1992a), but São Paulo's military police commander described the police operation as "perfect." Brazilian prisons, furthermore, are poorly maintained and managed, and need overall improvement in organization, administration, quality of training for personnel, and respect for human dignity. Denmark honors human rights with its institutional ombudsman; Brazil, on the other hand, casually violates human rights, and there is no internal agency charged with monitoring such violations. This has resulted in a lack of concern over human rights, especially for those who are disenfranchised. As Chevigny (1990) has noted, the elites and the polity as a whole in societies marked by extreme economic inequality may perceive a need for a show of violent force to discourage civil disturbances.

External organizations such as Americas Watch are monitoring human rights violations in Brazil, and it is hoped that pressure for change can be brought on those who regard violent response to deviants as a primary mechanism to induce conformity in society.

Discussion and Revision Questions

1. What are the major benefits of contrasting criminal justice systems?

2. What is a constitutional monarchy?

3. Compare and contrast unicameral and bicameral parliaments.

4. Why is protection of individual rights very significant in Denmark? What events led to emphasis on individual citizens' rights over societal rights?

5. The ombudsman in Denmark occupies a pivotal position in the maintenance of social order. Discuss.

6. Despite the fact that Denmark has a liberal prison system in the treatment of offenders, pre-trial detention continues to be very restrictive. Why?

7. Compare and contrast the organization and administration of prisons in the United States and Denmark.

8. Prisons in Denmark are designed to be small in inmate population. What are the administrative reasons for this approach?

9. What types of factories are found in Danish prisons?

10. Compare and contrast the rights of prison inmates in Denmark and the United States.

11. Compare and contrast women's prisons in the United States and Brazil.

12. What are the contrasting features of organization and administration of prisons in Denmark and Brazil?

13. What is the "Parrot's Perch" as used in Brazil?

14. Discuss in detail the rights of prison inmates in Brazil and in Denmark.

15. What do you understand by the term "death lottery" to mean as applied in Brazilian prisons?

16. Discuss and comment on the social conditions in Brazilian prisons.

17. The Brazilian penal policy is a shock to "Americas Watch." Discuss.

SECTION III
Africa

Obi N. I. Ebbe

Introduction

Much has been written about the Africa continent, but little scholarship has been done on the criminal justice systems of its nations. In this section we will help to supply such scholarship in three chapters, one dealing with the entire West African region and two others concentrating on Nigeria and Sierra Leone.

Because the United States, the African countries studied, and the former British West African region are all currently under legal systems derived from the common law tradition of England, this section can be seen as building on the preceding one. Most of English and American legal parlance and doctrine is applicable to the African nations studied.

On one hand, the small prison populations of Denmark are reminiscent of African prisons: as Arthur notes in Chapter 6, the prison system is alien to African nations, and contrary to Africans' traditional beliefs in reintegration. On the other hand, Brazilian prison overcrowding can be compared with overcrowding in some prisons in such countries as Nigeria, Sierra Leone, Ghana, Kenya, and Uganda.

An overview of policing and corrections in former British West African countries (Nigeria, Ghana, Sierra Leone, and Gambia) with references to the British East African countries of Kenya and Tanzania is presented in Chapter 6. Here John Arthur shows how the English system of policing and corrections intermingled with traditional African methods of social control, and generally examines the role of external geo-political forces in the development of modern penology in West Africa.

The criminal justice system of Sierra Leone is presented in Chapter 7, which provides a short history of Sierra Leone and an account of its laws and crime problems. In his capacities as a former High Court Judge of Sierra Leone, and with his skills as a social scientist, Thompson succinctly presents the organization and functioning of the police, courts, prisons, and juvenile justice of Sierra Leone.

Chapter 8 presents the judiciary and criminal procedures of Nigeria as an epitome of those in most of the former British colonies in Africa. Both the structure of the judiciary and criminal procedure are presented and critically discussed, with attention given to lay judges, chiefs, and village councils of elders who dispose of some serious and non-serious crimes through arbitration in customary courts at very little cost either to the offender or to the victim.

Asian countries also use arbitration in both criminal and non-criminal cases. That affinity between Africa and Asia will be examined in the next section.

6

Development of Penal Policy in Former British West Africa:

Exploring the Colonial Dimension

John A. Arthur

Introduction

The past two decades have witnessed an increase in the number of research studies focusing on crime patterns and criminal justice administration in Africa. Most of these studies have explained crime in Africa by noting the effects of social structural changes brought about by massive migration from the countryside to the cities, socioeconomic development, changes in family relationships and cultural values, economic inequality, and poverty on crime (Clifford, 1963; 1964; 1973; 1974; Clinard and Abbott, 1973; Opolot, 1976; 1979; 1980; 1981; Brillion, 1973; 1974; Ebbe, 1985; 1989; Igbinovia, 1984; Shelley, 1982; Owomero, 1987; Rogers, 1989; Arthur, 1991). Other researchers have explained crime in Africa and other developing regions of the world in terms of foreign colonization and the introduction of capitalist modes of production (Sumner, 1982; Odekunle, 1978).

While most of the studies have focused on the social processes and the structural determinants of crime in Africa, few studies have examined the social responses to crime and the cultural ideologies related to the punishment of criminal behavior. For example, there are few studies on penal culture and correctional practice in Africa, and research is sketchy on the external geo-political forces which shaped current penal philosophies in Africa. No sustained attention has been given to how colonial systems of criminal justice affected customary African standards and social control methods. Also, little is known about how modern Africa was affected by the major penological perspectives which developed in the eighteenth and nineteenth centuries, or about how the development of penal policies shifted or remained constant, or about what factors might account for shifts.

This chapter will examine the role British colonization played in the historical development of penal practices in former British West Africa, and will focus on Ghana, Nigeria, Sierra Leone, and Gambia. The common British colonial heritage of these countries will enable us to assess how foreign colonization affected the historical development of penal ideology and correctional administration.

We must remember from the outset that there are fundamental social, cultural, and economic differences among the nations of former British West Africa. It would not be methodologically sound to regard the four nations as a cultural monolith. Where applicable, we will note both variations and similarities in their social structure.

Knowledge of penal ideology in former British West Africa is important for several reasons. First, the study of penal policy is important for its own sake. In any modern society, criminal laws are enacted to embody, preserve, and enforce essential societal values. Punishment indicates the importance of the preservation of those norms. Second, knowledge about how external geo-political factors shaped the historical development of penal practices will help the studies of comparative criminologists, clarifying the cultural and political foundations of currently prevailing penal philosophies. A historical perspective can also help to specify crucial developments in crime, law, justice, and give direction for future change. Third, examining the development of prisons as socioeconomic and political entities in relation to the process of nation-building in Africa, we extend the frontiers of our discipline to include definitions and responses to crime in non-Western cultures. Modern criminologists must reinvigorate the field by introducing a cross-national perspective which it currently lacks. Comparing criminal justice in Africa with other nations will force us to construct new paradigms within which to view African culture, and enable us to avoid the insularity and parochialism otherwise characteristic of scientific criminology. Moreover, the answers to the questions we raise will help us both to understand the present penal policies of West Africa, and to formulate those of the future. Finally, the study of penal policy in West Africa will yield valuable insights about the cultural stresses influencing the social responses to crime, and the social structural contexts in which those stresses are produced.

The first section of this essay describes normative violations prior to British colonization, the pre-colonial systems of social control designed to preserve domestic tranquillity. The second section will examine the effects of the introduced British penal system on West African penal practices, comparing the resulting African system with penal policies developing at the same time in Europe, and especially in Britain.

The last section will highlight the major conclusions of this essay and indicate potential areas for further research.

Crime, Deviance and Social Control Prior to Colonization

Traditional societies in pre-colonial West Africa, like other societies, developed mechanisms for dealing with the problems of crime and deviance. Sanctions were imposed for normative violations such as witchcraft, sorcery, cattle raiding, theft, any sexual behavior outside the context of marriage, incest, murder, assault, and wounding.

As in other parts of Africa, social responses to violations of mores and acts of deviancy in West Africa were strongly anchored in the religions which permeated the entire fabric of traditional African society. Breaches of institutionalized norms were generally viewed as abominations requiring collective purification of the community, including the offender. As in other traditional societies, social sanctions were used to ensure domestic security and tranquillity.

A chieftain system based on legitimate order was the social institution primarily responsible for enforcing law among indigenous African ethnic groups. Under this system, the social regulation of normative violations came under the authority of chiefs, elders, a council of elders, and religious leaders, all operating within extended family and kinship authority systems. Political authorities settled personal disputes and conflicts within and between groups through authoritative allocation of legal rights and obligations. Thus, institutionalized mechanisms existed to ensure that individuals complied with the law. Social control depended on self-sanctioning, and on agents acting on behalf of the ruling local councils or political authorities.

Traditional African dispute settlement procedures included bilateral negotiations, binding mediation by persons mutually recognized by the disputants, and family arbitration. Thus, many violations of shared norms were settled within a communal context. In some cases, the victim(s) and the offender(s) would avoid one another until the bitterness ended. Occasionally, both might resort to more drastic punitive measures such as self-exile, suicide, or self-help. Self-help, as a punitive measure, occurs when an offender suspects that his problem with the society's norms is a result of his previous wrongs to the gods and to his ancestors. He then offers sacrifices to appease the gods and his ancestors. In conflicts where there was resort to community intervention, the whole community became actively involved in the settlement. Members of the community would assess the evidence, express opinions as to the rights and wrongs, and exhort the parties to resolve their differences (Kercher, 1981).

Imposed punishments were intended to protect the interests of the victim and the community at large, to regularize social exchanges, and to preserve important cultural elements. Punishments took several forms. Deviants were often subjected to informal sanctions such as gossip, ridicule or public humiliation. Property violations, including theft of agricultural produce and livestock, entailed restitutive compensations. Pre-colonial African society especially needed compensatory sanctions which would minimize offenses against its vital agrarian mode of economic production (Kercher, 1981). Pre-colonial African economics lacked the material conditions that would allow for the imposition of fines, so restitutive compensation was used as the social response to theft of agricultural produce and livestock.

For offenses of witchcraft and sorcery, the penal sanctions included outlawry, public humiliation, torture, ostracism or dedication to a Holy Shrine, and bodily mutilation. For habitual offenders, death by stoning or hanging was not uncommon. Witchcraft and sorcery were punished severely and swiftly for two main reasons. First, these violations went against established religious and political authority, and a failure to punish such violations was thought to prompt curses from ancestors and spirits. Second, these violations threatened social harmony and cohesiveness, and familial solidarity.

For serious violations such as wounding, sex-related norms, and theft or robbery, the common penal sanctions were equitable restitution to the victim, family, and the community at large. Sometimes severe or harsh punishments were used to bring an offender to normative compliance, but the main thrust of traditional methods in dealing with norm violators included restoring the basic harmony and solidarity which had existed within and between the concerned individuals and groups before the offense. The offender regained the graces of his or her community by making appropriate recompense for injuries sustained (Kercher, 1981).

Usually punishments were administered collectively by the agents of social control, the offender's family, and the community at large in order to ensure that the offender did not become alienated from the community. The focus was on the individual, not on the act that was committed. A punished offender had to be reintegrated into conforming society after the punishment was served.

In the predominantly Islamic areas of West Africa, the influence of Islam has had a profound effect on law and order. Islam means total surrender or submission to the will of Allah (God), and one's duties are defined in terms of the rules that believers must follow. Islamic influence is strong in northern Nigeria, Ghana, and to a lesser extent, in Gambia. In these areas, Muslim law and authority used severe punishments for offenses such as adultery, sodomy, intoxication, forcible rape, insults to the modesty of women, and thefts of agricultural tools and products.

Islamic judges maintained legal and extralegal control over the exercise of social regulation based on historical consensus. Thus, sanctions pronounced by these judges had firm roots in precedents, and the arbitrary or capricious use of judicial discretion by an individual judge could be challenged.

The most common forms of punishment in the traditional Islamic areas were death, torture, public humiliation, branding, and the forfeiture of one's property. These forms of punishment and their numerous variations have always been considered retribution for crimes. Flogging was common in Islamic West Africa, and was used primarily to preserve discipline and to punish crimes involving public disorder. For more serious offenses such as robbery and thievery, bodily mutilation and branding were common. For violation of adultery laws, proof of guilt or innocence was established from the testimonies of at least four witnesses or from an outright confession. If guilt was established and the offender happened to be married, the usual penalty was death by stoning.

The custodial confinement of offenders was therefore not an institutional feature of African penology and social structure. The idea of prisons and the use of incarceration was an imported phenomenon. The tribal systems of punishment found by the early colonizers used punishment to achieve social reintegration and restoration of the offender; that is, they practiced reparative rather than retributive justice. The indigenous African systems of law and order were adequate to the task of minimizing lawlessness and keeping disorderly conduct in check. Mechanisms of solidarity minimized crime and social deviance, families were held accountable for wrongful acts of individual members, and collective punishment solidified the sentiments and values of the law-abiding population. Both the offender and the victim were encouraged to settle their disputes within the context of family or communal relationships, or within the traditional, local, political and adjudicatory systems; and, in the case of bilateral negotiations, dispute settlement focused on getting to the root of the problem rather than on dealing with symptomatic behavior.

Offenders found guilty in criminal cases faced penal sanctions ranging from torture, death, and bodily mutilation to restitution, ostracism, banishment, and outlawry. But whatever the penalty, its main thrust was to restore solidarity, promote order and stability, and to assist in future reintegration of the offender.

The arrival of Europeans in West Africa, and the subsequent colonization of the area, had a manifold impact on the traditional forms of social control, dispute settlements, and penal practices. New adjudicatory and punitive systems were introduced giving powers to legislate, punish, and imprison to external civil authorities—the British colonial administrators. These new forms left a legacy of social and cultural dislocation in West Africa. Let us now examine in detail the dynamics and processes of British colonial intervention in West Africa, and the subsequent replacement of indigenous West African penal practices with incarceration.

Adoption of Incarceration and De-Africanization of Social Control

The development of modern penal systems in British West Africa must be examined within the nexus of British colonization and the political modernization of Ghana, Nigeria, Sierra Leone, and Gambia. British colonization and political control of these countries led to the replacement of the indigenous community-based systems of social control with a penal system alien to the region. Even though the British colonial administration claimed that they wished to keep African institutions intact and to allow them to function alongside those introduced from England, the powers of the chiefs and religious leaders eroded as the British succeeded in implementing their colonial domination. In cases where traditional laws addressed acts also considered criminal by the modern courts, the traditional laws gradually gave way.

The British colonial administration recognized the institutional effectiveness of the traditional African systems of social control and used them to shore up and legitimize their political and economic power bases. Traditional local authority councils were formed to assist in maintaining social and political order. Working through District Commissioners (DCs) appointed by the colonial governor, Britain was able to maintain a dual system of shared political governance composed of Africans on the one hand and appointees of the colonial administration on the other. In this way, traditional African patterns of social control were preserved, while matters with greater geo-political implications were resolved by the British colonial district commissioners.

Agitation for political enfranchisement and national independence weakened this dual political and social structure. Ghana, for example, attained political independence on March 6, 1957: political power fell back into the hands of the traditional local councils at the local community level, while Dr. Kwame Nkrumah, the President, assumed control over the central administration.

However, during the early years of independence, Ghana (and the other three countries as well) continued wholesale adoption of British law with only minimal changes. Ghana's criminal code after independence was essentially the same as it had been when under colonial status as the Gold Coast. The only major modifications occurred in laws pertaining to economic and political crimes such as smuggling of cocoa, profiteering, hoarding, illegal assembly, sedition, and subversion.

The post-independence penal code of Ghana establishes three broad types of offenses and punishment for each type. For capital offenses such as murder, treason, and piracy, death by hanging is sanctioned. Offenses falling under first degree felony (manslaughter, forcible rape, and

abetment of mutiny) are punishable by a term of life imprisonment. Second degree felonies (bodily woundings or inflicting intentional harms, robbery, and perjury) are punishable by a period of incarceration of up to 10 years (Marenin, 1989:146–151). Variable terms of incarceration may be imposed for misdemeanors such as assault, theft, unlawful assembly, corruption, and public nuisances.

The criminal law of Sierra Leone is not contained in a comprehensive code like that of Ghana, but is made up of a series of local ordinances (the Criminal Ordinance and the Criminal Law Adoption Ordinance) substantially similar to English statutes (Kurian, 1989). The criminal code of Nigeria during the colonial era was structured on uncodified principles of English criminal law, with offenses classified as misdemeanors and felonies. The latter were punishable by death or institutional incarceration for a minimum of three years, whereas misdemeanors attracted sentences ranging from 180 days to three years of incarceration.

The British colonial administration permitted northern Nigeria to keep its distinct penal code which was compatible with Islamic culture. The Islamic legal code, which deviates markedly from English legal codes, punishes such traditional Muslim offenses as adultery, drinking alcohol, and insults to the modesty of women. The northern penal code does not mention treason, sedition, customs violations, or counterfeiting. Statutory laws dealing with such activities have been enacted separately and appear as an addendum to the penal code.

Penal sanctions under both the criminal code in southern Nigeria and the penal code in northern Nigeria are usually harsh and calculated to achieve deterrence even though the concept of rehabilitation is acknowledged. Common penal sanctions include death, imprisonment, whipping, fines, and forfeiture of property. A death sentence cannot be passed on any offender in Nigeria under 17 years of age or on a pregnant woman. Before 1966, death sentences were carried out by hanging; since that time, the method has been public execution by a military firing squad.

By the end of the 19th century, a formal system of criminal justice in West Africa based on English jurisprudence had been successfully superimposed on indigenous systems and sanctions of the pre-colonial African societies (Kercher, 1981). The British legal systems not only redefined and reclassified crimes in West Africa, but also changed social perceptions of crime and deviance, arrest procedures, processing, adjudicating, and punishing of the offender.

As Korn and McCorkle (1959) aptly have described, the colonial system of punishment and traditional African methods of punishment differ fundamentally in their psychological consequences. Under the traditional method, great care was taken to ensure that punishment would not alienate the offender from the rest of society. Instead, the offender was made accessible to group influence and correction. Banishment, exile, or outlawry would be used only after the failure of repeated attempts at making the offender become law abiding. This contrasts sharply with the colonial legal system which emphasized the isolation and alienation of the offender from the rest of society. This way of punishing offenders assumed that society was best protected only when the offender was physically confined and isolated from the law-abiding public. It also used punishment to achieve specific and general deterrence.

The colonial criminal justice system essentially operated as an instrument of political and social control, and was designed to maintain law and order among diverse cultural groups and to punish law violators with little or no regard for the victim. Criminal acts were viewed as wrongs against the sovereign state. For most West Africans, these new forms of social control and penal philosophy required some adjustments.

English legal definitions shifted the West African understanding of crime and perception of the criminal. Crime was no longer viewed as an act that offended ancestors and the religious establishment, requiring purification for the entire community. Rather, the classical approach was taken: behavior is purposive and is based on hedonism, on the pleasure-pain principle, on free will and rationality. Punishment should therefore be assigned to crimes in order to make criminal behavior result in more pain than pleasure for those who break the law. The traditional African system of punishment had relied on the extended family of the offender, and was designed to ensure the gradual social acceptance and reintegration of the offender into the society after completing his or her punishment. However, the new legal system introduced by Britain weakened the relationship between the offender and his or her family by de-emphasizing the family's role in the punishment process. For the first time, the criminal faced social alienation from extended family and a stigmatization that became permanent, making rehabilitation and future reintegration difficult. This was the effect of shifting criminal responsibility from the family to the offender. Furthermore, although the family was no longer held responsible for the misdeeds of its individual members, crime still brought shame to the offender's family.

Let us now examine the economic process by which the British colonial administration succeeded in virtually replacing the pre-colonial African legal institutions with British legal institutions.

Industrial Production and the Development of Prisons

Two primary colonial objectives of the British in West Africa were to have unlimited and unchallenged access to abundant African natural resources and to gain protected markets for British manufactured goods. A secondary objective was to obtain cheap labor for processing exportable raw materials at West African factories and industries. The British largely succeeded in achieving these goals, realizing them by implementing a low wage labor economic system and taxation of labor.

When the British introduced their commodity and wage economy to West Africa, the following takeover of peasant land holdings forced peasants to seek employment in the foreign-owned agricultural plantations and industries and broke their ties with traditional modes of production. Wage labor, as a system where the laborer depends entirely on wages for subsistence, hardly existed in pre-colonial Africa (Shivji, 1982:41). The wage economy and the imposition of the poll and hut taxes in West Africa caused thousands of rural peasants to migrate to the urban industrial and manufacturing sectors to look for employment. Thus commenced one of the most notable and universal features of Third World economic development—the massive rural to urban migration of labor. Peasants had to migrate to the urban centers to find employment, so that they could pay the new taxes levied on them and at the same time earn enough money to buy imported consumer items (Todaro, 1969; Harris and Todaro, 1970; Amin, 1974; Caldwell, 1969; Todaro and Stilkind, 1981).

The concentration of population in the urban areas of West Africa and the establishment of agricultural plantations called for a new formalized system of social control by the colonizers to ensure maintenance of law and order. This was achieved through the application of English penal sanctions. As Humpheries and Greenberg (1981:213) have noted in their discussion of the dialectics of crime control, criminalization is one tactic among many that an exploiting class will attempt to use in controlling the exploited class, defining as illegal, and trying to punish, actions that threaten their interests. New catalogues of offenses were established, ranging from minor infractions such as misuse of employers' property,

using employers' property without permission, theft, intoxication, failure to commence work at the time agreed, and giving false address, to more serious violations such as desertion, willful neglect, destruction of property, and tax evasion. These offenses indicated British conceptions of the specific relationship between the owners of the means of production and wage earners. The punishment for minor offenses was a fine equivalent to half a month's wage, and for default of payment of the fine, one received imprisonment with or without hard labor for a term not exceeding one month (Kercher, 1981). For major violations, imprisonment and fines were used. Most British West Africans found these new laws and the penal sanctions that they attracted a new form of social control very much alien to African ideals of law and order.

These criminal definitions were put in place primarily for the benefit of the colonial administrators. Their application was a politically motivated attempt by England to redefine social relations, to establish mechanisms for protecting their political and economic interests, and to fend off French and German economic encroachment on their possessions in West Africa.

In matters of civil or tort liability, the British colonial administration allowed traditional West African legal systems to operate as institutions for dispute resolution. In northern Nigeria, under the colonial administration of Lord Lugard, this system became known as "indirect rule," a system whereby the British allowed northern Nigerian traditional rulers (Emirs) autonomy in matters of law and government. Three motives lay behind the British decision to allow African civil and customary laws to govern interpersonal relationships and thus coexist alongside British legal norms. First, the British found in the African chiefs, elders, and Emirs a well developed and centralized system of order maintenance which could help them achieve the goal of promoting and establishing social order and national integration, and simultaneously save them money and manpower in administrating the West African colonies. Second, the use of African legal norms in matters of civil and tort issues helped maintain good relations with the traditional chiefs and elders by giving them a sense of legitimacy and participatory governance. Third, West African legal institutions for resolving civil matters could be allowed to operate because they did not threaten the interests of Great Britain. The administration of laws dealing with economic activities such as production, marketing, and sale of goods were regulated by the British colonial administrators.

The new penal sanctions, then, clearly benefited and protected the economic interests of the British colonial administration. The new offenses and corresponding penal responses were not mere curbs for increasing crime rates and lawlessness; rather, they reflected British need to control the collective resistance of British West African labor and to ensure undisrupted economic activities. The new systems of social control basically protected Britain's economic control of its colonies. By the beginning of World War II, British West Africa had achieved immense industrial and economic development. Accumulation of capital brought about by global marketing of natural resources such as cocoa, gold, diamonds, cotton, hides and skin, and palm oil meant that funds could be appropriated for infrastructural development of railways, roads, and expansion of ports. To protect the free movement of goods and services, Britain established the West African colonial police force, a paramilitary force whose dominant role included the collection of the poll, hut, and land taxes for the colonial treasury. The perceived threats to social stability and British economic interests (emanating from mass revolts against British invasion, such as the Akasa raid in Nigeria and the Nigerian women's riot of 1929 against requiring women to pay taxes) demanded new strategies for social

control. In effect, the colonial masters had to set up forces to wedge the perceived future riots. The establishment of the Ports Authority police, the Post Office police, the Maritime police, and the Railways police was intended to achieve this goal. These formal agencies of social control were charged with providing protection to the local subsidiaries of the British mercantile companies in West Africa such as the United Africa Trading Company of the Gold Coast, the Royal Niger Company, the British South African Company, and the British East African Company.

When modern policing was introduced to British West Africa, it was intended for four important functions. First, it was an instrument of state power for the regulation of social conflict: the colonial police enforced the sovereign power of the state over the individual citizen. Second, it provided protection for the elites who worked for and represented the economic interests of Britain. Third, it formed a group of paramilitary organizations which could assist in the turbulent transition caused by the replacement of African institutions with British institutions. Finally, colonial police were not only useful for preserving the internal security of British West Africa, but could be deployed—as the forces in Nigeria and the Gold Coast (Ghana) actually were—to protect British interests in such places as Burma, the Congo (Kinshassa), Egypt, South Africa, and Sri Lanka (Tamuno, 1970).

The exigencies of trade (the need to have a steady supply of cheap raw material, and the need to secure a monopoly of market outlets for industrial products) were clearly the primary considerations that influenced the introduction and development of English systems of law enforcement and penal policy in British West Africa. The custodial confinement of law breakers in prisons became the new mode of offender disposal, and replaced religion as the basis of social control. In former British West Africa, like in Europe and North America, penal policies began with the onset of capitalism and later provided social and legal legitimacy to the institution of incarceration. The change from the peasant, agrarian economy to a semi-industrial manufacturing economy provided the legal context for the establishment of incarceration, a mode of punishment characteristic of capitalist societies. In turn, the changes in law gave Britain the legitimacy to control undesirable acts of labor, no matter how trivial. Social order had to be maintained to promote industrialization. Similar changes in the mode of economic production, the use of capital, and the rise of the factory system in Europe and North America also led to the emergence of the prison system (Melossi and Pavarini, 1981; Foucault, 1977). As Foucault (1977) pointed out, the development of capitalism provided another structural nexus between the prison and the economic mode of production. The capitalist mode of production is based on exploitation of the working class. Institutionalization of offenders (the prisoners) became a means of supply of cheap labor for the state and the statutory corporations. Thus, there is a structural connection between the prison system and capitalism. The development of the penitentiary system in colonial West Africa occurred along similar lines to those being developed in Europe: the driving force was the emergence of capitalism, which generated forms of criminality and systems of punishment akin to its own treatment of workers—that is, temporary deprivation of liberty or incapacitation of the offender.

Impact of Major Penal Philosophies on Corrections in West Africa

English rule and hegemony in the West African colonies was firmly established prior to the outbreak of World War II. The main objective of the British colonists was to reduce political agitation for self-determination to a minimum, and at the same time establish a stable political and eco-nomic base that would ensure the integration of West Africa into the world polity.

Criminal law, as introduced from England, became the instrument for maintaining law and order, with incarceration replacing the community-based punishments common in traditional African society. The penal system in British West Africa operated on a retributive philosophy, depriving offenders of their liberties and committing them to incarceration with hard labor.

In Ghana, the Ussher Fort and Nsawan maximum security prisons became the models and primary exemplars of British penal philosophy. Both resembled the late sixteenth-century Bridewell workhouses and houses of correction, providing for solitary confinement and labor, and neither classifying nor separating prisoners. Inmates were kept in filthy and unsanitary conditions, and men and women were held together in the same complex where they were neglected and brutalized.

In the case of Nigeria, the arrival of the English legal system in 1861 was followed by the establishment of the Broad Street Prison in the capital city of Lagos in 1872. According to Alemika (1983), the organization of the prison system in Nigeria lacks a clear-cut correctional philosophy to guide its operators, and this makes it difficult to fund improvements on the infrastructure of the prisons or to provide rehabilitation or vocational training for inmates. As Awe (1968) pointed out, prison policies and programs designed to improve the conditions of incarceration are not considered; furthermore, quality educational training for the custodial staff has been neglected consistently.

During the tenure of R. E. Dolan as Director of British colonial prisons in Sierra Leone, Ghana, and Nigeria (including those of other colonies as far away as Trinidad and Tanzania), some efforts were made to de-emphasize retribution in favor of rehabilitation by counseling and vocational-technical education. However, the colonial administration did not support Dolan's short-lived efforts.

To minimize inmate idleness, the newly established colonial prisons introduced work and religious instruction for inmate socialization. In all colonial prisons in both West and East Africa, the British colonial administration justified inmate work on grounds that it strengthened the work ethic and industry of the inmate and provided skills that might be useful on release; that the work component of punishment allowed the inmate to repay part of the expense of his or her upkeep; and that inmate labor and the prison industry allowed prisons to produce and market for profit items manufactured with inmate labor (Kercher, 1981).

Today, penal institutions in West Africa have retained the work component as part of penal philosophy. Inmates' handicrafts are marketed for profit, and government agencies are allowed to lease and use convict labor on penal farms or in government approved projects. Since the attainment of political independence, all four former British West African colonies have continued this tradition.

In 1895, the Gladstone Report on the condition of British prisons was released. This report provided direction and credibility for reforms aimed at social reintegration of inmates (Kercher, 1981), but it did not affect prisons in West Africa, which continued to employ a retributive rationale for punishment and a custodial model that emphasized security, discipline, and order. The principal goals of prisons under the custodial philosophy were incapacitation, retribution, and deterrence (general and specific). As a result, the prison system in the four countries completely encapsulated the lives of both the inmates and their keepers. Both the keeper and the kept were alienated by society, with the keeper controlling all aspects of the lives of the kept.

The major penological developments that occurred in Europe and North America in the nineteenth century were felt only slowly in the colonies. There have been four main reasons for the tardiness of the colonies in adopting modern penal reforms, as Kercher (1981), Clifford (1963), Awe (1968), and others have pointed out. First, Africa lacked well-organized philanthropic movements devoted to improving the conditions of prisoners and to remodeling penal institutions on humane and individualistic lines. Second, scientific research into prison conditions, causes of crime, and the study of criminal justice institutions in West Africa were and continue to be overshadowed by more pressing socioeconomic problems such as population growth and family planning, housing, food production, and health care. Third, the penal system and its problems have not yet acquired political legitimacy, perhaps because African societies still believe that the task of administering and caring for convicts should be a family responsibility rather than the responsibility of the state. Finally, there was disagreement in West African society about the goals of punishment. This disagreement was highlighted by the inability of the prison systems in West Africa to present to the public any credible equation between the heinousness of crime and just punishment. In 1952, half a century after the Gladstone Report, Ghana, Nigeria, Sierra Leone, and Gambia embraced the rehabilitative and reintegrative models of punishment. Nonetheless, reformatory penal policy had minimal impact on punishment in British West Africa. Although the Gladstone Report provided philosophical impetus for the introduction of innovations such as parole, probation, and the increasing use of alternatives to incarceration such as fines and restitutive compensation, these modified punishments were applied only to economic and property related offenses. For violent offenders, the penal policy remained retributive and bound to an inefficient, overcrowded, and poorly administered prison system featuring bad food, a lack of adequate medical attention for the inmates, and poor training and compensation for custodial staffs. Commenting on the appalling state of prison conditions, the Nigerian Law Reform Commission (1983:2) stated:

> Nigerian prisons are too congested, and poor ventilation is one of their glaring features; prisoners and detainees are cramped together in cells with no adequate accommodation provided. Hardened criminals are made to live together with first offenders and the type of treatment meted out to the latter by the former is unimaginable. Prisoners sleep in double decker beds with no mattresses and pillows provided. In these congested cells, not all prisoners are fortunate to be provided with beds. The unlucky ones are made to sleep on dirty, bare floors. The cells stink with hot, uninviting air oozing out at intervals from the cells to the immediate environment.

The prison system completely lacks social services support. As Alemika and Kayode (1981) and Kayode and Alemika (1984) have pointed out, reliable diagnostic information concerning the social history of offenders, their family background, and their prior criminal records are not readily available to assist judges during the sentencing stage. The prisons also lack treatment and counseling facilities. Under these conditions, recidivism rates have increased over time. The Nigerian Law Reform Commission (1983:2) further stated that:

> From all indications, the Nigerian prison system, as at present, is not geared toward the reformation of prisoners to enable them to live a more useful life. Instead our prison system appears more punitive and retributive, and therefore, is not in a position to help reform prisoners. Perhaps, this is why the rate of those returning to prison for the second, third, and even fourth term imprisonment continues to be on the increase.

Innovative ideas in punishment, such as those formulated in Cincinnati in 1870 and in the Gladstone Report of 1895, have lacked the institutional support of postcolonial prisons in West Africa. In effect, the major penal reforms of this century have had little or no significant impact on penal practices in former British West African countries. No pragmatic measures have yet been undertaken to assist the offender in acquiring skills that could lead to gainful employment upon release. Also, West African prisons lack adequate equipment and employ poorly educated, poorly trained, and poorly compensated personnel. Unable to meet the challenges posed by these problems, and hampered by the lack of a community-based system of corrections, the governments of the former British West Africa have had to continue using a retributive penal policy.

The English Penal Servitude Act of 1853, the Irish System of Ticket of Leave, and the Elmira Reformatory System mandated conditional release of inmates and accumulation of "good time credit" for good behavior. British colonial rule, however, never implemented conditional release of offenders; and, due to this lack of groundwork, parole and supervision of offenders within a community setting currently have not been instituted in former British West Africa.

The penal policy has helped to redefine West African social relationships to allow for capitalist economic production and ownership of property. But for West African society as a whole, the colonial intrusion on traditional forms of penal sanctions dislocated the social definitions, classifications, and perceptions, both of crime and of the criminal. Innovative correctional ideologies have not ameliorated the problems, despite a theoretical acceptance of rehabilitation, probation, parole, and community-corrections; in fact, no concerted efforts have been made to incorporate these into the existing penal frameworks. Substantial developments and reforms in penal and correctional systems did occur in England during the eighteenth and nineteenth centuries, but the British failed to support full introduction and implementation of prison reforms in the West African colonies.

Shifts in Penal Policy in Post-Independence West Africa

Since their attainment of political independence, the former British dependencies in West Africa have all undergone significant socioeconomic and cultural transformations. These changes in social structure have also brought changes in definition, classification, social perception, and response to crime. Describing postcolonial changes in penal policy will help to show how the newly independent West African nations adapted foreign colonial institutions to the reality of African traditional social structure and organization.

The types and rates of crimes have changed significantly in West Africa since independence. Given moderate levels of industrialization and increases in economic production in West Africa, property related offenses have increased. The most common form of crime in West Africa today is minor larceny or petty theft (Shelley, 1982; Clinard and Abbott, 1973; Opolot, 1981). The social perception is that minor property offenses are not as socially and economically disruptive as elite crimes such as political corruption and white collar crimes. While minor larceny brought penal sanctions of incarceration during the colonial era, sanctions for minor larceny in post-independence West Africa have shifted to fines, probation, restitution, forfeiture of property, public flogging, and community service. Law enforcement agents often are reluctant to enforce theft and economic malpractice laws, because they consider petty larceny necessary for the economic survival of a large segment of the urban underclass. For major crimes such as robbery, burglary, armed robbery, and murder, there has not been any major

shift in penal sanctions since colonial times, except that sanctions for robbery and burglary have become more severe. In both Ghana and Nigeria, penal sanctions for strong-arm robbery and unarmed burglary range from a minimum of seven years imprisonment with hard labor to life imprisonment, and armed robbery or armed burglary brings the death penalty by firing squad.

Political instability and weak economies have caused the four nations under study to create new categories of crimes to maintain control over their increasingly disgruntled citizens. Although the problems that confronted the fragile economies of these countries were economic and structural in nature, both Ghana and Nigeria (for example) attempted to ameliorate these problems by passing laws that proscribed offenses ranging from political crimes such as treason, sedition, unlawful assembly, and plotting to stage a coup to economic and business related crimes such as smuggling across international borders, foreign currency trafficking, hoarding, profiteering, and refusal to sell. However, the society at large does not perceive economic "criminals" as a threat to social stability. Rather, West African society considers these offenses inevitable and even necessary for survival in an economy characterized by frequent shortages of essential consumer goods. The legislative reaction to offenses such as hoarding, profiteering, smuggling, and the illegal exchange of foreign currencies has been less severe than the reaction to violent offenses. Punishments for economic offenses range from fines, loss of property, or community service, to imprisonment for a maximum of two years.

Shifts in penal policy have reflected the type of government or political administration in power. Military regimes or juntas have increased use of incarceration for minor offenses and the use of the death penalty for very serious offenses such as armed robbery, treason, or plotting to overthrow the government. In Ghana and

Nigeria, military governments increasingly have used house arrest, imprisonment without trial, and preventive detention to curb the activities of political activists who challenge the political legitimacy of military rule. Military regimes in both Ghana and Nigeria enforce law and order through the use of coercive and illegitimate power that does not recognize due process, constitutional or parliamentary provisions, social democracy, or equal protection. Punishments for criminal violations under the military regimes, especially for armed robbery, have tended to be very harsh, sometimes resulting in the burning to death of offenders by citizen vigilante groups before any intervention by law enforcement agents. However, in the midst of their attempts to administer severe justice, the military governments systematically overlook the massive corruption of appointed government officials who enrich themselves at the expense of ordinary citizens. In most cases, these military appointees have not been brought to justice, because they have the political backing of the ruling armed forces.

Civilian administrations have not provided ordinary citizens with much better fare. Under the guise of ensuring social democracy, fairness, and standards of equity, civilian regimes have also relied on the use of the police and army to administer social control. Like their military counterparts, the civilian regimes have used incarceration to achieve deterrence, rehabilitation, protection of society, and retribution.

Summary and Conclusion

Our primary goal has been to provide a concise sociological account of penology in colonial British West Africa, and to discuss the role of external geo-political forces in the development of modern penology in the region. We now will highlight the major findings of this essay and suggest directions for future research.

First, one can conclude that pre-colonial West Africa had a well developed system to ensure law and order and promote social stability prior to contact with Britain. This system of law and justice recognized the disruptive nature of crime and deviance, and therefore took specific steps to minimize them. The social response to law violations was based on the recognition that punishment must be used as a rehabilitative and reintegrative tool designed to ensure that the punished offender would still be regarded as a contributing member of society. Therefore, the punishment, no matter how severe, was collectively administered within the community. Only after repeated attempts at resocialization had failed did pre-colonial West African society resort to extreme forms of punishment such as exile, ostracism, death, bodily mutilation, and outlawry. Unlike the system of penal philosophy introduced to the region from England, which alienates the offender from society by custodial confinement and social stigmatization, pre-colonial West African society affirmed and stressed religion and the extended family network in the punishment process.

Second, the British penal policy of custodial incapacitation was new and alien to West Africans. The traditional system of social control became weakened as Britain took over administration of justice in her former colonies. Retributive justice replaced the traditional forms of punishment which were based on reparation. Incarceration brought a shift in social perceptions about crime and the criminal. Crime came to be perceived as a wrongful act against the state or a sovereign entity, and only the state was allowed to decide the form and measure of punishment. The role of the extended family network, as a partner in the collective punishment of the offender, was diminished, thereby making it more difficult than ever for an offender to reenter society.

Third, the British introduced their legal system to West Africa to protect companies doing business in West Africa, to ensure uninterrupted export and import trade in the region, and finally to promote a social climate of order and stability that would ensure access to and monopoly of West Africa's natural resources. Western styles of law and order entered West Africa not in response to any waves of crime encountered by the British, but because they served to suppress mass revolt, maintain systematic exploitation of the people, and protect the economic, religious, and political interests of the colonial masters.

Fourth, the use of incarceration as the basic form of punishment during the colonial era in British West Africa manifested the gradual replacement of the traditional subsistence mode of economic production with a capitalist mode of production. The penal policy of imprisonment was incompatible with the traditional subsistence economy and the communal system of land tenure that the British found in West Africa. But economic entrenchment under capitalism changed the relationship between capital and labor. This also led to a new formalized system of social control and regulation, with the state maintaining the right to define and punish crime.

Fifth, the major penological innovations which developed in Europe and America during the past two centuries have not had any major impact on penal policy in post-colonial West Africa. Although rehabilitation, parole, probation, and community correction are recognized as part of penal policy in the former British West African nations, no concerted efforts have been made to incorporate elements of the European models into post-colonial penal policies; nor have the systems inherited from England undergone any major and coherent transformation that is distinctively African. Penal institutions in the former British West Africa are poorly staffed, and their prisoners are poorly fed and lack adequate medical care. Policies and standards do not ensure that inmates have the basic necessities of life, and the penal system is still structured on the retributive model. West Africa currently has an antiquated penal system with no articulated philosophy.

Moreover, shifts in penal ideologies in post-independence British West Africa have been influenced by political and economic considerations rather than following a coherent and systematic penal policy more rooted in African social structure. Whether under military juntas or civilian regimes, penal ideologies have been retributive and have totally disregarded the rights of inmates.

Finally, more scholarship needs to address how external geo-political factors have influenced the development of penal policy throughout Africa. In West Africa specifically, the impact of French colonization on the development of penal policies could be assessed, especially in the former French colonies of Senegal, the Ivory Coast, Guinea, Benin, Burkina Faso, and Togo. Differences and similarities could be posed between British and French approaches to penal policy in West Africa, and the influence of Islam on current penal orientation could also be surveyed. Attention to these issues will clarify the important role played by criminal justice systems in nation-building and political modernization in Africa.

Discussion and Revision Questions

1. What are the main reasons why we try to understand penal ideology in former British West Africa?

2. What were serious offenses in former British West African countries in the pre-colonial times?

3. What are the essential features of traditional African dispute settlement?

4. Why were witchcraft and sorcery severely punished in pre-colonial Africa and Puritan New England?

5. Both Denmark and traditional African societies believe in a reintegrative model of offender disposal. Discuss. Compare and contrast each culture's approaches.

6. Criminal codes and imprisonment of offenders are colonial legacies to British West Africa. Discuss.

7. What was "indirect rule"?

8. What were the four purposes of colonial policing in former British West Africa?

9. What were the justifications for prison inmate labor in colonial Africa?

10. Compare and contrast punishment for violent crimes in West Africa and the United States.

7

The Criminal Justice System of Sierra Leone

Bankole Thompson

Introduction

From an American perspective, this study concerns one foreign criminal justice system, providing some knowledge about the practices of the West African state of Sierra Leone. The main motives for comparative and international criminal justice have been mentioned in Chapter One. To this account one might add that scholars have identified at least five possible models for studying criminal justice from a comparative perspective. These are (1) the anthropological-historical approach, (2) the institutional-structural approach, (3) the political-legal approach, (4) the social-philosophical approach, and (5) the analytical-problems approach (Terrill, 1984). Each model has its own strengths, and the nature of any particular criminal justice system may lend itself more easily to treatment by one of these models than by another. The socio-philosophical model, for example, would resolve such questions as: What are the prevailing views about the causes of crime and deviancy in a society? What philosophical approaches are used to resolve or cope with these views in the penal context? The institutional-structural approach, on the other hand, would seek a panoramic view, exploring the institutions, policies, and processes that give structure to a country's criminal justice system, and surveying the organization, structure, and function of the police, the courts, the correctional services and the juvenile justice process. It is this approach that we will take in examining Sierra Leone. Key features and elements of both substantive criminal law and criminal procedure in that country will be highlighted, providing grounds for a summary critique of its administration of criminal justice.

Brief History

Sierra Leone is a relatively small West African country with an area of 27,925 square miles, and a population of 3.7 million people. It is bounded on the west and north by Guinea and on the east by Liberia. The country is made up of many ethnic groups such as the Mendes, Ternnes, and Limbas. Most of the remaining population is composed of the Krios, or Creoles, who are largely Western in culture and still legally classified as "non-natives." The indigenous peoples are designated as "natives."

Throughout its modern history, and despite its British occupation, the country has retained the name Sierra Leone, thereby preserving its historical link with the Portuguese sailor, Pedro da Cintra, who sailed into a huge bay on the west coast of Africa in 1462 and named the surrounding country for the mountain ranges above that bay, which he believed resembled lions. Like most African countries, Sierra Leone blends Western cultural values derived from its British heritage with indigenous

African norms. Part of its history is enmeshed in the slave trade that attracted sea captains to the west coast of Africa in the sixteenth and seventeenth centuries. By 1792, the British government had established a settlement in Sierra Leone, and Lieutenant John Clarkson had become the first Governor of Freetown. The little settlement was administered by the Sierra Leone Company, which was formed in 1791.

In 1808 the settlement was taken over by the British government as a crown colony. The new colony became a base for the Act of Parliament (1807) abolishing the slave trade, with a naval squadron court set up in Freetown to try slave-traders. After the Napoleonic Wars, the other European nations agreed to abolish the slave trade, and the naval squadron court was supplemented by Courts of Mixed Commission. Thousands of slaves were freed as a result of these events, and most chose to settle in Sierra Leone. These liberated Africans—Krios or Creoles as they were called—came from all parts of Africa. By 1861, through treaties of cession, the colony had been extended to include the whole of the Sierra Leone peninsula, Sherbro Island, and various other small islands. In 1896 the surrounding territory was declared a British protectorate (Kaplan et al., 1976; Fyfe and Jones, 1968).

Sierra Leone's blend of cultures and historical background have enormous significance and implications for the present organization of its legal system, and for its criminal justice system in particular. One important result has been the country's dual system of justice, British oriented general law courts on one hand, and local or customary law courts on the other. We will examine the organization, structures and functions of these courts later in the chapter.

Crime Profile

Constructing crime profiles for most developing nations in Africa is, without exaggeration, a Herculean task. Many of these countries do not have accurate or reliable means to measure the amount of crime committed within their borders (Clinard and Abbott, 1973). This is true of Sierra Leone, where the only official source of indirect crime information is the *Annual Statistical Digest*. The *Digest* aims to present in one volume statistical data of interest to general users of official statistics, but while it covers a wide range of subjects, it does not give priority to factual crime reporting. No edition has ever reported crime facts. Other than information on road traffic accidents and casualties, the *Digest* does not provide data on amounts and types of crimes committed in Sierra Leone. Even in relation to road traffic accidents and casualties, there is some duplication of reporting. For example, the 1989 edition provides figures on one subject for the period, 1983–1987; and the 1990 edition, evidently attempting to consolidate data, covers that same subject for the period, 1979–1988.

On the rare occasion when statistical data relating to crime are reported in the *Annual Statistical Digest*, the method of compilation is penological, focusing on the number of persons committed to prison annually rather than on the numbers of crimes occurring yearly. The analysis proceeds on three levels. The first level enumerates (a) the number of inmates on remand and (b) the number of persons sentenced to imprisonment. Category (a) is broken down separately for each sex into those awaiting trial, those convicted but not sentenced, and others; category (b) is broken down separately for each sex into those sentenced to imprisonment without option of a fine, those in default of payment of a fine, and those sentenced to death (see Table 7–1).

The second level enumerates persons sentenced to imprisonment, classifying them by (i) sex and (ii) duration of sentence (see Table 7–2). The third level itemizes separately for each sex and year the number of previous convictions of persons sentenced (see Table 7–3). The *Digest's*

TABLE 7-1. *Persons Committed to Prison During the Year*

Type of Inmate	1979	1980	1981	1982	1983	1984	1985	1986	1987	1988
On Remand										
Awaiting Trial										
Male	16373	8119	16578	21367	18188	16887	18286	17358	14357	8409
Female	400	335	217	297	397	364	475	411	498	320
Convicted Unsentenced										
Male	3187	2835	2821	4150	2788	4868	4561	4418	4286	4251
Female	61	32	69	45	31	35	100	84	76	86
Other										
Male	52	52	294	1456	377	392	38	59	66	38
Female	1	2	--	3	9	1	--	3	6	2
Sentenced to Imprisonment										
Without Option of fine										
Male	18554	17232	17956	22194	19990	20643	16830	21198	18425	17549
Female	386	311	220	286	363	303	383	299	311	267
Default of Payment of fine										
Male	1002	842	752	549	384	308	303	350	324	346
Female	27	13	21	15	13	20	12	17	20	37
Sentenced to Death										
Male	2	--	--	--	9	4	3	2	12	--
Female	--	--	--	--	1	--	--	--	--	--

Source: Prisons Department, Freetown

Extracted from the 1990 edition of the *Annual Statistical Digest*

TABLE 7-2. *Persons Sentenced to Imprisonment: Analysis by Sex and Duration of Sentence*

Duration of Sentence (months)	1979	1980	1981	1982	1983	1984	1985	1986	1987	1988
Less than 3										
Male	553	513	419	411	210	131	146	131	138	173
Female	14	4	12	13	2	1	--	--	3	13
3 and less than 6										
Male	569	523	467	551	363	445	140	165	166	332
Female	14	5	19	6	9	10	6	3	3	15
6 and less than 12										
Male	624	610	681	664	619	665	331	240	256	266
Female	14	10	17	11	2	11	3	6	6	7
12 and less than 18										
Male	618	508	468	517	466	634	325	278	259	811
Female	12	5	6	4	6	13	5	2	6	5
18 and less than 24										
Male	404	311	270	266	363	458	297	225	184	209
Female	9	3	4	6	--	6	3	4	4	3
24 and over										
Male	376	222	288	278	349	488	470	367	325	363
Female	8	3	5	2	3	1	5	5	28	11
Sentenced to Death										
Male	2	--	--	--	9	4	3	2	12	--
Female	--	--	--	--	1	--	--	--	--	--

Source: Prisons Department

Extracted from the 1990 edition of the *Annual Statistical Digest*

TABLE 7–3. Persons Sentenced to Imprisonment Analysis by Sex and Number of Previous Convictions

No. of Previous Convictions	1979	1980	1981	1982	1983	1984	1985	1986	1987	1988
Males										
None	137	187	384	966	1046	1333	1510	1174	1385	1026
1–2	1300	900	1124	2924	1202	2718	3221	2336	1960	2917
3–5	800	900	925	1046	596	1061	479	933	924	327
6–10	641	700	587	640	308	143	250	34	76	19
11 and over	361	200	95	30	13	5	36	--	7	--
Females										
None	20	14	25	25	30	27	87	76	74	79
1–2	26	20	44	23	10	9	13	11	8	9
3–5	16	--	--	--	--	--	--	--	--	--
6–10	--	--	--	--	--	--	--	--	--	--
11 and over	--	--	--	--	--	--	--	--	--	--

Source: Prisons Department, Freetown
Extracted from the 1990 edition of the *Annual Statistical Digest*

penological approach to crime reporting has the serious limitation of not revealing either the seriousness of crime in Sierra Leone, or its demographical and ecological distribution.

Some criminologists doubt that the best available indices of crime rates are "crimes known to the police" (Hagan, 1987; Siegel, 1989), and the state of affairs in Sierra Leone would thoroughly justify this doubt. Poor police-community relations and a lack of adequate resources for the detection and investigation of crime allow numerous crimes to go unreported and undetected. In addition, strong socio-cultural attitudes and beliefs in traditional indigenous culture militate against the reporting and detection of crimes such as ritual murder and cannibalism. In the case of white collar and economic crimes, crime reporting and detection are constrained by political influence, status, power, and affluence. Another real constraint is fear of retaliation or reprisal by the offender in such cases as rape, incest, and assault with intent to ravish. Many in Sierra Leone, furthermore, believe the police force to be one of the most corrupt institutions in the country, and this can influence both how the police report crime and how they record it. Police have been accused of under-reporting of crime, and of deliberately obliterating evidence that a report was made and recorded.

Due to these constraints, this crime profile has been based largely on the ethnographic observations and perceptions of the author as a member of Sierra Leone society and a former Judge of that country's High Court. It will interpret empirical indicators such as (a) media accounts of crime, (b) government releases on the crime problem, (c) public concern over crime, and (d) pressures for legislative reform of the criminal law. Ethnographic observational data gathering is, of course, subjective; but such qualitative research can be used to substantiate criminological explanations for the causes and incidence of crime.

It is both fair and accurate to say that crime continues to escalate in Sierra Leone. The trend goes back to the late 1960s, and derives mainly from the major socio-economic changes that have taken place in that country since independence. Conventional crimes continue to be highly visible and are committed by both adults and juveniles. Specifically, one sees significant acceleration in murder, manslaughter, rape, wounding with intent, causing grievous bodily harm, child abuse, robbery with aggravation, robbery with violence, simple robbery, burglary, housebreaking, simple larceny, and receiving stolen property. Since the 1970s, the rise in violent crime has generated much anxiety, fear, and insecurity in the Sierra Leone population.

Any criminological inquiry into criminal behavior and tendencies in contemporary Sierra Leone, especially any dealing with personal or property crimes, must take into account the key role of socio-economic factors. Crime rates in Sierra Leone have no consistent correlation with punishment, whether viewed from a retributive, a deterrent, or a rehabilitative perspective. The level of criminality can be better explained and understood in the context of whether people: (i) protect, or have the means to protect, themselves from felonious acts; and (ii) secure, or have the means to secure, their property from damage or loss.

Crime rates may also have escalated in Sierra Leone because local government authorities are not able to provide the basic infrastructural security facilities which would allow citizens to go about their daily business without threats to their life, liberty, and property. Other factors include (a) the lack of discipline at home and at school, (b) unemployment and (c) housing conditions.

In the mid-seventies, armed robbery, robbery with aggravation, and robbery with violence reached peak levels in Sierra Leone and caused such widespread panic that the government resorted, for the first time in its history, to enacting the death penalty. Armed robbery and robbery with aggravation became offenses punishable by death, but the wording of the statute became problematic in application, with much legal controversy over its legislative intent—specifically, over whether the prescribed penalty of death by firing squad was mandatory or discretionary. Sentences imposed by the courts varied between these two schools of thought, and the matter was never judicially settled. Many of these crimes were perpetrated by two notorious youth gangs which acted under such names as "The Black December," or "The Black September." These gangs especially perpetrated felony murders, and two cases in particular provoked much public revulsion and made national headlines: the "Wellington Street Murder Case" and the "Mammy Yoko Street Murder Case." After full-scale police investigations, no effort was spared in bringing the perpetrators to justice.

Another personal crime rampant in some parts of the indigenous communities in Sierra Leone is ritual murder. From the author's knowledge (having himself successfully prosecuted charges of ritual murder), this type of homicide is committed out of some strong socio-cultural misperceptions that ritual killings promote the welfare of the group, family, clan or community and are instrumental in gaining power and leadership. Two recent and notorious cases of ritual murder in Sierra Leone were "State v. Alimamy Khazali" and the "Bureh Town Ritual Murder Case."

In addition to the increase in conventional crime, white collar, corporate and economic crimes predominate in Sierra Leone today, although statistics, as usual, are hard to come by. "White-collar crime" refers to offenses committed by individuals for self-enrichment in the course of their occupations and to offenses of employees against their employers. In this sense, the term is being used synonymously with "occupational crime" (Hagan, 1987); "corporate crime," on the

other hand, consists in offenses by the corporation itself. "Economic crime" refers to any non-violent, illegal activity which principally involves deceit, misrepresentation, concealment, manipulation, breach of trust, subterfuge, or illegal circumvention (Clifford, 1977). Empirical indicators show that white collar crimes became noticeable after independence, escalated in the seventies, and reached crisis proportions in the eighties.

Specifically, over the last two decades there has been a marked rise in crimes committed within and against the bureaucracies of Sierra Leone. Such crimes have especially detrimental effects on allocation and utilization of public resources, derived from both internal and external sources; and on socio-economic development, particularly in relation to agriculture, housing, trade, health, education, and similar projects. In the recent past, such funds have been embezzled practically into non-existence. White collar and economic criminality reached epidemic proportions in the late 1970s and early 1980s and culminated in the unearthing by the police of a huge fraud conspiracy within the civil service, later described as the "Vouchergate Fraud Cases."

It would be an oversimplification, then, to explain crime in contemporary Sierra Leone by reference to a single cause theory. Patterns of criminal behavior in that country rather seem to reflect a peculiar combination and interaction of these various factors: (i) the process of modernization and its socio-economic dislocations, (ii) traditional cultural attitudes and beliefs, (iii) social ties and networks based on the extended family system (these account in part for the high level of white-collar-type criminality), (iv) the inefficiencies of the criminal justice system, (v) non-legitimacy and political manipulation of the British style legal system, and (vi) lack of knowledge and interest in criminology as a social science.

Organization and Functioning
of the Criminal Justice System

In Sierra Leone, the task of preventing and combating crime is assigned to three institutions which together constitute the criminal justice system. They are the police, the criminal courts, and the prison system. Basically, their organization, structures, and functions are patterned after the English criminal justice system. In Sierra Leone, as in England, the police are the first agency with whom a person suspected of crime comes into contact.

The Police

It is difficult to understand the existing structure of the Sierra Leone Police Force without some historical insights into its origins. Right from its inception, the system of law enforcement in Sierra Leone has always been patterned after the British model of policing, though it would be incorrect to suggest that policing in the country currently functions at the same level of sophistication, expertise, and efficiency usually associated with the British model. Lack of modernization is one of the main weaknesses of law enforcement in Sierra Leone.

Conceptually, however, the Sierra Leone Police Force still much resembles its colonial beginnings. It dates back to 1829 when twenty-six constables, half of whom kept order by day and the other half by night, were appointed in Freetown. By 1836, the core of a modern civil police force, consisting of an inspector, three sub-inspectors, and sixty constables, had emerged. The senior officers were usually drafted from a pool of retired military non-commissioned officers or civilian volunteers. The force maintained law and order in Freetown and in the villages of what was then called the "Colony" (now the "Western Area").

In 1861, the British annexed Koya and Sherbro Island to Sierra Leone, thus making a greater measure of law enforcement and an increase in manpower necessary. The need was met by combined deployment of garrisoned troops and the police force. When the troops were withdrawn, the police became solely responsible for the maintenance of law and order in the colony. In order to provide the police force with some military training, the commanding officer of the garrison in Freetown was appointed Inspector General of Police, and the force was housed in police barracks, armed with carbines, and given uniforms of white tunics and slacks with broad leather belts. At that time, the numerical strength of the force was two hundred. As the colony expanded, the police force took on the additional role of guard duties at the frontiers. In 1891 they were relieved by the newly formed Frontier Police.

In October 1894, the civil police was designated the Sierra Leone Police Force for the first time in the government *Gazette*. With the formation of a police band in 1900, the total strength of the force reached six hundred. In September 1909, Superintendent Brook became the first Commissioner of the Force. He is credited with having formed a special riot squad to deal with civil disturbances.

In 1948, the force was enlarged to one thousand under a new police commissioner. Africans were promoted to the rank of assistant superintendent.

In 1951, the Sierra Leone Police Force became affiliated with Interpol. The riot squad was disbanded, and every police officer began to receive instructions in riot control. In September 1954, the force was extended to the main towns of the protectorate, replacing the disbanded court messenger forces. The first police woman was recruited in 1947. At independence, the police force had developed into a well-established, efficient law enforcement institution.

By late 1975 the overall numerical strength of the force (including all ranks) was about 3,900. The highest ranking officer in the force, Police Commissioner

Kaetu-Smith, like the military Force Commander, was a member of the legislature and a minister of state without portfolio, reflecting the high priority which the government placed on internal security and defense matters.

Unlike its British model, the Sierra Leone force is centralized, a true national police service, and its management and control has always been the responsibility of the central government. The force is organized into five geographical divisions, including one for the special protection of the country's diamond industry. Each regional division is sub-divided into a number of branches and departments which include mainly the Criminal Investigation Department (CID), a special branch, and a traffic division. The CID is the elite corps, responsible (like the U.S. Federal Bureau of Investigation) for the detection and investigation of serious crimes. In the 1970s and 1980s, the CID, under Commissioner of Police (later Inspector General) Bambay Kamara, was a highly organized and efficient branch of the force. Its detection and investigation of serious violent crimes used skills comparable to those employed by Scotland Yard.

Under specific statutory powers granted by the Police Act of 1964 and the Criminal Procedure Act of 1965, the police force in Sierra Leone has responsibility to: (i) maintain law and order and protect persons and property; (ii) prevent crime; (iii) detect and investigate crime; (iv) arrest criminal suspects with or without a warrant on reasonable cause; (v) control road traffic; and (vi) decide whether or not to bring charges against persons suspected of criminal offenses. In addition, pursuant to the Law Officers' Act of 1965 and under the direction of the Director of Public Prosecutions, they have responsibility for the conduct of prosecutions for less serious offenses, especially minor traffic violations. They also introduce evidence before magistrates' courts in preliminary hearings into felony charges. Some question whether the police in contemporary Sierra Leone make reasonable and fair use of their discretionary powers of arrest, search, seizure, and bringing charges against persons suspected of crime.

During the period of APC (All People's Congress, a political party) rule, policemen were frequently accused of abusing and misusing their powers of arrest, search, and seizure. It was also said that they solicited and accepted bribes or other favors from crime suspects or from agents or relations in exchange for leniency, and that they executed their duties in a manner that showed strong political biases and other extraneous influences. There are no empirical studies to support or refute these criticisms. Based on this author's official knowledge, the Sierra Leone police are not entirely without merit, and their errors and miscarriages in law enforcement can be explained in terms of (i) very low educational levels, (ii) lack of professional standards and ethics, (iii) very low wages, and (v) extremely low morale.

Recruits for the Sierra Leone police wisely have been drawn from all parts of the country. The majority of policemen in Sierra Leone have either elementary or junior high school educations, have passed a physical fitness test, and have graduated from the Police Training School at Hastings after six months' training. At the completion of their training, they are usually appointed constables and given housing in the barracks (those who cannot be accommodated in barracks receive special housing allowances). Post-independence governments have adopted a policy of recruiting senior high school and university graduates into the officer ranks. Recruits at this level still are sent to the United Kingdom for advanced training because no such facilities exist in Sierra Leone. After this training, they are appointed to the force as assistant superintendents for six months of practical work. Successful candidates are then promoted to existing vacancies or wait for openings. At the present time, the force is headed by an Inspector General, a Sierra Leonean lawyer who served at the officer level prior to passing the bar.

Apart from the regular police force, Sierra Leone has a Special Security Division (SSD). It is a reorganized and restructured version of the Internal Security Unit (ISU) set up in the early 1970s by the APC government. This force originally performed presidential guard duties, but later developed into a special countersubversive security force available for deployment during periods of internal disturbance and civil unrest.

The Criminal Courts

Scholars of Sierra Leone's legal history and constitutional law agree that the history of the administration of justice in the country dates back to the foundation of the settlement in 1787 by English philanthropists. Since that time, adjudication and judicial settlement of public disorders and private disputes has been administered according to the principles of English law. The first Chief Justice, Mr. Charles Stoddart, was appointed in 1788, and when Freetown was granted municipal status the mayor and aldermen of the municipality were constituted judges of the civil courts, while the governor and councillors were the colony's criminal court judges. Trial by jury, a core component of the adversarial system of justice, began during those early years of the settlement.

By 1925, courts of Tribal Rulers had developed, and also the Police Magistrate Court of Freetown, the Courts of the District Commissioners of the Bonthe and Headquarters judicial districts, the Coroner's Court, the Supreme Court, the Full Court of Appeal, and the Judicial Committee of the Privy Council (an English tribunal in London with final appellate authority for the British colonies).

The existing judicial structure reflects, as already noted, a dual system of justice, with general law (British oriented) courts and customary law or local courts. Both the historical and contemporary development of the general law courts have been shaped largely by the common law tradition of England. The local courts are essentially indigenous in character. Their evolution continues to be influenced by the country's tradition of customary norms and values, though efforts are being made to modernize their procedures. Like the English courts, the general law courts of Sierra Leone are organized on the basis of jurisdiction (by geography, subject-matter, and hierarchy) and on the basis of venue, with adjudicated cases confined to specified political boundaries (a metropolitan or urban area, a village or group of villages, a district or group of districts). Judicial business in Sierra Leone reflects the familiar English common law bifurcation between civil and criminal disputes.

The criminal courts are the linchpin of the criminal justice system and have responsibility for the trial, conviction, and sentencing of persons accused of crime. In addition to the geographical limitations on their jurisdictions, the powers of criminal law courts may be either limited or general in terms of subject-matter, and either original or appellate. Presently, the country has a five-tier court system exercising criminal jurisdiction.

Local Courts

At the bottom of the hierarchy are the local courts with limited jurisdiction. These adjudicate minor criminal cases, especially those involving customary law issues where the maximum penalty is imprisonment for one year or a fine of six hundred leones or both. Elders of the local area who are proficient in customary law preside, and their decisions are subject to review by the Customary Law Officer, who acts not formally as a court but in a quasi-judicial capacity. Despite the absence of statistics, it can be said that these courts dispose of a significant volume of minor criminal cases involving customary law throughout the country, because the vast majority of Sierra

Leoneans are rural people who willingly live their daily lives in accordance with customary law.

Magistrate Courts

Next in the hierarchy are the magistrates' courts. They too are courts of limited jurisdiction, but have both original and appellate functions. They are courts of record and judges of both facts and law, and in their capacity as original courts, they perform three main roles. These roles are based on the modern classification of criminal offenses into: (1) indictable offenses that must be tried on indictment before a jury (all very serious crimes are in this category); (2) indictable offenses that can be tried either on indictment or in magistrates' courts; (3) offenses that are both indictable and summary; (4) summary offenses in which the defendant can demand trial on indictment; and (5) summary offenses triable only in magistrates' courts.

On the basis of the foregoing classification, the first and chief role of magistrates' courts in Sierra Leone is the hearing and disposition of lesser criminal charges punishable by a maximum imprisonment of three years or a fine not exceeding one thousand leones or both. This summary function was extended in 1973 to include perjury or subornation of perjury under the Perjury Act of 1911 and reckless driving as defined in the Road Traffic Act of 1964.

Summary jurisdiction, a second role of the first instance magistrates' courts of Sierra Leone, comes into play when a person is charged with an offense punishable by a maximum penalty of seven years or a fine not exceeding three thousand leones. If the court so determines, the defendant can opt at preliminary hearing to be tried summarily instead of on indictment. The magistrate will then hear and dispose of the case in accordance with the summary trial law.

In the course of a summary trial, magistrates' courts may commit a defendant to be tried on indictment if the circumstances of the case so warrant or on the grounds of some aggravating or compelling factor. This function is especially useful when statutes create offenses which specify the maximum penalty for conviction summarily and the maximum penalty for conviction on indictment. Legislation of this type clearly makes the crime both summary and indictable, but leaves the courts with no guidance for determining whether a particular case should be tried summarily or on indictment. In one case, the legislature of Sierra Leone conferred special jurisdiction on magistrates' courts in 1977 and 1981 over offenses committed within the country's territorial waters, or in any port, harbor, wharf, or airport. They now have power to try persons charged with such offenses and punish them, on conviction, with a maximum of five years' imprisonment or a fine of up to twenty-five thousand leones or both. This is an example of legislation making a crime both a summary and an indictable offense because it gives the court discretionary power to determine whether to try the case summarily or on indictment. (A magistrates' court cannot exercise this power if it is staffed by lay justices of the peace.)

The magistrates' courts also play a third key role, holding preliminary investigations into felony charges. This is a very important task, because it determines whether a person charged with the commission of a serious crime is to face trial in the High Court or have the charge dismissed. Decisions are made on the basis of whether there is sufficient or *prima facie* evidence to warrant a committal. Where there is no such evidence, the court will dismiss the case and discharge the defendant. The procedure is analogous to that of the preliminary hearing and the grand jury in the United States. Magistrates' courts in Sierra Leone have, since their inception, committed for trial or indictment for such charges as treason, sedition, murder, manslaughter, wounding, causing grievous bodily harm, rape, robbery, burglary, larceny, forgery, and conspiracy to defraud.

Unlike some countries, there are no separate Justice of the Peace Courts in Sierra
Leone, but these lay officials do play an important role within the country's criminal
justice system. They sit in a magisterial capacity, and, generally, carry out the same
functions as legally qualified magistrates.
Their sentencing power, however, is limited: they cannot impose fines in excess of
three hundred leones or imprisonment for
more than a year. One important aspect of
the criminal jurisdiction of lay magistrates
is adjudicating juvenile offenses (a subject
addressed later in this chapter). It is
thought that non-legally qualified magistrates bring to the administration of juvenile criminal justice a much needed lay
perspective.

There are not less than twenty-five magistrates' courts in Sierra Leone, one in each
of the six districts which make up the
Northern and Southern Provinces respectively, three in the Eastern Province, and
about ten in the Western Area. (The uncertainty in the number of magistrates'
courts in Sierra Leone today is a result of
the creation of new magisterial districts by
the new regime of a military government
that assumed power on April 29, 1992.)
They carry the bulk of the criminal workload within the country's criminal justice
system. Respect for the law and confidence in the legal system in Sierra Leone
often are linked with the adjudication of
cases in the magistrates' courts. This is because their function as appelate courts
provides the first intersection between the
customary justice system and the general
law courts system. As District Appeal
Courts, they hear and determine appeals
from decisions of local courts, ascertain-
ing whether the court below applied the
relevant rule of custom correctly to the
facts of the case and whether, on the whole,
the case was heard fairly. In exceptional
cases the *de novo* procedure allows them
to rehear an entire case, admitting additional witnesses who did not testify in the
lower court. Appeal to the magistrates'
courts is automatic following an automatic

stay of execution of the decision of the
lower court for a period of fifteen days.
Unlike procedure in local courts, attorneys have a right of audience before
District Appeal Courts, which consist of
the magistrate for the district sitting with
two assessors selected from a list of experts
in customary law drawn up by the District
Officer. District Appeal Courts dispose of
a substantial number of criminal appeals
emanating from the local courts. In light
of the review jurisdiction of the District
Appeal Courts, it is debatable whether the
review authority of the Customary Law
Officer over the decisions of local courts
is desirable or necessary to retain.
Magistrates are appointed by the Judicial
and Legal Service Commission and are (except for lay magistrates) legally qualified
and salaried.

The High Court

The next court in the hierarchy of criminal courts in Sierra Leone is the High
Court. By far the most important forum in
the structure, the High Court together with
the Court of Appeal and the Supreme Court
constitute the superior Court of Judicature
of the State of Sierra Leone. The High Court
is a court of records with general jurisdiction. Its powers are original, appellate, and
supervisory. As an original court, it hears
and determines all types of criminal cases,
especially those involving treason and
such serious felony charges as sedition,
murder, manslaughter, rape, robbery, burglary, larceny, forgery, and conspiracy to
defraud. The cases are usually tried by
judge and jury; and, exceptionally, by
judge alone (on the *ex parte* application of
the Director of Public Prosecutions). The
work of the High Court is centered in the
Western Area, but there is a High Court for
the Southern Province, another in the
Eastern Province, and an itinerant High
Court Judge for the Northern Province. In
exercising its original criminal jurisdiction, the court is constituted by a single
judge or by a judge and jury.

The High Court also hears and determines appeals from decisions of magistrates' courts, given either as trial courts of limited jurisdiction or as District Appeal Courts. The appeal procedure reviews the decision of the lower court to determine whether relevant law was correctly interpreted and applied to the facts of the case, and scrutinizes the records of the lower court's hearing to ensure that the proceedings were conducted fairly and properly. The High Court may also inquire whether the court below wrongly admitted or excluded evidence. As an appellate tribunal, the court can (a) dismiss an appeal, (b) overturn a conviction and set aside its sentence, (c) dismiss an appeal and leave a sentence unaltered or impose a substitute sentence, (d) order a retrial, or (e) substitute an alternative conviction (e.g., attempt to commit the crime, or commission of a different crime) for the conviction given in the lower court.

When the court hears appeals from a District Appeal Court, it is designated a Local Appeals Division of the High Court and constituted by a single judge with two assessors selected by him or her from a list of experts in customary law drawn up by the Customary Law Officer.

In its supervisory capacity, the High Court has authority in any given case 1) to force a magistrates' court to accomplish an act which is legally required of it by an order of *mandamus*, 2) to require a magistrates' court to send up the records of its proceedings for review by an order of *certiorari*, or 3) to require the court below to refrain from proceeding with a matter not within its jurisdiction by an order of *prohibition*. The most important additional order in the supervisory legal armory of the High Court is the writ of *habeas corpus*, by which it can inquire into the legality of the detention of any person in Sierra Leone.

In the Western Area, the High Court is continuously in session except for the vacation period which runs from July 17 to September 17. In the provinces, the sessions are not continuous, varying from two to three a year. In the Western Area, two or three courts sit separately, and there may be three courts sitting simultaneously; in the provinces, only one court sits. The cases—most of them committed by the magistrates' courts after a preliminary hearing—come before the courts in an order known as the "criminal calendar" for each session.

Exceptionally, there may be cases on the "Criminal Calendar" which have been sent up for trial on ex-officio *ex parte* information from the Attorney General and Minister of Justice or from the Director of Public Prosecutions. This procedure is often invoked in cases with a political complexion, like treason, and in huge fraud cases involving heavy financial losses to the government. It is also used in felony murder cases, where an expeditious trial best serves the ends of justice. Virtually all serious crimes are tried by the High Court. High Court judges are legally qualified and are appointed by the President on the advice of the Judicial and Legal Service Commission, subject to the approval of Parliament. Such appointments are usually made from the pool of State Attorneys employed by the government and from members of the private bar. An attorney who currently aspires to High Court judgeship must have at least 10 years' professional standing (formerly it was five years). All Superior Court judges hold office pending good behavior. They may opt to retire at age 60, but must retire at age 65. The High Court consists of at least 10 judges.

Court of Appeal

The Court of Appeal is the intermediate appellate tribunal in the general law courts system in Sierra Leone. As a criminal court, it hears and determines appeals from decisions and orders of the High Court. Because it is practically the final appellate court for most criminal appeals arising out of decisions of the High Court, especially in exercise of its original jurisdiction over felony cases, its workload is tremendous. In most cases, appeal is automatic. As a review tribunal, the court determines whether the High Court interpreted and applied the law applicable to the facts of the case correctly; and, after an examination of the records of High Court proceedings, whether the trial was conducted properly; or, in the case of an appeal, whether it was heard fairly. It can also inquire into whether evidence was improperly admitted or excluded.

After hearing an appeal, the Court of Appeal can (a) dismiss the appeal, (b) overturn the conviction and set aside the sentence, (c) dismiss the appeal and leave the sentence unaltered or impose a substituted sentence, (d) order a retrial, or (e) substitute an alternative conviction (e.g., attempt to commit the crime or commission of a different crime). When dismissing an appeal, the court can claim that, though there is merit in the point or points of law raised on appeal, yet no substantial miscarriage of justice occurred. As in England, but not as in America, this statutory power safeguards against the use of legal technicalities to overturn convictions on appeal, especially where the evidence overwhelmingly points to the guilt of the defendant.

The Court is constituted by three Justices, with the most senior presiding, for the normal business of hearing an appeal; but by a single Justice in respect of interlocutory matters. Justices of Appeal are legally qualified and are usually appointed from the pool of judges on the High Court bench on the basis of seniority rather than merit. In exceptional cases, an appointment may be made directly from the team of government lawyers or the private bar. As already noted, all superior court judges in Sierra Leone are appointed by the President on the advice of the Judicial and Legal Service Commission, subject to the approval of Parliament. Current aspirants for the position of Justice of Appeal must have at least 15 years' professional standing (formerly it was seven years). The Court of Appeal consists of at least eight Justices.

Supreme Court

The Supreme Court of Sierra Leone is the highest judicial organ in the country. Its jurisdiction is mainly appellate and limited to the hearing and determination of civil and criminal appeals from the Court of Appeal. In exercise of its criminal appellate jurisdiction, the Court hears and disposes only of a limited number of appeals largely dictated by the Court itself and the Court of Appeal. In Sierra Leone, a defendant who is dissatisfied with a decision of the Court of Appeal in a criminal appeal can either opt by right to appeal the decision directly to the Supreme Court or, if the case involves a substantial question of law or is of public importance, he or she can seek permission from the Court of Appeal itself to appeal its decision. He or she can also obtain special permission from the Supreme Court to appeal against any decision of the Court of Appeal. But in recent times the Court has insisted that defendants not under an imposed death penalty first apply to the Court of Appeal for permission to appeal its decision before they file an appeal in the Supreme Court or seek its special permission to do so. By this practice, the Court limits itself to hearing and determining only those criminal appeals that raise substantial questions of law or are of significant public interest. Because of this limitation, the court disposes of only five to 15 criminal appeals a year.

The Supreme Court also exercises supervisory jurisdiction over all other courts in the country through procedures similar to the *certiorari, mandamus,* and *prohibition* proceedings of the English House of Lords and the United States Supreme Court. It also has original jurisdiction, to the exclusion of all other courts, (i) in all matters relating to the interpretation and enforcement of the constitution and (ii) where any question arises whether an enactment is *ultra vires.* Also, any citizen of Sierra Leone who alleges that any of his or her constitutional rights or freedoms has been, or is being, or is likely to be, violated, can apply directly to the Supreme Court for redress. These two functions are far reaching, but they certainly fall short of the substantive judicial review power which the U.S. Supreme Court possesses; nevertheless, they do act as significant due process safeguards.

The court is constituted for regular judicial business, whether appellate or original, by five Justices, including the Chief Justice (or, in his or her absence, the most senior Justice) acting as president. When hearing interlocutory matters, a single Justice sits. Justices of the Supreme Court are legally qualified and are usually appointed from Justices of the Court of Appeal, emphasis being placed on seniority rather than merit. Exceptionally, an appointment may be made from the team of government lawyers or the private bar.

The Chief Justice and other judges of the Supreme Court are appointed by the President on the advice of the Judicial and Legal Service Commission and subject to the approval of Parliament (the advice requirements are recent additions). The position of Chief Justice is pre-eminent, with the candidate being chosen from among persons qualified to be Supreme Court justices. Present candidates for the position of Justice of the Supreme Court must have at least 20 years of professional standing (formerly it was 10 years). The Supreme Court consists of at least five Justices. During the period of APC rule, those appointed to the position of Chief Justice would be judges with considerable political leverage.

The Prison System

Like the other components of the criminal justice system, correctional institutions in Sierra Leone are fashioned after the British model with variations appropriate to local conditions. The main correctional facility in the country—the Freetown Central Prison—is indeed a relic of outmoded English penological theory, with an architectural design reminiscent of correctional institutions in late-eighteenth-century England. Since independence, there has

been no major attempt to alter or modify the architectural design of that correctional institution.

The administration of correctional services in Sierra Leone falls within the responsibilities of the Minister of Social Welfare, but the services are centered in Freetown, the capital city, under the direction and supervision of the Director of Prisons. There are several provincial correctional facilities, including Bo, Makeni, Kabala, Kailahun, Sefadu, Mafanta, and Masanki. Ideally, and by statute, prison inmates are to be grouped and segregated according to sex, age, those awaiting trial, and those already convicted. Except for the Freetown facility, there are no correctional facilities in the country providing for complete physical segregation of male and female inmates, and females sentenced in the provinces ought normally to be transferred to Freetown, but in practice this does not happen. In a developing society like Sierra Leone, where economic resources are very scarce, funds for the improvement of correctional institutions will necessarily receive very low priority. Hence, the system does not reflect the traditional English classification of prisons into local, short-term training, medium-term training, and long-term training. In 1976 the National Development Plan envisaged the expansion of the main provincial facilities to accommodate more inmates. There was also provision for the development of industries in the Freetown Central Prison. But these plans were never fully implemented because they lacked adequate funding.

The key philosophy underlying the prison system in Sierra Leone is that inmates must either work or learn basic skills, the emphasis being on rehabilitation. Judges in Sierra Leone, however, focus on retributive justice in their sentencing practices. During the period of incarceration, inmates are taught such trades as carpentry, tailoring, shoemaking, printing, bricklaying, weaving, and painting. Courses are also given in basic reading and writing. Funds are not presently available to secure necessary new and additional equipment and machinery for teaching these trades and skills.

As with the police force, recruits in the prison service are drawn from all parts of the country. The majority of prison personnel have either an elementary or a junior high school education, and have passed a physical fitness test. As an incentive for highly educated persons to enter the prison service, successive governments since independence have adopted recruiting policies favoring senior high school and university graduates. After some in-service training, these specially recruited officers are appointed to the rank of assistant superintendent, with the opportunity of being promoted to ranks such as Chief Superintendent, Assistant Deputy Director, Deputy Director, and Director.

Prison sentences in Sierra Leone range from one month to life imprisonment depending on the nature and gravity of the offense. Persons convicted of treason, murder, armed robbery, and robbery with aggravation may be sentenced to death.

There are also special correctional facilities for juvenile offenders. The issue of prisoners' rights in Sierra Leone has never raised much controversy, except as a result of criticisms emanating from Amnesty International on the issue of political detainees.

Juvenile Justice

In Sierra Leone, juvenile justice is regulated by the Children and Young Person Act of 1945. The juvenile justice process in the country is based on the British model, and focuses on rehabilitation with a social welfare emphasis. Two main goals are pursued—first, to fulfill the needs of juveniles for care, protection, and supervision. When a juvenile is found wandering, and seems not to have any home, settled place of abode, or visible means of existence, he or she may be brought before a juvenile court in Sierra Leone as one in need of care

and protection. The second main goal of the juvenile justice agencies is to protect society against juveniles who violate the criminal law and threaten the fabric of society. A juvenile found guilty of an offense punishable, in the case of an adult, with imprisonment, may be committed to the custody of an approved school until age 18 or for a shorter period of time.

The agencies responsible for addressing the problem of juvenile delinquency in Sierra Leone are the legislature, the courts, the police, prosecutors, defense attorneys, prison, probation officers, approved schools, and remand homes. The Children and Young Persons Act of 1945 and following amendments give statutory provisions defining the scope of the legal authority of these agencies, prescribing procedures for the determination of guilt and for the hearing and disposing of juvenile cases. The term "juvenile," is defined to include both the "child" and the "young person," a child being under age 14 and a young person being between ages 14 and 17.

As in most countries, the bifurcation of the system of justice into juvenile and adult proceedings in Sierra Leone manifests itself in two sets of institutions and procedures with distinct goals and objectives: one set addresses juvenile delinquency and the other adult criminality. This is part of the British common law heritage. But although the juvenile justice system does have formal goals and procedures, its processes tend in practice to be more flexible and informal due to the large element of discretion granted to agencies handling juvenile cases.

On the whole, juvenile proceedings differ from adult proceedings in certain significant respects. The age boundary between the juvenile justice system and the criminal justice system for adults is 17 years. Generally, the language of adult proceedings, with its denunciatory connotations and stigmatizing effect, is not used in juvenile proceedings. When a juvenile is adjudged guilty or not guilty, reference is not made to a "conviction," a "sentence," or an "acquittal," but to an "order" (the only exception is homicide, in which case a juvenile is tried as an adult). Unlike in the United States, magistrates hearing criminal charges against juveniles (who are not charged with adults) sit in different buildings or rooms from those used for ordinary court sittings. Except for homicide, a child is not sentenced to imprisonment. The same applies to a young person, unless the court finds no other statutory disposition suitable. Again, except for homicide, policy dictates that an imprisoned young person should be segregated from adult prisoners.

The entire panoply of due process safeguards afforded the defendant in adult criminal proceedings are not available in juvenile proceedings. Juvenile court hearings take place *in camera* (meaning, in a judge's private room or place; in a private place, not in public), and only members and officers of the court, relatives of the defendant, parties to the case, their attorneys, and other persons directly concerned are allowed to be present. Other persons cannot attend except with the permission of the court. The court can grant special permission to credentialed representatives of the press to attend. Strict statutory requirements preclude the disclosure of the name, school, or any other identifying information of the youth except with the permission of the court.

When a juvenile is adjudged as having committed a crime, the court will hear evidence of the juvenile's character, antecedents, home life, occupation and health so as to determine what disposition should be made in the juvenile's best interest. So long as a juvenile has been adjudged guilty of an offense other than homicide, the court may make such custodial or noncustodial orders as: (i) a conditional discharge on the juvenile's own recognizance, with or without sureties, to be of good behavior; (ii) a fine, compensation or costs order against the parent or guardian, or against the juvenile, where the parent or guardian cannot be located or did

not condone the crime; (iii) that the juvenile be repatriated to his or her home or district of origin; (iv) a release to the custody of a fit person or institution; and (v) a release to the custody of an approved school. The court may also order that any custodial or noncustodial measure be supervised by a court appointed probation officer.

Juvenile courts in Sierra Leone also dispose of cases involving status offenses, acts done by juveniles which, by virtue of the offender's status as a child or young person, may require care, protection and supervisory jurisdiction from the juvenile justice system. Status offenses include begging or receiving alms; wandering without home or settled place of abode; and falling into such bad associations as the company of a reputed thief or a common prostitute. This jurisdiction also extends to cases where the juvenile is a victim of acts such as parental abuse, neglect, abandonment or being in the custody of a parent or guardian who is criminally disposed or who is violent and alcoholic. Juveniles who are so victimized may be made wards of the court. In such cases, the court may order (i) that the juvenile be sent to an approved school; (ii) that the juvenile be committed to the care of a fit person, whether a relative or not, or to an institution; or (iii) that his or her parent or guardian guarantee to give him or her proper care and guardianship.

As in England and the United States, there are both pretrial and trial juvenile procedures in Sierra Leone. Pretrial procedures are called referrals, and are essentially an intake process. Although no supporting statistics are available, it is evident that referrals to the juvenile court in Sierra Leone have increased over the years because of the country's economic decline. Most referrals come from the police. Parents and relatives rarely make referrals except as a last option, an attitude rooted in both the European and the African strands of Sierra Leone culture and tradition. A delinquent child brings moral opprobrium on the family, and it is thought that rehabilitation can be handled better within the fam-

ily than by legal and institutional procedures. After a referral, the court must make
three key decisions: (i) whether to detain an
arrested juvenile pending investigation of
the case, or to release him or her on bail on
his or her own recognizance or that of his
or her parents or guardian; (ii) whether or
not to file formal charges against him or her;
and, when it has been decided that the juvenile is in need of care, protection, and supervision, (iii) whether to file a formal
petition for any appropriate statutory order.
The fact that juveniles are not afforded the
same comprehensive set of due process
rights has not been controversial in Sierra
Leone. Essentially, juveniles are afforded
the right to bail; the right to cross-examine
prosecution witnesses; the right of appeal;
and the right to an attorney—but unlike in
the United States, not at the expense of the
State.

Some key aspects of trial procedures
have already been covered in this section
especially as regards to *in camera* nature
of juvenile proceedings, and the specific
orders which the court can make both in
exercise of its criminal jurisdiction and in
the context of the adjudication of status offenses. When a juvenile is charged with a
criminal offense other than homicide, the
substance of the charge is explained to him
or her in simple language. The court then
gives him or her an opportunity to explain
or else to admit to the allegation. If the juvenile's statement amounts to a plea of
guilty, the court will record that the charge
is proved. If the allegation is not confirmed,
or the explanation does not amount to a
guilty plea, the court will proceed to hear
the evidence of the prosecution witnesses.
At the close of the evidence of each witness, the court will ask the witness any
questions necessary and desirable to establish the truth of the allegation or test the
witness's credibility. The juvenile is also
given the opportunity to question the witness, and the court will make sure that this
is done, particularly when the juvenile is
unrepresented. When all the prosecution
evidence is in, the court will hear defense

evidence including any further statement
the juvenile may wish to make, if it finds
that a sufficient or *prima facie* case has
been made against the defendant.

In Sierra Leone today, there are three
penal facilities for juveniles. They are probation, approved schools, and remand
homes. They function under the control
and supervision of probation officers and
managers who are in turn supervised by the
court.

Conclusion

Criticisms of the social control mechanisms of criminal law and of criminal justice systems are inevitable because their
application concerns the extremely delicate and sensitive issue of marking boundaries between individual liberty and the
punitive power of the state. In many countries criminal law and criminal justice
processes are perceived as conservative,
and in the developing state of Sierra Leone,
it would be difficult to contest this gener-
alization. One historical reason adduced
for the current lack of a Sierra Leone criminal code is the opposition of a legal profession that has always prided itself in
uncritical adherence to the inherited common law system. The state of affairs is all
the more anomalous for the fact that Sierra
Leone has a permanent Law Reform
Commission whose specific functions are
to eliminate anomalies found in the law, to
repeal obsolete and outdated enactments,
to consolidate enactments, to introduce
and incorporate new areas of law, and to
modernize and update the law. In spite of
a truly elaborate and comprehensive mechanism for the reform of law in Sierra Leone,
some key catalysts for law reform are missing, to wit, a lively public opinion, an importunate press, and an insistent academic
legal community.

It is arguable, therefore, that criminal law
and the criminal justice system in Sierra
Leone are seriously in need of refurbishing.
This is necessary, if they are to achieve their

avowed goals and objectives as a social control mechanism, adjusting and responding to the rapidly changing socio-economic realities and attendant criminogenic effects in a developing society with a strong common law heritage. For instance, unlike in the United States and in England, there has been no major effort either to devise a rational body of criminal law or to reform in the light of new realities some of its underlying principles and specific offenses. Sierra Leone has no counterpart to the U.S. Model Penal Code or the English Theft Act of 1968. Change is needed, and a legion of issues critical to the functioning of the criminal justice system ought to be addressed; but for our purposes it will suffice to identify the main ones. They are: (1) whether or not the criminal jurisdiction of the local courts, whose adjudications are not based on due process, ought to be preserved; (2) the role of the jury in trials on indictment; (3) the effectiveness of the criminal justice system as a whole in dealing with crime; (4) the growth of white collar crime, and (5) the goals of juvenile justice.

With regard to whether the criminal jurisdiction of the local courts should be preserved, undoubtedly the ideal for any country is to have one law and one judicial system for everybody (Roberts-Wray, 1959). The bifurcated legal system of Sierra Leone preserves normative disparities by keeping the customary law jurisdiction and the general law jurisdiction separate, and such disparities can inhibit modernization and progress towards industrialization in a developing country. However, two potentially compatible forces are at work in the modern socio-legal setting of Sierra Leone. On one hand, inherited English law is undergoing constant adaptation and modification in response to the changing socio-economic realities of a pluralistic society which includes both the values of Western liberal democracy and indigenous African norms and beliefs. On the other hand, customary law rules are being refashioned and reformulated to ensure the rights and obliga-

tions of persons of indigenous culture. These complementary forces eventually may lead to the integration of the general law system with the customary system of justice (Thompson, 1991). The problem with this idea is that we cannot successfully eliminate a society's cultural values and standards entirely.

The second critical issue arising from the administration of criminal justice in Sierra Leone today concerns whether juries in trials on indictment perform their important duty effectively. The issue has neither been seriously addressed in recent times in the country, nor has it evoked much public concern. Nevertheless, in one or two isolated cases in the post-independence period jury verdicts have been suspected of being tainted or perverse, and the press has questioned the usefulness of the institution. This problem should be addressed, not by searching for a better system of trial, but by considering new rules for jury eligibility and qualification. It is well-known in Sierra Leone that the level of education of persons who qualify for jury service and who actually do serve as jurors seriously compromises the system. The need for reform here cannot be over-emphasized.

The criminal justice system of Sierra Leone, as presently organized, is clearly incapable of dealing with the country's escalating crime rates. The law, the courts, the police, and the correctional services currently do not have sufficient resources to address all the manifestations of criminal behavior. Street crimes, white collar crimes, corporate and economic crimes are epidemic. The criminal investigation department's various operational crime units certainly need increased manpower and logistical resources to do their jobs.

Furthermore, there is the malfunctioning of the heavily burdened criminal courts. Again we encounter the recurrent theme of scarcity of resources: criminal justice is not accorded a high place in governmental priorities. The courts have excessive caseloads, heavy backlogs, and protracted delays both in trials and in the hearing of appeals. The High Court typically spends three to six months adjudicating some ordinary felony cases; and two to three years can pass while trying difficult and complicated fraud cases. Cases on appeal never get determined more quickly than two to four years after they have been listed. On the trial level, vital witnesses, especially medical experts, may leave the country during protracted judicial delays, making prosecution when the case comes up for trial impossible. This happens frequently in homicide cases, where law requires the medical cause of the victim's death to be established conclusively. In the provinces, witnesses may not be able to attend trials due to scarcity of public transportation. It also should be noted that the criminal courts are often criticized for allegedly poor quality of justice and for failure to resist politicization of the criminal justice process.

The growth of white collar crime in Sierra Leone manifests not only a lack of political will to fight this brand of criminality, but also a lack of expertise in the criminal investigation department's fraud unit to unravel the complex financial malpractices that take place inside and against bureaucracies and corporate bodies. The difficulty is compounded by the powerful political connections often wielded by businessmen engaged in questionable commercial practices, and by the semblance of legitimacy they acquire from corrupt accountants and tax consultants.

Finally we address the critical issue of the goals of the juvenile justice system in Sierra Leone. As in most countries, juvenile justice in Sierra Leone can be properly characterized as the neglected sister, the "Cinderella" of the two justice systems. But Sierra Leone, unlike the United States and Britain, shows no concern about the future direction of juvenile justice. There has been no move to improve its process or to redefine its goals in the light of new realities, nor

have rises in juvenile deviance provoked any significant impetus in that direction.

Discussion and Revision Questions

1. Why are many crimes unreported and undetected in Sierra Leone?

2. What is ritual murder?

3. Which crimes predominate in Sierra Leone today?

4. Patterns of criminal behavior in Sierra Leone reflect a combination and interaction of many factors. What are these factors?

5. What is one of the major obstacles to effective law enforcement in Sierra Leone?

6. Name six major roles of the Sierra Leone Police Force.

7. What are the major criticisms against the police in Sierra Leone?

8. Compare and contrast the U.S. Supreme Court and the Supreme Court of Sierra Leone.

9. What is the main philosophy underlying the prison system in Sierra Leone?

10. Compare and contrast correctional ideology in Sierra Leone and Denmark; Sierra Leone and the United States.

11. Name five ways in which a juvenile offender can be treated in Sierra Leone.

12. Compare and contrast juvenile courts in Sierra Leone and the United States.

13. Thompson raised five issues of critical concern in the Sierra Leone justice system. What are they?

14. What is the role of the Law Reform Commission in Sierra Leone?

8

The Judiciary and Criminal Procedure in Nigeria

Obi N. I. Ebbe

Introduction

Criminal law creates both crime and the criminal; and crimes and criminals create in turn judiciary and criminal procedures. For indigenous Nigerian society, then, where all such criminal justice concepts are alien, there could be no judiciary and no criminal procedure. This will descriptively analyze the emergence of a Western judiciary and criminal procedure model in a formerly stateless society; how the new judicial system currently exists in symbiosis with customary law and procedure; and factors that have influenced the operation of the Western and Nigerian customary models.

Studying Nigerian judiciary and criminal procedures provides answers to why societies evolve from simple to complex, why rules change over time, and what impact a dual system of judiciary can have on societal order.

This chapter will give a brief history of how the concepts "crime" and "criminal law" emerged in Nigeria, and will also provide arrest and prosecution rates and offender disposal records. The account is based on this author's own ethnographic observations as a native of Nigeria, on his formal and informal knowledge of Nigerian history, and on a review of relevant literature on Nigerian judiciary and legal history.

Pre-English Legal System

Before its colonization in 1849, Nigeria was a stateless society made up of isolated clusters of "gemeinschafts" or communities. Some larger communities had kings, Emirs, Obas, chiefs, an elder, or a council of elders who judged disputes in the community. Relative order and solidarity prevailed in communities without a criminal or penal code.

Offenses in stateless Nigeria were conceived as abominations, taboos, offenses against the earth or deities or ancestors, and minor interpersonal victimizations. The highest authority in each community settled all interpersonal victimizations. Abominations, taboos, and offenses against earth, deities, and ancestors could be tried and disposed by the community as a whole according to the customs of the tribe. But none of these offenses was technically a "crime"; and the concept of criminality did not emerge in Nigeria until 1861.

The Emergence of the English Legal System

In 1849 the British annexed Lagos and declared it a colony (Lagos was the capital of Nigeria until 1992). In time, the British gained control over the whole of Nigeria, whose several parts were the colony and protectorate of Lagos, the protectorate of

Southern Nigeria, and the protectorate of Northern Nigeria. In 1861 a legislative council was created to control friendly and unfriendly populations, and to regulate business activities which included agents from many European and African countries (Burns, 1929; Niven, 1957; Dike, 1959; Arikpo, 1967).

The British consuls and the Royal Niger Company, who set up the legislative council, also established Courts of Justice and an armed constabulary to enforce laws and regulations. Between 1861 and 1874, ten different courts were created, only four of which were concerned with criminal matters: the Supreme Court/Police Magistrate Court, the Court of Civil and Criminal Justice, the West African Court of Appeal (WACA), and the Privy Council (Elias, 1963). The laws enacted by the colonial legislative council were based on laws, values, standards, and customs in England. It was during this period that the concept of "crime" emerged in Nigeria. In 1900 the British government took over direct administration of Nigeria from the Royal Niger Company, retaining all of the courts, laws, and regulations of the previous administration.

Nigeria has two codes of law and procedure, the Criminal Code and the Penal Code. How and why the two codes emerged will be discussed below.

The Criminal Code

In 1904, Lord Lugard, the colonial Governor of the Northern Protectorate of Nigeria, introduced a Criminal Code for the Northern Protectorate only (Elias, 1954; 1963; 1967; Nwabueze, 1963; Okonkwo and Naish, 1964; Adewoye, 1977). It was modeled closely on the code introduced into the State of Queensland, Australia, in 1899; and the Queensland Code was in turn based on a Criminal Code drafted by British Criminal Law attorney Sir James Fritzstephen, in Jamaica in 1878 (Arikpo, 1967; Oloyede, 1972). The Southern Protectorates of

Nigeria were amalgamated in 1906, and in 1914 the Southern Protectorates were amalgamated with the Protectorate of Northern Nigeria. Lord Lugard subsequently made the Criminal Code of 1904 applicable to all of the protectorates in Nigeria.

The Nigerian Criminal Code and its antecedent colonial documents were based on the values of the English common law tradition and not on the values of the people governed; furthermore, the members of the central Legislative Council who drafted and approved the Nigerian Criminal Code of 1904 were all of British origin (Elias, 1954; Ebbe, 1985a). Therefore, the first Nigerian Criminal Code was determined by the interests and standards of British officials, and by what would constitute a crime in Great Britain (Lugard, 1913). The Criminal Code provoked conflicts of norms among the citizens of Nigeria because it criminalized some customary practices and normative standards of the Nigerian people. For example, Section 370 of the Nigerian Criminal Code prescribes seven years' imprisonment for any person who marries another while his or her marriage partner is still living (Elias, 1954; 1972b; Ebbe, 1985a). According to this section of the Criminal Code, "Bigamy is the contracting of a second marriage during the lifetime of one's 'first' wife or husband. Section 35 of the Marriage Act declares such a second marriage as void, and there [are] penalty provisions in Section 47 and 48 of the Marriage Act" (Elias, 1954; 1972b). Section 370 of the Criminal Code was interpreted to mean that second marriages under Customary Law henceforward would be illegal.

The introduction of a bigamy statute into Nigeria was a gross error, and would not have been featured in the Nigerian Criminal Code if it had been based on "customs, customary beliefs, ideals, values, and taboos" of Nigerian society, as consensus theorists assumed. Culturally and traditionally, polygamy is a cherished tradition in Nigerian culture: a Nigerian who marries a second or a third wife gets a handshake, and a pat on the back, like a man who has scored a touchdown in American football. Furthermore, the Islamic Maliki Law, to which 49 percent of Nigerians are subject, allows its members a maximum of four wives (Ebbe, 1985a). After 35 years of political independence from Britain (1960–1995) and some amendments to the criminal code, Nigerians still have difficulties with its alien-based standards.

The Penal Code

In 1959, the current Nigerian Criminal Code ceased to apply to Northern Nigeria. Throughout the colonial era, the courts in the Northern region of Nigeria had been without personnel with professional training in English criminal law, and the British judges had experienced difficulties with the Emirs regarding offense and punishment differences between Islamic (Maliki) Law and English criminal law. As a result, a panel of jurists introduced a Penal Code that would take into account the interests, values, and standards of the Muslims (Adewoye, 1977; Nwabueze, 1963). The new Penal Code was based on the Sudanese Penal Code, because the Sudan's Muslim laws were similar to those of the Maliki Code in Northern Nigeria (Elias, 1967).

The Northern Nigerian Penal Code law was intended to apply to all persons living in Northern Nigeria, thus solving some of the problems associated with having different laws for different groups. Occasionally a non-Muslim had been brought before an Islamic Alkali Court, with the defendant not even knowing the illegality of some acts in the Emirate (Karibi-Whyte, 1964). The Penal Code made the region's laws applicable to everybody; but because the majority of the people living in the region were Muslim, the Penal Code Law avoided any conflict with the dictates of the Holy Koran (Elias, 1967).

Customary Law

After the Criminal Code became applicable to the whole of Nigeria in 1916, most criminal cases were still governed not by the Code but by "Native Law and Custom." In Southern Nigeria customary law was unwritten, but Northern Nigeria had written customary law and even schools of jurists such as the Maliki School (Nwabueze, 1963; Allott, 1963). This created problems, especially in Northern Nigeria, where Maliki law and English law were frequently incompatible (Okonkwo and Naish, 1964). In Maliki law, for instance, the capital offense of homicide included any assault ending in death, regardless of intention. What the colonial criminal code considered manslaughter was interpreted as murder under Maliki law (Okonkwo and Naish, 1964).

It is not surprising, then, that colonial authorities attempted to abolish customary law in 1933 by dropping clauses protecting it in Section 4 of the Criminal Code.[1]

British administrators, however, realized that total abolition of the Maliki law would cause an intolerable backlash; therefore, Section 10 of the Native Courts Ordinance allowed customary law to continue, provided that its punishments did not involve mutilation or torture and were "not repugnant to natural justice, equity, and good conscience" (Elias, 1963).

Since independence in 1960, both the Criminal Code and the Penal Code of Nigeria have been amended many times to reflect the norms, values, and standards of the Nigerian people (Karibi-Whyte, 1964; Elias, 1972b; Ebbe, 1985a). Also, some Nigerian customs that were criminalized by the colonial administration have again been legalized. For example, by a 1970 decree, the anti-bigamy law was declared null and void (Elias, 1972b; Obilade, 1969; Ebbe, 1985a).

The post-independence legislatures have given more regard to customary law and its administration than the colonial regime. Indigenous Nigerian administrators understand and sympathize with the culture of the people and their traditional justice system more than the colonial administrators; and many customary laws were restored and others strengthened after the colonial regime (Keay and Richardson, 1966).

Today, Nigeria operates a tripartite system of criminal law and justice. First, there is the Criminal Code, based on English common law and legal practice; second, the Penal Code, based on Maliki law and the Muslim system of law and justice; and finally, Customary law, based on immemorial customs and traditions of the people. These native laws and customs are conventional and unwritten in Southern Nigeria, while in Northern Nigeria, they are written.

In order to understand the judiciary and criminal procedure in Nigeria, we will now discuss the nature of that country's crime problem.

The Crime Problem

The crime problem in Nigeria emanates mainly from modernization. By the time colonial rule ended on October 1, 1960, Nigeria had become the largest and most populous center of Western, Asian, and Middle-Eastern trade in sub-Saharan Africa. Nigerian cities had many racial and ethnic groups, with the pre-colonial gemeinschaft structure, or what Durkheim (1964) called the "mechanical solidarity" type of structure, having given way to an "organic solidarity." After sixty years of direct British administration of Nigeria, English laws, values, and education had been embraced by the greater part of the Nigerian people.

The heterogeneity of city population made English law seem most suitable for a country of Muslims, Christians, and African religions. However, such multiracial, multi-ethnic, and multi-religious communities with laws of alien origin as a control mechanism, led inevitably to cultural conflict and crime (Sellin, 1938).

Crimes in Nigeria today are classified by seriousness (with felonies being very serious and misdemeanors less serious). They are also separated by the Nigerian police into offenses against persons, offenses against property, other offenses (crimes without victims), and offenses against local ordinance.

Felonious offenses include armed robbery, arson, auto theft, burglary, child-stealing, counterfeiting, conspiracy, drug offenses, forgery, fraud, kidnapping, murder, aggravated assault, rape, smuggling contrabands, theft of something of high value, strong-arm robbery, and treason. All other offenses are misdemeanors.

For the purpose of criminal prosecution, any person of seventeen years or older is an adult. Young persons 12 to 16 years old are treated as juveniles, while ages 7–11 are regarded as children. The offenses of both children and young persons are handled by juvenile courts. The magistrate of a county and a layman and a laywoman constitute a juvenile court—i.e., an ad hoc informal court (Ebbe, 1988).

Drug offenses in Nigeria include possession or selling of cocaine, heroin, or marijuana. Unlike in the United States, all barbiturates and amphetamines are legal drugs which can be purchased easily as over-the-counter medicines.

Tables 8–1 and 8–2 show the rates of crime based on police records from 1986 to 1989, in terms of number of crimes reported (which includes crimes reported by citizens, crimes observed by citizens, and crimes observed by the police), percentage of cases solved by the police, and rate of crime per 100,000 population. Table 8–1 and 8–2 do not include attempted offenses; nor do they include "offenses against local ordinance," for which much data is missing.

Systematic record keeping on crime data in Nigeria is still very cumbersome for the Nigerian Police Force (NPF), but Police Force Headquarters is making some effort toward achieving that goal. The number of robberies and burglaries recorded by the

Table 8–1. *Rates of Crime Based on Offenses Known to the Police—1986–1989*

Types of Offenses	1986			1987		
	Number of Crimes Reported	Cases Solved Percent	Crime per 100,000	Number of Crimes Reported	Cases Solved Percent	Crime per 100,000
1. Armed Robbery	1,217	66.7	1.52	1,436	57.2	1.77
2. Assault (Aggravated and Simple Assault)	56,832	85.4	71.18	52,117	61.6	64.31
3. Auto Theft	5,139	41.7	6.43	6,288	36.4	7.75
4. Burglary	11,223	41.6	17.81	15,319	41.2	18.90
5. Counterfeiting	541	48.4	0.67	581	42.9	0.71
6. Drug Offenses	316	42.8	0.39	422	46.9	0.52
7. Forgery	283	39.7	0.35	189	41.3	0.23
8. Fraud	387	29.3	0.48	287	35.2	0.35
9. Manslaughter	738	65.2	0.92	618	54.9	0.76
10. Murder	984	54.7	1.23	849	61.5	1.04
11. Rape	1,238	49.4	1.55	1,116	42.2	1.37
12. Smuggling	449	28.5	0.56	364	39.8	0.44
13. Stealing (Theft)	68,322	48.5	85.57	69,767	45.0	86.09
14. Strong-Arm Robbery	826	49.9	1.03	944	49.9	1.16
TOTAL	151,495	----	189.76	150,297	----	185.47
POPULATION	70,835,000			81,035,000		

Source of Data: Annual Reports of the Nigerian Police Force 1986–1989 and Nigerian Year Book 1986–1989. The rates of crime are computed based on the police reports, and the country's population was estimated from the 1991 Nigerian census report of 88,569,226.

Nigerian police constitutes only about 30 percent of the robberies or burglaries committed in the country, because many such crimes are not detected or reported. Furthermore, over 60 percent of crimes that should appear in police records are disposed without record at informal, customary criminal justice courts of the chiefs or councils of elders. Police crime record data from Nigeria can be used only with the full realization of its incompleteness.

The definitions of the crimes listed in Tables 8–1 and 8–2 are similar to English and American definitions, but the American concept of date rape is not a rape in Nigeria. Additionally, unlike in some states in the United States, in Nigeria a husband can never be said to have raped his wife.

From the state of the crime problem presented here, one can see that Nigeria has become more complex than in the precolonial period. It was unavoidable under such an amalgamation of ethnic groups, regions, and religious denominations, that an English-based judiciary and criminal procedure should be introduced.

Table 8–2. Rates of Crime Based on Offenses Known to the Police—1986–1989

Types of Offenses	1988			1989		
	Number of Crimes Reported	Cases Solved Percent	Crime per 100,000	Number of Crimes Reported	Cases Solved Percent	Crime per 100,000
1. Armed Robbery	1,529	46.5	1.83	1,398	44.9	1.61
2. Assault (Aggravated and Simple Assault)	55,334	62.4	66.31	54,116	53.0	62.97
3. Auto Theft	6,291	42.8	7.54	5,282	47.6	6.14
4. Burglary	13,862	41.8	16.61	12,678	49.3	14.75
5. Counterfeiting	488	37.7	0.58	472	41.7	0.54
6. Drug Offenses	593	45.9	0.71	588	45.2	0.68
7. Forgery	326	51.8	0.39	336	46.1	0.39
8. Fraud	457	43.3	0.54	492	37.8	0.57
9. Manslaughter	629	65.3	0.75	543	49.4	0.63
10. Murder	838	61.6	1.00	928	54.7	1.07
11. Rape	963	44.2	1.15	1,032	47.7	1.20
12. Smuggling	291	35.4	0.34	287	42.5	0.33
13. Stealing (Theft)	72,368	50.3	86.73	69,454	49.9	80.82
14. Strong-Arm Robbery	851	50.8	1.01	865	46.6	1.00
TOTAL	154,820	----	185.55	148,462	----	172.76
POPULATION	83,435,000			85,935,000		

Source of Data: Annual Reports of Nigerian Police Force 1986–1989 and Nigerian Year Book 1986-1989. The rates of crime are computed based on the police reports, and the country's population was estimated from the 1991 Nigerian census report of 88,569,226.

Judicial System

Administration and Organization

There are two classes of courts in Nigeria: federal courts and state courts. Federal courts include the Nigerian Supreme Court and the Federal High Court. In the states, there are a variety of courts. Unlike in the United States, the states in Nigeria have no Supreme Court. The State High Court is the highest court in most states, although some have a High Court of Appeal.

We will first discuss the federal courts and then proceed to the State Courts.

The Supreme Court

The Nigerian Supreme Court was established under the Constitution of the federation Order-in-Council, 1960, and revised by the Republican Constitution (1963). The Republican Constitution did not ensure the independence of the judiciary, but did provide for a Supreme Court with the Chief

Justice of Nigeria and at least five other judges. The Supreme Court is the Final Court of Appeal and a superior Court of Records. It has exclusive jurisdiction on constitutional matters, and its judges are appointed by the President of the Republic.[2]

The Nigerian Supreme Court today has powers similar to those of the United States Supreme Court. Under the 1979 Constitution the Supreme Court and its judges became independent of the president and the legislature, and presidential appointments were made subject to the approval of both Houses of the Legislature (Kasumu, 1978). There are thirteen judges in the Nigerian Supreme Court including the Chief Justice. The judges must be certified lawyers who had served as judges at the federal or state court levels for a minimum of ten years.

Unfortunately, the presence of a military Head of State in Nigeria can adversely influence the roles and decisions of the Supreme Court. We will discuss the Supreme Court's procedure for hearing appeals in a later section on criminal procedure.

Federal High Court/Federal Court of Appeal

The Federal High Court is composed of a Chief Justice and at least five other judges, all of whom are appointed by the President of the Republic. The Federal High Court is a Superior Court of records, hearing cases involving the federal government versus individuals or states, or states versus states. Appeals from its decisions go to the Supreme Court. The Federal High Court may sit in any one of the states as an Assize Court, especially where the parties come from the same state. A case involving persons of different states may be filed in a Federal High Court in Lagos or Abuja. The court has both original and appellate jurisdiction in offenses involving violation of federal law

such as smuggling contraband, counterfeiting, and possession of marijuana or narcotic drugs (drug appeals and currency offenses are now tried by special tribunals). Ten years of experience on the bench is required before a lawyer is appointed judge of the Federal High Court. The Federal High Court hears appeals from state high courts and states' courts of appeals.

State Courts

All of Nigeria's 30 states have powers under the constitution to establish state courts of appeal for the determination of appeals brought from a state high court (Elias, 1967). Where a state has a court of appeal, decisions from its high court cannot be brought directly to the Nigerian Supreme Court. Instead, appeals must first be made to the State Court of Appeal and from there to the Supreme Court.

The Court of Appeal (Western States)
In the western states, a court of appeal was established by the Court of Appeal Edict, 1967 (Elias, 1972b). The provisions of the Edict were given effect under Section 127 (2) of the Constitution of the Federation by the Constitution (Western Nigeria Court of Appeal) Order, 1967. The court consists of the president and four justices of appeal, and receives appeals from high courts of western states. It has jurisdiction in questions concerning the interpretation of the state constitution, civil matters, murder, and all felonies requiring over five years of imprisonment.

The Courts of Resolution (Northern States)
The Court of Resolution of Northern Nigeria was established by the Court of Resolution Law (1960)[3] for the purpose of resolving any conflict of jurisdiction between the State High Court and the Sharia Court of Appeal.

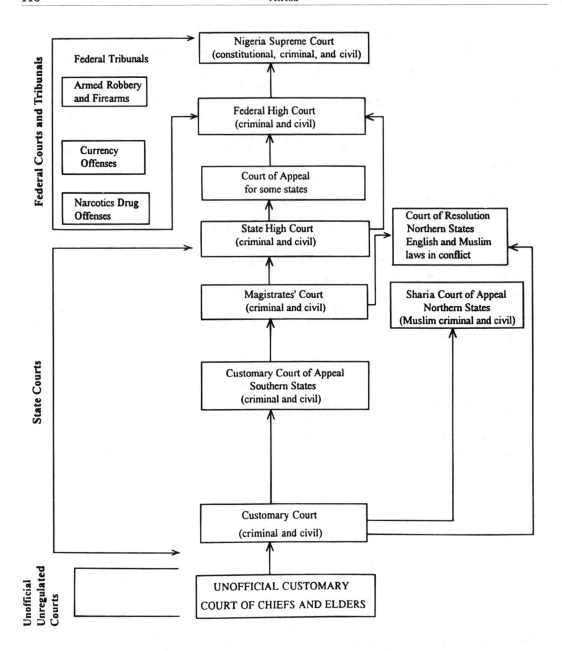

Figure 8.1   Structure and Organization of the Court in the Federal Republic of Nigeria

Today, the Court of Resolution of each northern state consists of the chief justice of the state (who is the president), the Grand Khádi, one judge of the high court nominated by the chief justice, and one judge of the Sharia Court nominated by the Grand Khádi.[4] No appeal can be made from the Court of Resolution to any other court.[5]

The Sharia Court of Appeal (Northern States)

The Sharia Court of Appeal was established in the northern states in 1960 for hearing appeals from customary courts where Muslim personal law is involved. The Sharia Court of Appeal consists of a Grand Khádi and not less than two other judges well versed in Sharia law. The judges are appointed by the president after consultation with the Advisory Judicial Committee. Appeals from an upper area court in cases involving Muslim Personal Law go to the Sharia Court of Appeal. Appeals from the decision of the Sharia Court of Appeal on questions regarding the interpretation of the Constitution of the Federation, or that of a state, or questions about violations of fundamental constitutional rights, go to the Nigerian Supreme Court.[6]

The High Courts
The Federal Constitution of 1954 empowered the Regional Legislatures to establish courts for their respective regions, and in 1955 each region established a High Court, Magistrates' Courts, and Native or Customary Courts. When the regions were broken into 30 states, each state was granted power to establish its own courts in accordance with the Federal Constitution.

Under the Constitutions of 1960, 1979, and 1992, the High Court of each state consists of the Chief Justice of the state and other judges. Each State High Court is required by law to have six or more judges (except in the state of Lagos, which requires five or more). The Chief Justice is appointed by the State Governor. The other judges are also appointed by the Governor, but the appointments have to be in accordance with the advice of the state Judicial Service Commission. During Nigeria's military regimes, the Chief Justice of each high court and the other judges of the court were appointed by the Supreme Military Council after consultation with the Advisory Judicial Committee.

Each high court is a Superior Court of Records having original and appellate jurisdiction. Since the Nigerian Civil War destroyed most of the customary court buildings in the Eastern States, customary courts have been abolished there, and the high courts now have original jurisdiction in their land causes and matters arising under customary law.

Magistrates' Courts
There are different grades of the Magistrates' Court from state to state. The Public Service Commission of each state is empowered to appoint magistrates, and there are grades of magistrates and magistrates' courts which vary from state to state. The magistrates are all certified lawyers with at least five years of experience on the bench. In the Eastern States, especially in the Ibo areas, the cases that used to be brought to the Customary Courts now go to the Magistrates' courts.

Customary Courts
All judges of customary courts, including Sharia Courts, are lay-judges without formal legal training. They are supposed to be persons who, by their age and experience, have a deep knowledge of the customary laws of their clans.

In the northern states, the Customary Courts are known as Area Courts. Area Courts are of four types, Upper Area Courts, Area Courts Grade I, Area Courts Grade II, and Area Courts Grade III. The Area Courts are established by the chief justice of each of the states, and their judges are appointed by the State's Public Service Commission. Appeals go from an Area Court Grade I to II or III, or to the Upper Area Court having jurisdiction. Appeals from Upper Area Court go to the Sharia Court of Appeal in cases involving Muslim Personal Law, and to the High Court in other cases (Aguda, 1974; Elias, 1967; Nwabueze, 1963).

In Midwestern States, all Customary Courts are now of the same grade. Customary Courts are established by the Chief Justice subject to the approval of the State Governor. The Chief Justice has the power to appoint persons as presidents or members of a Customary Court on the recommendation of the Advisory Judicial Committee (Elias, 1972a).

In the Western States, Customary Courts are graded as A, B, and C; there was formerly a D grade which has been abolished. The Judicial Service Commission was empowered to appoint presidents of grade A and B courts presided over by legal practitioners. On the abolition of the Judicial Service Commission, the Local Government Service Board was empowered to appoint, dismiss, and exercise disciplinary control over all members of Customary Courts (Aguda, 1974).

All the courts discussed above have powers of criminal jurisdiction except some district courts in the northern states.

Special Courts

Special Criminal Offenses Tribunals Special criminal offenses are those for which trials cannot be originated in any of the courts discussed above. Such crimes are tried at special tribunals, including (a) The Armed Robbery and Firearms Tribunal (1970), (b) The Currency Offenses Tribunal (1974), and (c) The Illegal Drugs and Narcotics Tribunal (1986).

The Nigerian government set up these tribunals because people known to have committed these certain offenses were not paying the price for their crimes in regular criminal courts due to pettifogging legal arguments of defense lawyers. Each one of the tribunals is composed of five to seven officials such as retired court judges, senior military officials, retired senior police officers, or retired senior civil servants, most with no degree in law. The defendant is allowed to call witnesses and to have a defense attorney, and there is no prosecutor; the trial session consists of the defendant and his or her defense attorney facing a panel of unbiased judges. This system and its operation could be said to be the spirit of the Nigerian customary criminal procedure haunting the government's English judicial system. In effect, the adversarial system is disregarded in these tribunals in favor of the inquisitorial approach: instead of the accused being convicted only when evidence proves that he or she committed the offense beyond a reasonable doubt, the accused has to prove to the tribunal that he or she did not commit the offense.

Penalties for each of the three offenses are established by decree, with very little discretionary power given to the judges in sentencing: any person convicted of any of the tribunal offenses receives death by a firing-squad. It was only in November 1992 that Nigerian Head of State Ibrahim Babangida commuted the death penalty to life imprisonment for any person convicted of narcotics drug smuggling or possession. Whether a person convicted of narcotics drug smuggling has a prior criminal record is immaterial to the life sentence, and Nigeria has no parole system.

Juvenile Court The juvenile court in Nigeria began in Lagos in the 1940s as a brainchild of British colonial authorities. After World War II it was introduced into the Western, Eastern, and Northern regions (Ebbe, 1988). Today the court is composed of a magistrate who is the president of the court, a layman, and a laywoman.

Juveniles adjudicated as delinquent either are sent to approved schools, sent to remand homes, or placed on probation. A juvenile accused of murder is tried as an adult in a criminal court. If convicted, he or she is sent to a medium security prison until he or she attains the age of 17 or 18.

Criminal Procedures

To both Nigerians with some Western education and to those without Western education, the English system of criminal procedure can be a nightmare. It is not easy to adapt criminal procedures to a society for which any such system is culturally alien. In fact, in some rural towns and villages in Nigeria today, it will offend the whole town or village if any member of the community calls the police over any criminal victimization by a community member, or brings a lawsuit against any member for damages. This attitude has prevailed since colonial days. Most villages want to handle all criminal victimizations within the village in a traditional manner.

Nigeria is a country divided between literates and illiterates, with the literates holding firmly to Western ways and systems of justice; therefore, the English system of criminal procedure probably has come to stay despite its difficulties and despite local opposition. The controversiality of the English criminal procedures, however, has made police operations in Nigeria very cumbersome and often ineffective.

Rights of the Accused

When the accused is indigent and incapable of providing a defense attorney, he or she is protected against self-incrimination by a public defender.

There has been no jury trial in Nigeria since the eclipse of the colonial administration of justice (Aguda, 1974). If an accused is brought before a magistrate's court and pleads guilty during questioning, the court will immediately refer him or her to a psychiatrist to determine whether he or she is in full control of his or her mental faculties. If he or she is found to be normal, the magistrate will then give sentence according to law without regard to his or her pleading guilty. (The court accepts the defendant's guilty plea, but—unlike the American plea bargaining situation—there is no reduction in the severity of punishment for the offense.)

Arrest and Investigation

Suspects come to the attention of the police through victims or crime-scene observers, or suspects may be caught by the police on patrol. The police officer with greatest seniority at the station thoroughly investigates the case, and may take any one of the following three actions:

a. Dismiss the case because of insufficient evidence.
b. In trivial cases, simply warn the suspect and discharge him or her on grounds that:

i. The suspect has no prior criminal record.
ii. The crime has no victim.
iii. The offender has agreed to compensate the victim.
c. When the suspect is a juvenile (less than 17 years old), refer the case to a juvenile court or discharge the juvenile.

If there are grounds to detain the suspect, the police officer will do so and initiate an investigation of the case. If the investigation report shows that the suspect actually committed an offense, the case reports for the accused person are transferred to the office of the Director of Public Prosecution (DPP). If the DPP finds inadequate evidence to charge the case to court, he or she dismisses it. If there is enough evidence to charge the accused of a crime, he or she places charges against the suspect in a Magistrates' Court.

A person charged with a misdemeanor is entitled to bail unless the DPP and the court see good reasons for not granting it. In felony cases, however, granting bail is at the discretion of the court. Should the offender fail to show up on the day of trial, the bailer is held liable. Bail can be granted by the court on recognizance with or without sureties to appear before the court. The court can deny bail and require an offender to be remanded in custody awaiting trial in a medium or maximum pre-trial security prison. Law allows magistrates to detain a suspect for 30 days, but in practice detainees may be in prison awaiting trial for six months or even a year. Bail may be denied on the following grounds:

a. The suspect refused arrest.
b. The suspect is a recidivist.
c. The suspect committed the crime while on bail.
d. The suspect is arrested for murder, rape, armed robbery, narcotics drug smuggling, counterfeiting currency, or any other heinous crime.

e. The suspect is an apparent danger to the public.
f. There is a need to protect the offender.
g. The suspect is an unruly juvenile.

It is noteworthy that in the area of public prosecution, there are deviant factors that can make the police or the DPP not charge an offender with a legal violation. These are the interests and influences of top officials or politicians in the executive branch of the government, justice department, corporate executives, and of wealthy businessmen. These individuals can order or lobby the police or the Director of Public Prosecution not to take a case to court, or cause a case to be dropped when it is already charged to court.

As in Britain, most criminal prosecutions are police prosecutions. The DPP and department prosecute only in more serious cases, particularly murder, armed robbery, and narcotics drug trafficking (Aguda, 1974). When the police prosecute, the prosecution may be in the name of the officer of the Nigerian or native authority police; or in the name of the Commissioner of Police of the state (for example, *Obi Okonkwo v. Commissioner of Police*); or in the name of the native authority of the area in which the offense was committed, or against whose rules the offenses were committed (for example, *Bobo Ikemefuna v. Orlu Urban Council*; or *Jim Jones v. The Inspector General*). In contrast, in the United States the accused is prosecuted in the name of the State or the People (e.g., *The People v. O. J. Simpson*).

There is no plea bargaining in the Nigerian criminal justice system. The defense in a criminal trial may claim self-defense or insanity (Brett and McLean, 1963), but intoxication is not a defense unless coupled with duress. Minor criminal cases that require negotiated settlements are referred at the discretion of the magistrate to a customary court that has jurisdiction over the parties involved in the case. In practice, if it is clear, unequivocal, and beyond a reasonable doubt, that the defendant

committed the crime charged, Nigerian criminal procedure will not entertain denial of due process (e.g., failure to read Miranda rule or judges rule to the accused) as a defense in court. This constitutes a major difference between Nigerian and American criminal procedure.

Tables 8–3 and 8–4, which show offender disposal records for 1987 and 1988, indicate that most persons convicted of offenses in Nigeria are not incarcerated. Instead, they receive non-prison sentences, including warning, compensation, service at public projects, a fine, or time in a labor camp. Most arrested persons are not prosecuted, but most of those prosecuted are found guilty of the offense(s) charged (66.9% in 1987 and 81.2% in 1988). Rates of conviction are particularly high for murder, armed robbery, rape, burglary, counterfeiting, forgery, fraud, auto-theft, strong-arm robbery, and drug offenses. Assault charges (except for premeditated aggravated assault) are less likely to lead to a sentence of imprisonment. Assault and battery are a traditional means of settling differences between friends in Nigeria, and social changes have increased their frequency despite the fact that the British criminalized them; thus, they do not lead to incarceration of the offender in most cases today.

Dismissal or Discharge

Every criminal court in Nigeria, whether a court of first instance or a court of appeal, can dismiss a case and discharge the accused, if it finds no reasonable grounds to put the accused on trial or convict him.

It is provided, however, that the dismissal of a complaint or the discharge of the accused is not the same as an acquittal (The Criminal Procedure Act, Cap. 43 of the Laws of the Federation of Nigeria; Aguda, 1980). Also, if an accused has been tried by a court of competent jurisdiction for a crime and convicted or acquitted of the crime, he or she will not be tried again for the same offense; nor will the same facts be used to charge him or her with any other

Table 8–3. *Offender Disposal Records (1987)*

	No. of Persons Arrested	No. of Prosecutions (%)	No. Discharged (%)*	No. Imprisoned (%)*	Death Sentences (%)*	Non-Prison Sentence (%)*	Found Guilty (%)**
1. Murder	716	441 (61.6)	38 (8.6)	147 (33.3)	256 (58.0)	----	91.4
2. Manslaughter	618	339 (54.9)	102 (30.1)	237 (69.9)	---	---	69.9
3. Armed-Robbery	1,012	579 (57.2)	66 (11.4)	125 (21.6)	388 (67.0)	---	88.6
4. Rape	1,116	471 (42.2)	113 (24.0)	358 (76.0)	---	---	76.0
5. Burglary	12,867	5,301 (41.2)	1,809 (34.1)	3,492 (65.9)	---	---	65.9
6. Stealing/Theft	31,281	14,077 (45.0)	2,163 (15.4)	4,722 (33.5)		7,192 (51.1)	84.6
7. Assault (All types)	33,019	20,341 (61.6)	9,874 (48.5)	1,316 (6.5)		9,151 (45.0)	51.5
8. Smuggling	263	105 (39.9)	16 (15.2)	89 (84.8)	---	---	84.8
9. Counterfeiting	522	224 (42.9)	21 (9.4)	203 (90.6)	---	---	90.6
10. Forgery	121	51 (42.1)	19 (37.3)	32 (62.7)	---	---	62.7
11. Fraud	169	60 (35.5)	22 (36.7)	38 (63.3)	---	---	63.3
12. Auto Theft & Snatching	4,063	1,479 (36.4)	173 (11.7)	1,306 (88.3)	---	---	88.3
13. Strong-Arm-Robbery	623	311 (49.9)	58 (18.6)	188 (60.5)	---	65 (20.9)	81.4
14. Narcotic Drugs Offense	422	198 (46.9)	86 (43.4)	66 (33.3)	46 (23.2)	---	56.5
15. Other	814	464 (57.0)	132 (28.4)	152 (32.8)	----	180 (38.8)	71.6
TOTAL	87,626	44,441 (50.7%)	14,692 (33.1%)	12,471 (28.1%)	690 (1.5%)	16,588 (37.3%)	66.9%
POPULATION	81,035,000						

Source: Nigerian Police Force Annual Reports 1987

*Percentage of those prosecuted.

**Percentage of those prosecuted found guilty of the offense charged.

Table 8–4. Offender Disposal Records (1988)

	No. of Persons Arrested	No. of Prosecution (%)*	No. Discharged (%)*	No. Imprisoned (%)*	Death Sentences (%)*	Non-Prison Sentences (%)*	Found Guilty (%)**
1. Murder	876	540 (61.6)	42 (7.8)	189 (35.0)	309 (57.2)	----	92.2
2. Manslaughter	518	339 (65.4)	131 (38.6)	208 (61.4)	----	----	61.4
3. Armed-Robbery	1,214	565 (46.5)	33 (5.8)	238 (42.1)	294 (52.0)	----	94.2
4. Rape	912	403 (44.2)	98 (24.3)	305 (75.7)	----	----	75.7
5. Burglary	10,961	4,582 (41.8)	914 (19.9)	3,553 (77.5)	----	115 (2.5)	80.1
6. Stealing/Theft	43,119	21,689 (50.3)	1,224 (5.6)	8,731 (40.3)	----	11,734 (54.1)	94.4
7. Assault (All types)	35,866	22,380 (62.4)	7,361 (32.9)	4,406 (19.7)	----	10,613 (47.4)	67.1
8. Smuggling	213	76 (35.7)	24 (31.6)	38 (50.0)	----	14 (18.4)	68.4
9. Counterfeiting	364	137 (37.6)	11 (8.0)	113 (82.5)	----	13 (9.5)	92.0
10. Forgery	229	119 (52.0)	15 (12.6)	104 (87.4)	----	----	87.4
11. Fraud	332	144 (43.4)	9 (6.3)	135 (93.8)	----	----	93.8
12. Auto Theft & Snatching	4,158	1,821 (43.8)	53 (2.9)	1,768 (97.1)	----	----	97.1
13. Strong-Arm-Robbery	541	275 (50.8)	37 (13.5)	189 (68.7)	----	49 (17.8)	86.5
14. Narcotic Drugs Offense	517	237 (45.8)	26 (11.0)	135 (57.0)	76 (32.1)	----	89.1
15. Other	966	493 (51.0)	113 (22.9)	117 (23.7)	----	263 (53.3)	77.0
TOTAL	100,786	53,800 (53.4%)	10,091 (18.8%)	20,229 (37.6%)	679 (1.3%)	22,801 (42.4%)	81.2%
POPULATION	83,435,000						

Source: Nigerian Police Force Annual Reports 1988

*Percentage of those prosecuted.

**Percentage of those prosecuted found guilty.

crime "for which a different charge from the one made against him might have been made before the court by which he was earlier on acquitted or convicted" (Aguda, 1980; Brett and McLean, 1963). Such a second trial would amount to "double jeopardy," also prohibited by law in the U.S. criminal justice system.

However, if an accused was tried for a crime and convicted or acquitted by a court that has no competent jurisdiction in the matter, he or she can be subsequently charged with and tried for the same offense without regard to the decision of the court where he or she was first charged and adjudicated (The Criminal Procedure Act, 1960; Brett and McLean, 1963; Aguda, 1980).

Right of Appeal in Criminal Cases

Both Federal and State constitutions in Nigeria provide for rights of appeal from subordinate courts to the appropriate High Court and from the State High Courts, in their original and appellate jurisdictions, to the Federal High Court or to the Federal Supreme Court on constitutional grounds. The constitutional provisions are the same, *mutatis mutandis*, for all of the 30 states in Nigeria and for the capital territory of Abuja.

Appeals to Magistrate's Court

At the customary court level, if a convicted party does not countenance the decision or order of a Grade A or Grade B District Court or a Customary Court of Appeal, he or she can appeal to the Magistrate's Court or the State High Court within 30 days from the date of the lower court's order or decision (similar appeals are allowed six or seven months to be lodged in the United States and three days in China). The cases appealed must involve a prison sentence or a fine exceeding N250 (two hundred and fifty naira) on conviction.

An appeal from a decision or order of a Magistrate's Court goes to the High Court of the state where the Magistrate's Court is located. The appellant must give the Registrar of the Magistrate's Court notice of appeal indicating the grounds on which his or her complaints are based.

If the appellant is in prison custody, the magistrate may "release him from custody on his entering into a recognizance, with or without securities," and at a reasonable cost that the magistrate thinks expedient to secure the appellant's appearance (Nigerian [Constitution] Order in Council, 1960; Brett and McLean, 1963). The magistrate will not grant a release from prison custody if:

a. The appellant has previously served a sentence of not less than six months' imprisonment; or
b. The magistrate has a reason to believe that if released from prison, the appellant is likely to commit an additional crime; or
c. The appellant is likely to abscond or disappear.

The magistrate has the discretionary power to release the appellant from prison custody or not to do so. However, if the magistrate refuses to grant the appellant a release from custody, the appellant can apply to the State High Court, which also has the power to grant a release or refuse to do so. If the High Court grants the release request and the appellant fails to show up on the day of the appeal hearing, the High Court may take any one of the following actions:

a. Issue a warrant for the appellant's arrest;
b. Dismiss the appeal or order the appeal hearing to be postponed, and order that, if the appellant is caught, he or she should be remanded in custody;
c. Order that the appellant's security or securities be forfeited in total or in part.

The High Court in Criminal Appeals

The High Court, in its appellate jurisdiction in criminal cases coming from the Customary Courts and Magistrate's Courts, can respond to the appeals as follows:

a. It can, after reviewing the matter, confirm the decision or order of the lower court and dismiss the appeal;
b. If it sees that there is sufficient ground to interfere with the decision of the lower court, it can set aside the earlier decision and (1) acquit the appellant; or (2) retry the appellant on the same charge and/or on a new charge that might have been disclosed by the evidence, and then sentence the appellant as it deems just; or (3) order a retrial of the appellant on the same charge or on any new charge disclosed by the evidence; or (4) modify or substitute the decision or order of the lower court where the appeal was filed (Brett and McLean, 1963; Aguda, 1980).

An appeal court may not entertain an appeal made only because the decision reached by the lower court is "challenged on the ground of its being contrary to the weight of the evidence," *Aladesuru and Others v. R.* (1955), 39 Cr. App. R. 184, p.c. (Aguda, 1980). However, the Court of Appeal can hear the case, if it can be shown that the decision or order of the court of trial is "unwarranted, unreasonable, and cannot be supported having regard to the evidence," *Chivo Adi v. R.* (1955), 15 W.A.C.A.G. (Aguda, 1980).

The Appellate Jurisdiction of the Nigerian Supreme Court

The Federal Supreme Court has exclusive jurisdiction to hear and determine appeals from State High Courts and the Federal High Court. In addition to civil matters, the Supreme Court has final say (1) in all criminal cases brought before the High Court sitting at first instance; (2) in any criminal decisions addressing alleged violations of the constitutional rights of the accused; (3) in instances where a death sentence has been imposed by a High Court, or decisions "in which the High Court has affirmed a sentence of death imposed by some other courts" (Aguda, 1980; Brett and McLean, 1963).

The Supreme Court allows an appeal against conviction from a High Court if it thinks that the decision reached at the lower court "should be set aside on the ground that it is unreasonable and cannot be supported having regard to the evidence"; or it believes that a wrongful decision was made based on a question of law applied to the case; or "on the ground that there was a miscarriage of justice" (Brett and McLean, 1963).

If the Supreme Court allows an appeal against a conviction, it may set aside the conviction and order that the appellant be acquitted. Also the Supreme Court may order that "the appellant be retried by a court of competent jurisdiction" (Brett and McLean, 1963).

A defendant in a criminal case who wants to take a case to the Supreme Court must "give notice of appeal or notice of his application for leave to appeal" (Aguda, 1980; Brett and McLean, 1963) according to the rules of the court and within 30 days. In some circumstances, 15 days may be added to help the appellant prepare.

The Supreme Court may, at any stage, appoint counsel to help an appellant. When the Supreme Court upholds the decision of the High Court, the appellant serves the sentence imposed by the High Court that led to the appeal.

Appeals may also reach the Supreme Court from the Special Tribunals for cases of armed robbery, which draws the death penalty; or for cases of counterfeiting currency and narcotic drugs trafficking, which draw a life sentence without parole.

Penalties and Sentencing

Sentencing Process

Nigeria has no pre-sentencing hearings. The Magistrate or a high court judge, in a state court, can sentence an offender to terms of imprisonment according to law on the very day the case is tried, if the accused is found guilty of the offense. Only rarely does a judge or Magistrate postpone sentencing until a later date.

Only judges can give sentences. Victims have no sentencing role; nor do psychiatrists or social workers, although they may be involved in pre-trial investigations.

Types of Penalties

Persons found guilty of misdemeanor offenses may be fined, warned, granted probation, or, as in Singapore, be given corporal punishment or a community service order. Persons found guilty of felonious offenses may be sentenced to some years of imprisonment, served either in a maximum security prison or in a medium security prison, depending on the gravity of the offense. Less serious felonious offenders are sent either to minimum security prisons or to a labor camp.

Nigeria has the death penalty for murder, armed robbery, treason, and serious currency offenses. Until November 1992, illegal drugs and narcotics smuggling was disposed by death penalty. The punishment is now life imprisonment, which in Nigeria means that the offender will be released from prison only in a coffin. Once again, there is no parole program in the Nigerian criminal justice system.

House-arrest, banishment, and exile are no longer used in the Nigerian criminal justice system. House-arrest, however, may be applied to a political dissident.

Capital punishment is carried out publicly by a firing squad of soldiers with the offender tied to a stake. Sometimes the audience is an angry crowd of crime condemners; sometimes it is a sympathetic crowd.

Discussion

Every aspect of the Nigerian criminal justice system is still developing, partly because most of Nigeria's laws are based on alien customs and traditions, and partly because federal governments in Nigeria fall like ripe apples. Every new regime brings new decrees, a new constitution, and new organizational structures, and what criminal codes declare to be illegal acts depends on who occupies the seat of power. Changes in Nigerian law reflect changes in its ruling classes.

Contrary to Thompson's idea about Sierra Leone (Chapter 7), Nigeria does show that multiple systems of criminal justice, the English legal system, the Islamic legal system, and the customary legal system, can co-exist and work in relative harmony with each other. The Muslim courts and the customary courts are very close to the people and are understood by the common citizens, because the legal arguments in those courts are based on immemorial custom, tradition, revelation (Sharia); that is, on the values and standards of the people. Cases are disposed of in these courts cheaply and expeditiously. But the English legal system, although entrenched in the Nigerian constitution, still appears alien and threatening to the majority of the people.

The English-based legal system has many loopholes through which a criminal can escape. It is a phenomenon of the urban areas, and so is crime: criminals take refuge and operate in the cities because customary law and its informal control mechanisms are too far away to apply. Finally, frequent military interventions in the governance of Nigeria weaken the independence of the judiciary and generally disrupt the normal course of the criminal justice system.

The judiciary in Nigeria is highly politicized. Arcane societies which unite some members of the judiciary, the military, and top civilians create disintegration and insincerity within the judiciary. In effect, partisanship has nullified the rule of law and due process, and the entire society has become disorganized. The military regime and violent criminals maintain their power through cold-blooded assassinations of persons who oppose the military clique; consequently, some murders are not truly investigated because they were ordered by top military commanders or their civilian cronies. The judiciary has failed to challenge the illegal regimes and their atrocities because many important members of the judiciary are party to political conspiracies and self-defeating political agendas.

Under this state of affairs, an offender who reaches the courts and gets convicted is one who has no money and no "godfather" in the military or among the top civilian population. Nigeria's criminal justice system has shortened *prima facie* cases against offenders with "godfathers," but for the poor and unconnected has become a nightmare.

Conclusion

In nations without viable political systems, justice is denied; and Nigeria is such a nation. The Nigerian Constitution becomes obsolete with each change of government, and a new one is created in its place; the masses become disorganized and the judiciary is rendered powerless before the military. Worst of all, the Nigerian Supreme Court refuses to declare an act of the military junta or government unconstitutional. In effect, the military junta has criminalized any behaviors that fail to serve its interests. The Nigerian criminal justice system will never be reliable until the military undergoes an improvement of manners, adopts respect for human dignity, and submits to rule of law.

In summary, the advent of the English legal system in Nigeria in the late nineteenth century created new forms of crime and criminals. Contemporary Nigerian criminal law is based on English law, cus-

tomary law, and Maliki law summed up in the criminal code and the penal code. Of course, customary law still stands apart from the two codes, making Nigeria effectively operate a tripartite system of criminal law and justice.

Nigeria has two classes of courts, federal and state, with the Nigerian Supreme Court being the highest court of the land. The 1979 Constitution gave the Supreme Court powers similar to those of the United States' Supreme Court, but the Nigerian military regimes have reduced the court to impotence. The most important lesson to be learned from the Nigerian criminal justice system is the use of lay judges, chiefs, or a village council of elders as mediators in disposing some serious crimes at very little cost to the victim, offender, or taxpayers. This customary court approach also reduces the number of undecided cases in the files of Magistrates' Courts and High Courts.

Finally, as long as the military continues to abuse the constitution drafted by a preceding regime, Nigeria will continue to be an unjust society, and a raped democracy.

Notes

1. Section 4 of the Criminal Code originally stated that "no person shall be liable to be tried or punished in any Court in Nigeria, other than a native tribunal, for an offense except under the express provision of the Code or some other Ordinance, or some law, or of some Order-in-Council made by his Majesty for Nigeria or under the express provisions of some statute of the Imperial Parliament which is in force in, or forms part of the law of Nigeria" (Okonkwo and Naish, 1964; Elias, 1967). It was amended to read that "no person shall be liable to be tried or punished in any Court in Nigeria for an offense except under the express provisions of the Code or . . . under the express provisions of some statute of the Imperial Parliament which is in force, or forms part of, the law of Nigeria" (Okonkwo and Naish, 1964; Elias, 1967).

2. Constitution of the Federal Republic of Nigeria 1963, Sec. III(2).

3. Northern Region Law Report, 94 of 1960.

4. Court of Resolution Law, Cap. 28, Law of Northern Nigeria, 1964 Revision Section 3(1).

5. Ibid.

6. Constitution of the Federation Sec. 119, Act No. 20 of 1963.

Discussion and Revision Questions

1. What are the two codes of law in Nigeria?

2. The Nigerian Criminal Code of 1904 was determined by alien norms. Discuss and Comment.

3. What is the consensus theorists' view of criminal law?

4. What is Maliki Law?

5. What is Sharia Court?

6. What is meant by the statement that "Nigeria operates a tripartite system of criminal justice?"

7. Compare and contrast the judiciary in Nigeria and the United States.

8. What are the common features of the Nigerian judiciary and the Sierra Leonean judiciary?

9. On what grounds can bail be denied an accused in the Nigerian Criminal Justice System?

10. What are the functions of the Director of Public Prosecution (DPP) in the Nigerian Criminal Justice System?

11. What are the defenses available to one accused of a crime in Nigeria?

12. What factors will make a magistrate choose not to release an appellant from detention when his or her appeal is pending?

13. Under what circumstances can the Nigerian Supreme Court allow an appeal against conviction from a High Court decision?

14. What are the capital offenses in Nigeria?

15. What factors politicized the Nigerian judiciary and made it unreliable in upholding the rule of law and due process standards?

16. Compare and contrast treatment of offenders in pre-colonial Nigeria and in contemporary Denmark.

SECTION IV

Asia

Obi N. I. Ebbe

Introduction

Little more is known about the criminal justice systems of Asian countries than is known about those of countries in Africa. This section attempts to remedy this lack, and to show that Asian countries, with their large populations and checkered history, have insights useful for contemporary social control.

Like the African countries presented in Section III, Asian countries maintain both formal and informal systems of criminal justice. At the informal judicial level, both exclude lawyers from the adjudication process, use village councils and lay judges, and reach a verdict through consensus, mediation, and arbitration. Imperial China (221 B.C.–1911) and many other Asian nations also resemble sub-Saharan Africa by having had no written laws until the turn of this century (Situ and Liu, Chapter 9).

The criminal justice systems of such Asian countries as Japan, Malaysia, Singapore, Taiwan, and Hong Kong have been influenced decisively by European systems of justice through the colonization of the eighteenth and nineteenth centuries. Japan, however, followed a different pattern, with Western influence entering through the United States occupation after World War II, and through earlier voluntary copying of some European criminal justice methods, especially in the area of corrections (Johnson, Chapter 12).

There are five chapters in this section. Situ and Liu present "An Overview of the Chinese Criminal Justice System" in Chapter 9. They emphasize the influence of Confucianism, an oriental religion which denied individual rights, in the criminal justice system of China. Highlights in this chapter include the various hierarchies of courts, absence of judicial precedence (*stare decisis*), the right of the police to administer punishment to offenders in certain circumstances, absence of private legal practice, use of lay judges, substantive rather than procedural justice, and the system and rules of people's mediation.

Chapter 10 analyzes typical Chinese criminal procedure more deeply. Despite its population and size, China has a centralized court system, and this chapter documents its detailed structure, organization, and the functions of the various courts including the highest, the Supreme People's Court. The salient features of the Chinese courts and criminal procedure include: holding criminal trials at the work unit or college where the defendants work or are resident; the use of assessors in criminal cases just as in colonial and post-colonial Africa, but unlike in African countries, assessors in China have equal power with the judge in adjudication of a case; verdicts delivered to the defendants in writing; death sentences with two-year suspensions (to be commuted to life imprisonment if convicts repent); the necessity of appealing most convictions within ten days, and capital offenses within three days; the similarities and differences between the role of the Chinese Procurator and that of the Prosecutor in the United States and the Director of Public

Prosecution (DPP) in Nigeria, Sierra Leone, and Britain; the absence of presumption of innocence; formal court verdicts by majority vote rather than by consensus; the active investigatory and inquisitorial role of the court judge in China; the ideology of correction through re-education and reform-through-labor; and the possibility of ex-convicts losing their communities.

"The Police System in the People's Republic of China" is presented in Chapter 11. The police in China are under the Ministry (Department) of Public Security. This chapter describes the internal structure and organization of the police department, and the role of the police in the judicial process and social arena. Important features of the Chinese Police System include centralization and multiple bureaus; the use of neighborhood police to educate the masses on crime prevention and the law; unlike in Brazil, police being "prohibited from extorting confession from an accused by torture, threats, enticement, or deceit of any other illegal nature"; public security committees similar to the Guardian Angels in America; mass legal education; and the conservative role of the police as a tool and ally of the government (compare Sierra Leone, Nigeria, and Ghana; Thompson, Chapter 7, and Arthur, Chapter 6).

In Chapter 12 Distinguished Professor Emeritus Elmer H. Johnson presents the operation and administration of prison industries in Japan. This chapter analyzes how prison labor played a significant role in the development of modern Japan, how the factory system of correction instills discipline in the inmates, and how factory labor evokes a friendly atmosphere between inmates and wardens and among the inmates themselves. Important features in this chapter include: a comparison of centralized Japanese prisons with the decentralized system in the United States; the self-sustaining economies of Japanese prisons, which (as in Denmark) shift the financial burden of keeping inmates behind bars from taxpayers to inmates, who sell their prison factory products to contractors; an outline of the advantages of Japanese inmates' industrial labor (Japanese prisons being congregate cells unlike the American Auburn plan)—the silent cell system—daily work quotas for inmates at the factory, assembling shopping bags by physically unfit inmates who are incapable of working at the prison factory; why the Japanese prisons accept the behavioral standards of the industrial prison; an account of prison retail stores and prison annual trade fairs; why prison industries declined in the United States; and the absence of opposition to the Japanese prison industries from the Japanese public.

The last chapter in this section discusses community corrections in Japan in historical terms. Japanese arguments for reducing imprisonments of offenders to a minimum are presented, and (as in pre-colonial African societies) community corrections are extolled as superior to imprisonment. This is an essay on community rehabilitation that respects the ex-offender. Important features in this chapter include the low imprisonment rate in Japan compared to the United States; the Japanese courts' ability to suspend a prison sentence after having imposed it; the dependence of community corrections on private citizens; the role of patronage societies in corrections; the use of volunteer probation officers and hostels; and (as in sub-Saharan Africa) the holding of villages accountable for the crimes of their members.

9

An Overview of the Chinese Criminal Justice System

Yingyi Situ and Weizheng Liu

Introduction

In China, as in any other country, the criminal justice system is a particular sector of the national political system. Thus its development is greatly affected by changes in Chinese government. During the past century, China has experienced a number of social revolutions that changed an established legal system, and created a new one. Until the late 1970s, all attempts to establish a stable legal system failed due to the frequency of these social revolutions. The last such upheaval, the Great Proletarian Culture Revolution initiated by Mao Tse-tung, then Chairman of the Chinese Communist Party, ended with Mao's death in 1976. Since 1978, a new generation of Chinese Communists has begun to establish a more formal and stable criminal justice system, one more modern than Mao's from an international point of view.

Although the legal codes, institutions, and procedures of the Chinese criminal justice system have been altered constantly in the past hundred years, one striking characteristic has remained constant in Chinese legal tradition: the society has been regulated not by one, but by two judicial systems. The first is a formal system composed of governmental institutions. The second is an informal system based on community vigilance. Both mechanisms influence revisions in the Chinese criminal justice system.

This chapter will provide a brief history of the Chinese criminal justice system, and then review its present formal and informal characteristics.

Chinese Legal Tradition

Chinese legal tradition can be traced as far back as twenty-one hundred years ago, when one of the warring states began to use law as an instrument for maintaining social order (Chen, 1973:7). However, a sound, formal legal system based upon written law was never established in Imperial China (221 B.C.–1911) due to resistance from the dominant Confucian philosophy. This ideology emphasized social obligations and self-sacrifice. It required that individuals or groups in conflict resolve their differences through discussion and compromise (Brady, 1982). Under the state philosophy of Confucianism, legal procedures were not designed to protect individual rights, or to give litigants redress, but served to discourage them from litigation, which was regarded as an extreme form of self-assertion (Brady, 1982; Lubman, 1983). The defendant, witnesses, and litigants alike were tortured, made victims of extortion, and humiliated in a casual and routine fashion throughout the judicial or penal processes (Brady, 1982). As a consequence, fear of encounters with the legal system prevailed.

Traditionally, the administration of law was handled by a governmental magistrate at the county level. The magistrate served as a general administrator of the area. He was a Confucian scholar, untrained in legal matters, and never regarded enforcement of the law as a function or specialty of the government. He would prefer that conflicts be resolved informally (Lubman, 1983).

Given the relatively large size of each magistrate's jurisdiction and the official animus against litigation, laws were rarely applied to local communities. Below the county level, groups—landlords, the village heads, the merchant guilds, the clan (which united all descendants from common ancestors) and the family—played a significant role in settling both civil and criminal cases.

The informal justice process usually was called mediation. The first line of settlement was the family or clan. Clan mediation was usually accomplished by the older males or local gentry who provided the clan's political leadership. Mediation between members of different clans was accomplished by the local government of the village. In such a case the locally appointed village constable or village headman often decided the course of compromise and/or punishment (Brady, 1982:38–39). The determination of wrongs and negotiation of punishments through mediation was not bound by legal codes. Like official courts, the informal justice followed the contours of power and wealth. Thus the decisions of clan, guild, or village mediator-elites considered both the facts of the case and the wealth, prestige and political power of the conflicting parties (Brady, 1982:39).

Imperial history ended in 1911, when the Qing dynasty was overthrown. The post-imperial Republic of China was spotted with warlordism, civil wars, war against the Japanese, exploitation from abroad, and corruption within the regime. The Kuomintang (Chinese Nationalist) attempts to reform the legal system were limited to the cities, and compromised by corruption and ineptitude. The long-standing imperial social heritage and the disorder of the Kuomintang's ruling period kept China from developing a sound legal system during the first half of the twentieth century.

The ouster of the Kuomintang regime in 1949, and its replacement by the People's Republic, marked the beginning of a new and more interesting era. After seizing power, the Communist government immediately abolished all the laws of the Kuomintang, because it believed that those laws represented only the interest of the bourgeoisie, landlord classes, and feudal society. During the first thirty years of the Communist regime, the abolished laws were not replaced by new codes but by a mixture of statutes, rules, decrees, orders, Party regulations, and directives that were subject to changes based upon the ruling Party's whims. Political policy of the Party was the major guideline for the adjudication process.

The judicial system developed since the mid-1950s in Communist China adapted formal to informal tradition. The formal justice system was composed of three branches: the public security organ (the police), the people's court, and the people's procuratorates. A suspected offender would be arrested by a Public Security Bureau, formally indicted by a Procurator, and convicted by a hierarchy of courts. Although on paper the judiciary was formally distinct from other Party and state apparatus, in practice it remained essentially subordinate to the Party. Since the Civil War days, the Communist Party has enjoyed judicial power in its base areas. At that time, all arrests and death sentences to be carried out were examined and approved by the area's Party committees. After the founding of the People's Republic of China (PRC), the Party continued this tradition. In serious cases, guidance from the Party committee was the major basis of adjudication: examinations and approvals by Party committees were required (*Encyclopedia of New China*, 1987).

The informal justice system (popular justice), which applied the forms for popular tribunals and mass movements, provided two functions. The first function was to apply punitive sanctions to "class enemies," thus handling "antagonistic contradictions." The second function handled "non-antagonistic contradictions" among working classes by "criticism and self-criticism" and mediation (Mao, 1966).

For the first thirty years of Communist rule, the informal or popular justice took precedence over bureaucratic justice: the Communist Party continued its radical revolutionary policies until 1978, shortly after Mao's death. The revolution finally fell into chaos during the Great Proletarian Culture Revolution (1966–1976), when bureaucratic justice was essentially abolished. Popular justice meant suppression of class enemies: landlords, rich peasants, capitalists, counter-revolutionaries, "bad elements" (all kinds of law breakers), rightists (those who disagreed with the Party's radical policies), "revisionists" (those Communist governmental officials who advocated professionalism), and intellectuals. This proletarian dictatorship was operated by radical Communist leaders and supported by radical students, poor peasants, and unskilled workers. Millions of "class enemies" were arrested and prosecuted by the "revolutionary organizations." They were tried without defense attorneys by "people's Tribunals," convicted and sentenced without a right to appeal.

The "cultural revolution" ended in 1976 with Mao's death and the arrest of his fellow radical Party leaders. Since then the pragmatic Party leaders have begun to restore and develop a formal legal system, but allowed it still to remain under the control of the Communist Party.

In 1979, the National People's Congress adopted the People's Republic of China's first code of criminal law and criminal procedure law. In the same year local Party organizations' power of examination and approval of cases was limited by abolish-

ing their political-legal committees. The judicial institutions began to exercise more independent power. From 1976 to 1979, several important legal institutions and systems were established: the Legal System Commission of the Standing Committee of the National People's Congress, a legislative institution; the Ministry of Justice; the People's Procuratorate; the People's Courts; a lawyer system; a notarization system; and legal personnel training institutions.

In short, prior to the 1980s, the Chinese legal system underwent many changes because of evolution of the political system. But the development from a feudalist society to a semi-feudalist, semi-colonial country, and then to a communist nation did not alter two characteristics of the Chinese criminal justice system. First, the tradition of combining both formal and informal mechanisms into an indistinguishable control entity has remained constant. Second, a well-developed formal legal system never appeared. Only in the 1980s did the Chinese criminal justice system enter a new constructive era.

We will now review the contemporary formal and informal justice systems in the People's Republic of China.

Formal Justice System[1]

The present formal Chinese justice system is composed of public security organs, state security organs, people's procuratorates, people's courts, and judicial administrative departments. The public security organs are responsible for investigation of crime, detention of suspects, formal arrest and pretrial custody, and preparatory examination. State security organs are charged with cases involving counterrevolutionary organizations and espionage operations. The people's procuratorate is responsible for approving arrests, conducting procuratorial control (including investigation), and initiating public prosecutions. The people's courts are responsible for adjudication. Finally, the judicial administrative departments are responsible for the execution of court judgments and decisions.

Court System

The people's courts in China consist of a unified, hierarchical system of four courts: basic people's court, intermediate people's court, higher people's court and the Supreme People's Court. Additionally, there are special courts with special jurisdictions. The basic people's courts, established in each autonomous county, include criminal tribunals, civil tribunals, and economic tribunals. Most ordinary civil and criminal cases are handled in first-instance cases by the basic people's courts, although law requires that certain sorts be heard directly by the higher people's courts. In large geographical jurisdictions, the basic people's courts can establish separate people's tribunals according to the specific circumstances. The judgment and decisions of the people's tribunal carry the same weight as those of the basic people's courts.

The intermediate people's courts maintain criminal tribunals, civil tribunals, and economic tribunals; and they establish other tribunals when necessary. The cases handled by the intermediate people's courts are of four categories: a) first-instance cases within their jurisdictions, such as counter-revolutionary cases, cases in which there may be a sentence of life imprisonment or death, and cases involving foreigners; b) first-instance cases transferred from the basic people's courts; c) appeals and counter-pleas made by people challenging the judgments and decisions of the basic people's courts; and d) cases protested by the people's procuratorate at the corresponding level.

The higher people's courts include criminal tribunals, civil tribunals, economic tribunals, and other tribunals established when necessary. Cases handled by the higher people's courts are of five types: a)

first-instance cases within their jurisdiction, including the major criminal cases which affect an entire province; b) first-instance cases transferred from the lower people's courts; c) appeals and counterpleas made by people dissatisfied with the judgments and decisions of the intermediate people's courts; and e) cases protested by the people's procuratorate at the corresponding level.

The Supreme People's Court (seated in Beijing) includes criminal tribunals, civil tribunals, and economic tribunals, and other tribunals set up when necessary. Cases handled by the Supreme People's Court include: a) first-instance cases exclusively within its jurisdiction, including major criminal cases with an impact on the entire country; b) cases appealed and counter-pleaded by people dissatisfied with the judgments and decisions of higher people's courts and special people's courts; and c) cases protested by the Supreme People's Procuratorate according to supervisory proceedings. Judgments and decisions of first-instance or second-instance cases made by the Supreme People's Court all constitute judgments and decisions of the last instance, and become legally effective the day they are announced. The primary function of the Supreme People's Court is to exercise leadership over lower level courts.

Special courts, established according to law for special departments or special cases include military courts, maritime courts, and railway transportation courts. They handle cases within their own organizational systems. The military courts handle cases of violation of military codes and criminal cases involving servicemen. The maritime courts handle cases related to maritime affairs and businesses. And the railway transportation courts handle criminal cases which occur along rail lines and aboard trains, as well as cases of economic disputes related to rail transportation.

In China's unified, hierarchical court system, courts at higher levels oversee the administration of justice by those at lower levels. The Supreme People's Court, the highest judicial organ, supervises the administration of justice by local courts at different levels and by special courts. Its judgments and rulings are final. Few cases are tried at first instance by the Supreme People's Court.

The people's court is composed at each level of judicial officers: the president, vice-president, presiding judges, deputy presiding judges, judges, and a number of assistant judges. Judicial officers are elected and appointed by the organ of the state power. The presidents of different levels of courts are elected by people's congresses at corresponding levels. Vice-presidents, presiding judges, deputy presiding judges, and judges are appointed and dismissed by the standing committees of the people's congresses at corresponding levels. Assistant judges are appointed and dismissed by the courts at the same level. Assistant judges can act for judges at the suggestion of the president of the court and with the approval of the judicial committee. The courts are accountable only to the people's congresses at corresponding levels.

China's judicial organization includes special judicial committees which are set up at different levels of the people's courts. These committees do not try cases directly, but discuss and make decisions on the most important or difficult cases handled by collegiate benches of judges. They are also responsible for reviewing judicial actions and making recommendations on judicial work. The judicial committee exercises collective leadership over the judicial activity within each people's court. Members of the judicial committee are appointed or dismissed by the standing committee of the people's congress at the request of the president of the court. Membership on the judicial committee is generally delegated to highly qualified professionals in the judiciary system who have considerable legal and political experience. Their meetings are presided over by the president of the court, and they follow the principle of majority rule.

Cases of minor criminal offenses and private prosecution can be tried by one judge. Adjudications of serious criminal cases in the first instance are conducted by a collegiate bench composed of one to three judges and two to four people's assessors, depending on the nature of the case and court level. Adjudications of appeals are final, and are conducted by a collegiate bench composed of three to five judges. The people's assessors are lay people elected or invited temporarily. Citizens who have reached the age of 23 and are eligible to vote and stand for election may be elected as people's assessor. In carrying out their duties at the people's courts, people's assessors are component members of the courts in which they participate and enjoy equal rights with judges. When the collegiate bench conducts its deliberations, if opinions diverge, the minority defer to the majority, but the opinion of the minority is entered in the record. At the discretion of the presiding judge, major or difficult cases can be submitted to the judicial committee for discussion and decisions. The collegiate bench is obligated to carry out decisions made by the judicial committee.

The courts try cases and pronounce verdicts publicly. Cases which are not subject to an open trial as specified by law include those involving state secrets, privacy, personal secrets, and juvenile delinquency.

The accused in a criminal case has a right to self-defense. He or she has the right to argue the case, explain his or her innocence, or request mitigation or relief of punishment. The accused also has the right to hire a lawyer. The defense attorney can also be recommended by the accused's employer or by a citizen allowed by the court. Also, the accused can ask a close relative or guardian to defend his or her case in court. In such necessary cases as a trial with a public prosecutor, the court can appoint a lawyer for an accused with no one to speak in his or her favor.

Basically, the Chinese court system is an inquisitorial one in which the burden of proof rests on the accused, and the judge takes the leading role in the proceedings. Facts such as hard evidence, testimonies by witnesses, and the defendant's confessions are the basis for decisions made by people's courts. During the examination of facts, the defendant enjoys few of the due process rights which are commonly recognized in adversarial court systems such as that of the United States. The presumption of innocence, the exclusionary rule, protection against self-incrimination, the right to a jury trial, and protection against "double jeopardy" are alien to the Chinese courts.

Unlike such common law courts as those of the United States, Britain, Canada, Nigeria, or Ghana, the Chinese courts do not enjoy the power to make law. Judicial precedent, therefore, does not figure in the Chinese system of justice. Consequently, Chinese judges handle cases flexibly, according to the needs of the state at any given time, and do not strive for doctrinal consistency (Leng, 1982).

Procuratorate

The people's procuratorate is set up at levels corresponding with those of the people's courts. At all levels, a people's procuratorate:

a) exercises its procuratorial power in cases of treason, national separatism, and serious sabotage of the implementation of state policies, laws, and governmental decrees;
b) investigates those criminal cases which it directly handles;
c) examines cases handled by public security organs to decide whether or not to issue arrest warrants, and whether or not to initiate and prosecute cases;
d) supervises investigative processes to ensure that the public security organs conform to the law;
e) supervises prosecution processes to ensure the legality of the judicial activities of the people's courts;

f) reviews the legality of court judgments;
g) supervises the execution of judgments in criminal cases; and
h) monitors the activities of prisons, detention houses, reformatories, and reform-through-labor establishments.

People's procuratorates exercise a very important function in criminal cases. They approve arrests made or to be made by public security organs and determine whether or not to initiate prosecutions. It is also their responsibility to ensure equal treatment for criminal defendants as well as to discourage interference by other governmental agencies, officials, or private persons.

Public Security Organs

Public security organs (police) carry out the following main tasks: a) investigation, detention, and making arrests; b) securing the populace and maintaining public order; c) safeguarding state organs, enterprises, and other institutions and establishments; d) executing administrative punishment; and e) handling administrative routines, such as residence registration and citizen exit and entry.

The public security organs are both hierarchical and local in organization. The Ministry of Public Security of the central government directs the national police force through its provincial and local bureaus. In time of emergency, every local police officer can be mobilized through this vertical command system. In the meantime, public security organs at different levels are under the horizontal supervision and leadership of government agencies at the same levels. For example, the Ministry of Public Security is under the leadership of the State Council and the Beijing Public Security Bureau is a department of the Beijing Municipality.

The formal structure of the current system is described by a leading official of the Ministry of Public Security as follows:

The Ministry of Public Security is under the State Council, and the Social Security Bureau is a professional bureau under the ministry and consists of a criminal investigation department, and an institute of forensic science and technology. The public security bureaus of the provinces, municipalities directly under central government, and autonomous regions have social security and criminal investigation departments. The public security bureau at the prefecture level has a social security and criminal investigation section, and the public security bureau at the county level, a social security and criminal investigation team. In cities, the public security bureaus have their social security and criminal investigation divisions or sections. At the grass roots, are located their police stations (Brewer et al., 1988).

In the police's hierarchical system, the most effective organization in social control may be the neighborhood police station. The neighborhood police handle all kinds of activities such as criminal investigation, peace keeping, residence registration, legal education, foot or bicycle patrol, and visiting offenders and their families within the jurisdiction. The police motto holds that the local police officers belong to the people, are not functionally and structurally separate from the masses, and should be active in community affairs (Johnson, 1978). In order to promote good relations between the police and the masses, the neighborhood police officers serve the people in kindly ways such as: sending sick to the hospital; helping the lost find their homes; shopping for the aged; removing garbage around the community; taking part in mediation to resolve conflicts; educating the young and the potential offenders. They also listen to people's comments and opinions in order to provide them with better services. In return, the neighborhood police require the residents to cooperate in crime prevention

and investigation, and in watching out for potential offenders and strangers.

According to the Security Administration Punishment Act, which was first passed in 1957, republished in 1980, and amended in 1987, the police have the power to order and carry out "administrative punishment" in cases of minor crimes and public-order offenses by means of warnings, fines, and detention in police cells. The maximum fine is 400 yuan (the average monthly salary was about 100 yuan in 1987), and the maximum detention period is 15 days. A dissatisfied defendant has the right to appeal his sentence, first to a higher level in the Public Security Bureau, and ultimately to the courts. In minor cases the police alone carry out apprehension, adjudication, and correction without reference to the procurator, the courts, or the correctional institutions (Bracey, 1989b). The Security Administration Punishment Act made the police the most powerful organ in the Chinese criminal justice system.

State Security Organs

State security organs are secret police bureaus handling cases of counter revolutionary (i.e., anti-communist and/or anti-current government) organizations and foreign espionage. Little is known by the public of their organizations and tasks. Their subject matter jurisdictions are claimed to be similar to those of the public security organs in criminal cases (*Encyclopedia of New China*, 1987).

Lawyers

Traditionally, China had no formally recognized "lawyer system." An experiment in legal profession was conducted in the mid-1950s, but was discontinued after only three years. The system was reestablished in response to the 1979 code of criminal law and criminal procedure law. By

1993, there were about 4,100 law firms and offices with 50,000 lawyers in China (Zhang, 1993).

The function of lawyers is to offer legal aid to state organs, institutions, people's organizations, enterprises, and citizens in order to ensure the correct implementation of state laws. Furthermore, the lawyers are to protect the interests of the state, collectives, and the lawful rights and interests of citizens. Lawyers are allowed the following scope of operations:

a) to accept engagements from state organs, institutions, social organizations, and enterprises to act as their legal advisers;

b) to accept the authorization of parties to civil cases and act as agents taking part in prosecution;

c) to accept the authorization of parties to criminal cases or appointments of people's courts and act as defenders;

d) to accept the authorization of private parties in private prosecutions, injured parties in public prosecutions or their immediate family members, to act as agents and take part in prosecutions;

e) to offer legal aid upon the authorization of parties involved in disputes, and to act as agents taking part in mediation or arbitration; and

f) to answer questions on law, and to draft indictments or complaints and other legal documents on behalf of parties to a lawsuit.

In China, private legal profession is not permitted. Lawyers work either for government legal-advisory offices or in lawyer associations. Judges and procurators receive separate legal training and are not lawyers. In a criminal lawsuit, lawyers are not seen as defenders of individual rights or as protectors of opposition to the government. A lawyer is first and foremost responsible to the court, not to the client. If the client has confessed to his lawyer that he committed a crime, the lawyer must plead his client guilty of the offense: it is a criminal act in China for a lawyer to shield a guilty client. Since the notion of presumption of innocence is not accepted by the government, "seeking truth from the facts" has become the standard in criminal cases. Under this principle, a lawyer who has discovered that a client committed a criminal act cannot plead *"not guilty"* for him or her. The most the defense attorney can do in such a case is ask for leniency. Thus, as indicated by Ingraham (1987), Chinese lawyers emphasize substantive justice much more than procedural justice.

Corrections

The judicial administrative organs are responsible for all correctional activities except for juvenile work-study schools used for reforming minor juvenile offenders, and police jails used for short-term administrative punishment. The Ministry of Justice of the central government, and bureaus and departments of justice at various levels, have been judicial administrative organs since 1983, replacing the Ministry of Public Security.

China has more than six hundred correctional institutions with 1.1 million inmates (Chen, 1993). Correctional institutions include provincial and municipal prisons, reform-through-labor camps, and juvenile reformatories, where convicts serve fixed term imprisonments, life imprisonments, or death sentences with a suspension of two years. Most serious offenders are assigned to reform-through-labor camps.

Punishment and rehabilitation are both included in Chinese corrective philosophy, and both are carried out by the policy of reform-through-labor. This policy is based on the belief that people are basically good, albeit corruptible; that bad examples and bad company can lead individuals astray; that education is the best tool for systemic and individual reform; and that people are malleable throughout their lives (Bracey, 1989a; Munro, 1977).

The process of reform-through-labor relies on combining labor production with political education. All prisoners with the physical ability to do so are required to work. The prison administration operates factories and farms, and obtains sub-contracts from outside enterprises. Inmates are not paid beyond a small regular allowance, since labor is one way to repay society for their wrongdoing. The products of prison labor are turned over to the state. The length of labor is generally limited to nine or ten hours daily. During the busiest production seasons, the length of labor is twelve hours a day, at most (*Encyclopedia of New China*, 1987:186). Juvenile convicts are organized to do appropriate light labor, taking into consideration their age and health needs.

In both juvenile and adult institutions, political education is used to rehabilitate and reform. Political education includes legal education such as study of laws and regulations, and moral education in socialist ideology (e.g., positive attitudes toward work, acceptance of collectivism) and social ethics. Self-criticism and mutual criticism are an important part of the process. Everybody is supposed to confess his or her crime and make self-criticism in public. Juvenile inmates, as well as adults, may receive cultural education at their own level—from elementary school through college. Vocational education is available in most of the institutions.

By their policy of meting out rewards, correctional institutions give convicts a chance to perform meritorious services to atone for their crimes. Convicts with good records are given oral commendations, are offered material rewards, have their terms of imprisonment reduced, or are granted parole. On the other hand, those who either refuse to repent or refuse to accept reform-through-labor are punished. Those found to have committed additional criminal offenses or new sorts of crimes during their term of reform-through-labor are referred to the people's procuratorate.

Often the Chinese correctional system has been regarded as a humane, natural, and practical model for the West (Allen, 1987). However, it is necessary to realize that Chinese authorities' patience has not been unlimited. Their intolerance can be found in three different situations. First, if the correctional officers' genuine commitment to help inmates bears no fruit, they may terminate further efforts. Second, "punishing one to warn a hundred" is an accepted correctional principle, and its implementation has resulted in the execution of thousands of habitual criminals and dangerous offenders who committed crimes ranging from murder, rape, and bribery to political dissension. Third, in the political and judicial campaigns against various specific offenders, severe penalties can be imposed on convicts without allowing for the possibility of reform. These campaigns are usually launched by the central or local governments and are designed to "frighten the criminal, encourage healthy trends, give publicity to the legal system and educate the masses" (*Questions and answers*, 1986:147).

According to a 1983 decision of the Standing Committee of the National People's Congress, sentences are allowed to overpass the maximum punishment fixed in the criminal code during campaigns against some offenders (Xu, 1992:18). For instance, in the current campaign against smuggling illegal immigrants into foreign countries, the legal secretariat of the Party's Central Committee declared that in order to stop such illegal activity effectively, the organizers of smuggling must be punished severely, and the death penalty is one of the alternatives (Ren, 1993).

Thus, both rehabilitation and punishment are considered philosophies of Chinese correction, and the Chinese correctional system is capable of being lenient on one hand and severe on the other.

From the above discussion, one can tell that the functions of formal Chinese criminal justice institutions are designed to support each other when handling criminal cases, and to provide checks and balances. For example, the procuratorate supervises investigations by the public security organ, examining and approving arrests and prosecutions. It also oversees trials and deliberations of verdicts by the court. Also, if the public security organ disagrees with a procuratorial decision such as not to arrest or to sue, it can ask for reconsideration. If its suggestion is rejected, it can ask for review by the procuratorate at a higher level. If the court finds the facts are unclear or insufficient to support the procuratorate's prosecution, it can return the prosecution to the procuratorate for a supplement. If the case is not important enough to follow up, it can ask the procuratorate to retract its suit or refuse to accept it.

One must also realize the importance of the relationship between the Chinese Communist Party (CCP) and the Chinese criminal justice system. Although the CCP has separated considerably from the state legal system since 1978, Party policy still plays a key role in judicial work. The justice system does not enjoy actual judicial independence in most significant cases. Under the principle of "strengthening party leadership," which is considered one of the four cardinal principles for modernizing China, one cannot expect the influence and control of the CCP to disappear in the near future.

Informal Justice System [2]

More than in most other nations, informal justice is an organic part of the entire Chinese criminal justice mechanism. The formal system and the informal system are connected with each other and are often fused. The teachings of proper behavior and the controlling of law-breaking run a parallel course through formal and informal methods (Krase and Sagarin, 1980). The current policy of comprehensive treatment for social order focuses not only on formal judicial measures, but on informal combining of all political, economic, executive, educational, cultural, and judicial methods. The implementation of informal justice relies heavily on the activities of neighborhood public security committees (PSCs), people's mediation committees, and the security departments of enterprises and institutions.

According to the 1982 Chinese Constitution, each urban neighborhood committee and rural village committee is made up of a public security committee, a people's mediation committee, and other public affairs committees (Article 111). These unofficial organizations are grounded in citizen participation through a network of committees composed of unpaid, elected representatives who are usually retired governmental cadres and workers.

The public security committee (PSC) can be used by local police for mobilizing the residents to participate in crime prevention. In 1992, there were more than 1.17 million public security committees nationwide and more than twelve million PSC members (Xu, 1992). The major functions of the PSC are:

a) to assist the judicial organs in criminal investigations by (e.g.) cordoning off the scene of a crime, informing the police of any suspect, conducting surveillance of the defendant prior to trial, and supervising the convicts on suspended sentences or parole, or when they are out of custody for medical treatment;
b) to patrol, inspect, and safeguard the neighborhood. In the daytime, safety sentries are posted in key areas, and at night, foot patrol is widely used;
c) to identify and advise potential offenders. The PSC analyzes and identifies those who have criminal histories and are potential offenders in the neighborhood. PSC members are assigned as advisors to potential offenders in order to help them re-

solve usual problems such as residence registration, employment, marriage, and family. The advisors also educate and discipline potential offenders to drive them back into conventional society;

d) to investigate and determine the causes of some minor offenses such as petty larceny and fist-fighting. In this case, the PSC plays the role of police and judge. Punishment could be a written self-criticism;

e) to popularize legal concepts and advise citizens to observe the law; and

f) to help mediators to settle civil disputes and prevent such controversies from developing into criminal offenses.

The PSC has yielded positive results by discovering, controlling, halting, and preventing crime. In 1988, 35,985 criminals of all kinds were apprehended by PSC members and other informal justice organizations in three municipalities—Beijing, Shanghai, and Tianjin. The PSC also helped the police uncover 19,193 criminal cases (Xu, 1992).

Another important informal justice agency is the people's mediation committee (PMC). According to the 1982 Constitution of PRC, Article 111, there must be a people's mediation committee under each neighborhood committee in urban areas and under each village committee in rural areas. People's mediation committees may also be set up in enterprises and institutions. By the end of 1988, there were about one million mediation committees in China with 6.37 million mediators (Si, 1989).

The history of mediation in China can be traced back two thousand years to when the principles of Confucianism reformed the Chinese people's behavior. The Confucians believed that criminal punishment could not bring people to awareness of high morals in human society; educating the offenders and the general public in moral principles, on the other hand, could

assure knowledge of the correct way to behave. Therefore, only the most serious offenses would be left for the formal justice authority to deal with by punishment. The vast majority of civil disputes and less serious criminal offenses were disposed of locally, most of them through mediation that was regarded as a form of moral education.

Although some changes have occurred in the structure and process of nonjudicial conflict management, the basic principles of out-of-court mediation of conflict have remained in contemporary dealings between persons and organizations.

People's mediation committees operate under the guidance of local governments and local people's courts, and the legal assistant of local government is in charge of mediation committee affairs. Members of the people's mediation committee are elected by the people living or working in the PMC's jurisdiction. They are volunteers and "solid citizens"—retired or current workers and petty officials, usually older and respected, maintaining close links with the masses, enthusiastic in promoting public welfare, and having some legal knowledge.

The system of people's mediation is a necessary element in mass self-government, self-control, self-administration, and self-education. The mediator works at the request of the people involved in a conflict and can also intervene directly in a conflict without being requested to do so. Because the mediator lives in the community, he or she is usually able to respond to the incident quickly. The service is free. In settling a dispute, the mediator is not entitled to use any forceful administrative or legal measures. The basic method of response and intervention is reasoning and persuasion. During mediation, laws and policies are explained to the parties concerned. Public morale is discussed and the interests of each party are balanced, commonly resulting in compromise. In the 1980s, about 7 million conflicts were resolved annually through mediation (Si, 1989).

Entering mediation is based on the principle of voluntariness. Not every disputing party must go through the process of mediation. If one of the parties refuses to enter mediation, or if the mediation effort fails, or if one of the parties decides to bring the case up again after having first accepted the results of mediation, he or she can file a lawsuit directly at a court or request the local government's decision. However, according to the "People's Mediation Committee Organic Rules" (1989), once the parties concerned enter mediation and once a mediated agreement is reached, each party should carry out the agreement. In other words, the mediated agreement has the force of law, and any violation of the agreement may result in a lawsuit (Ai, 1989).

The people's mediation committees are responsible for settling ordinary civil disputes and minor criminal cases. They also familiarize the people with laws and government policies. Ordinary civil disputes occur over such issues as neighborhood relations, housing, debts, marriage, family, compensation for losses, inheritance, division of family property, provision of livelihood for aged parents, and support of children after a divorce. Minor criminal cases include such offenses as minor physical injury, maltreatment, petty larceny, encroachments, scuffles or fist-fights, and slander. Generally, the people's mediation committee procedures are quite casual, unhurried, and nonstandardized. However, there is some formality: keeping of records, preparing of agreements, and standardizing of the physical arrangements of the mediation sessions (Clark, 1989). Results of mediation are filed and written agreements may be issued at the request of the interested parties.

In addition to the resident neighborhood and village PSCs and PMCs, security departments are also set up in such large enterprises as factories, companies, universities, and government bureaus, as part of the informal criminal justice system. The personnel of such security departments are generally full-time professionals, many of them with military or police experience. When necessary, they can carry weapons for enforcing the law. Functions carried out by the security departments are quite similar to those carried out by the public security committees; they assist the police in investigating crimes inside the enterprise; they handle some minor offenses, both investigating and punishing; they safeguard properties of the enterprise; they supervise probationers and parolees in the enterprise; and they popularize laws and regulations, advising employees to observe the law. Working together with other formal and informal judicial agencies, the security departments play a very important role in crime prevention and in settling minor offenses.

All of these informal justice mechanisms have significantly regulated behavior, controlling crime and maintaining social order, but they are not informal justice in the sense often meant by Western criminologists. These committees and departments are part of the local administrative structures mandated by Chinese Executive Laws, and they are guided by the Communist Party and its governmental policies. Thus, in China, the state remains ultimately in charge of both the formal and the informal justice mechanisms. It not only implants its ideology in these informal agencies, but actually controls their operations. These organizations are informal in the Western sense only by their use of persuasion, reasoning, and administrative methods to settle disputes and combat crime, instead of mobilizing the police, going to court, and sentencing an offender to imprisonment.

To summarize, Chinese society historically has been regulated by two criminal justice systems. The formalized bureaucratic justice based on the centralized government emphasized punishment and reforming the convict. Popular, informal justice is rooted in community associations and emphasizes mediation and education. Basically, formal justice deals with the serious offenders, punishing them for their misconduct, and reforming them into "new people"; while informal justice manages minor and potential offenders, helping them to resolve problems that may result in criminal activity, and educating them by promoting laws and public morals. The two systems complement each other, sharing a common aim: shouldering and pressuring the deviant back into tracks set by the society's norms and the nation's power base.

Notes

1. The discussion of the formal criminal justice system in this section draws heavily on *The Criminal Law and the Criminal Procedure Law of China* (1984); "The Criminal Procedure Law of the People's Republic of China" (1982); the *Encyclopedia of New China* (1987); Felkenes, "Courts, Sentencing, and the Death Penalty in the PRC" (1989); McCabe, "Structural Elements of Contemporary Criminal Justice in the People's Republic of China" (1988); and Min Zhang and Shan Changzong, "Inside China's Court System" (1990).

2. The major sources for this section include our personal experiences; Y. Fang, "Public Security Organization" (1988); Clark, "Conflict Management outside the Courtrooms of China" (1989); and the *Encyclopedia of New China* (1987).

Discussion and Revision Questions

1. Why did imperial China have no written constitution?

2. Compare and contrast individual rights in China and Denmark.

3. What are the three branches of the formal justice system in China?

4. Why were the Kuomintang laws abolished in 1949?

5. What are the two main functions of the informal justice system in China?

6. What is meant by popular justice in China?

7. What is the modus operandi of popular justice in China?

8. What are the four categories of cases handled by Intermediate People's Courts in China?

9. What cases are handled by the Supreme People's Court?

10. Describe briefly the role of Chinese judicial committees in the criminal justice system.

11. What are the functions of the Procuratorate?

12. What are the functions of neighborhood police?

13. Compare and contrast customary courts in Nigeria and the Chinese informal courts.

14. Compare and contrast the role of lawyers in American and in Chinese criminal justice systems.

15. What are the functions of Public Security Committees?

16. Briefly explain the following:

    a. Urban Neighborhood Committee;
    b. Rural Village Committee;
    c. People's Mediation Committee.

10

The Court System in the People's Republic of China With a Case Study of a Criminal Trial

Robert Davidson and Zheng Wang

Introduction

The American and Chinese approaches to social control are enforced by two very different philosophical and experimental perspectives (Rojek, 1985). Indeed, they differ so fundamentally that they invite comparison in order to promote a better understanding of each. This chapter will attempt such a comparison focusing on the basic structure, organizational dynamics, and philosophies of the Chinese judicial system. In order to illustrate how the system works, a case study of criminal trial also will be provided. Finally, a summary on the trial will be given from a comparative perspective.

The present court system in China was first designed after the founding of the People's Republic of China in 1949, but has been remodeled several times since. Under Article 17 of the Common Program[1], "laws and decrees promoting the people shall be enacted, and the people's judicial systems shall be established" (Important documents, 1949:1–20). Later, the Ministry of Justice was set up, with the court system being one of the functions within the Ministry. On September 20, 1954, the first adopted Constitution announced that the court system would be separated from governmental supervision under the Ministry of Justice and under an independent system, the Supreme People's Court. September 28, 1954 saw passage of Organic Law of the People's Court , which laid out the present court system.

Overall Structure

According to the Organic Law of the People's Courts of the People's Republic of China, the judicial authority of the state is exercised through the Supreme People's Court, local people's court's, and special people's courts.

Special courts include military, maritime, railway-transportation, forestry, and other courts. The military courts handle cases of violation of military duties and criminal cases involving servicemen in the Chinese People's Liberation Army. The maritime courts deal with cases related to maritime affairs. There are eight maritime courts in the eight coastal and island river ports. Railway-transportation courts handle criminal cases which occur along rail lines and aboard trains, as well as cases of economic dispute related to rail transportation.

The major court system in China is divided into two levels: the Supreme People's Court at the national level and the

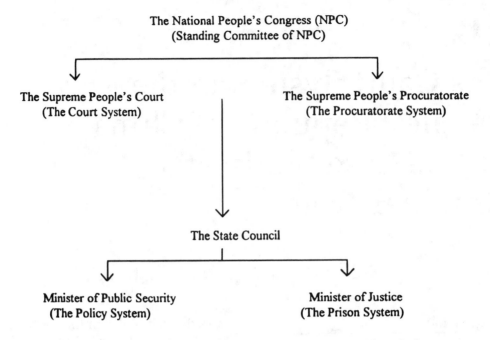

The National People's Congress (NPC)
(Standing Committee of NPC)

The Supreme People's Court
(The Court System)

The Supreme People's Procuratorate
(The Procuratorate System)

The State Council

Minister of Public Security
(The Policy System)

Minister of Justice
(The Prison System)

Figure 10.1   The Legal System of the People's Republic of China

local people's courts at the divisional levels. The local people's courts are subdivided into another three levels: the Higher People's Courts at the provincial, autonomous region and autonomous city level; the Intermediate People's Court's at the municipal or prefecture level; and the Basic People's Courts at the Urban district level or rural county level (also called the District People's Court).

There are five autonomous regions in China, each occupying an area inhabited predominantly by minority peoples. Their governments have the same basic responsibilities as the provincial governments in economic affairs, but enjoy more favorable national policies.

Three of China's largest and most important cities, Beijing, Shanghai, and Tianjin are called autonomous or centrally administered cities. They are not subject to provincial governments, but under the direct supervision of the central government or the State Council. Therefore, each of these three cities has a Higher People's Court, an Intermediate People's Court, and several District People's Courts.

Prefectures lie within autonomous regions, and county levels. Their main function is to provide a convenient administrative division for minorities who occupy areas larger than counties but smaller than provinces.

China's judicial system is a highly centralized (unified) and hierarchical organization. The Constitution gives the Standing Committee of the National People's Congress (NPC) judicial as well as legislative control of the country. The Standing Committee interprets the Constitution and various statutes, it enacts and amends statutes, and also supervises the work of the Supreme People's Court, the Supreme People's Procuratorate, and the State Council. This is unlike the United States, which limits constitutional interpretations to the highest judicial organ (the U.S. Supreme Court).

The Supreme People's Court is the highest judicial organ in China. It supervises the administration of justice by the various local courts, although these local people's courts also must answer to the Standing Committee of the NPC at corresponding

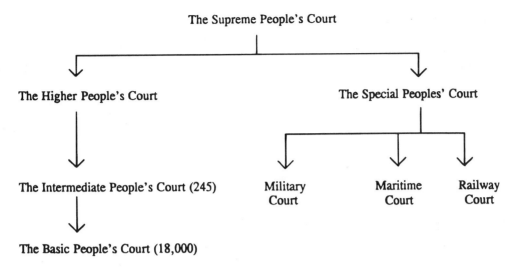

The Supreme People's Court

The Higher People's Court

The Special Peoples' Court

The Intermediate People's Court (245)

Military Court   Maritime Court   Railway Court

The Basic People's Court (18,000)

Figure 10.2   The Court System of the People's Republic of China

levels. The Supreme People's Court has several important functions. First, it explains how laws and decrees should be specifically applied in judicial procedures. Such explanation by the Supreme Court usually occurs in two ways: in response to petitions from local courts and in notices issued to local courts in the region (Gong, 1989). Second, the Supreme People's Court deals with cases that will have significant impact on the whole judicial system of the country. When the Supreme People's Court decides a case, its judgment or order is final. Third, it hears appeals from Higher People's Court. Finally, it approves death sentences.

Few Cases are tried directly by the Supreme Court. Since 1949, first instance trials have included only the cases of Japanese war criminals and the Lin Biao and "Gang of Four" cases. The court operates at four levels, consisting of four subcourts (also called divisions, chambers, or tribunals): the criminal court, the civil court, the economic court, and the administrative court. On certain occasions and for special purposes an additional court is set up.

The different levels of criminal court have jurisdiction over criminal cases. The criminal court within the Higher People's Court at the provincial level serves as a court of both first and second instance. As a court of first instance, it decides major cases that have an impact on the entire province. As a court of second instance, it receives appeals from the criminal court of the Intermediate People's Court at the municipal or prefecture level.

The criminal court within the Intermediate People's Court hears the criminal cases of major crimes in the jurisdiction, such as murder, rape, robbery, bombing, arson, and grand larceny. Like the Higher People's Court, the Intermediate People's Court also serves as a court of second instance.

The criminal court within the Basic People's Court tries misdemeanor and minor felonious cases, such as theft, assault, and violations of public order. This level of the courts carries the heaviest workload in the judicial system. In recent years, some district courts in Beijing, Tianjin and some other larger cities have also established neighborhood-based courts. These courts not only handle cases in their permanent offices, but also make a circuit of localities to try the cases on the spot. The procedure has allowed them to handle large numbers of civil disputes. Today, they handle some 70–80 percent of the civil cases and economic disputes accepted by those district courts (Zhang and Shan, 1990).

Every court is composed of a president, two or more vice-presidents, one chief judge (presiding judge of a given division), several deputy judges, judges, and assistant judges. The court president is elected by the people's congress at the corresponding level, while other members are appointed and dismissed by the standing committees of those congresses. Assistant judges can act for judges at the suggestion of the president of the court with the approval of the judicial committee, and they are appointed and dismissed by the courts at the same level.

Every court at every level must set up a judicial committee to deal with the most difficult or major cases. Instead of trying cases directly, the committee first discusses and then decides the most important or difficult cases submitted by collegiate benches of judges. Its members are appointed by the Standing Committee of NPC at the corresponding level, upon the recommendation of the president of the court. The procurators at the corresponding levels have the right to attend the committee meeting as observers.

Major Procedures

The people's courts at various levels in China abide by the following procedures in their judicial responsibilities.

Pretrial

The court should send a copy of the indictment to the accused at least seven working days before the trial, and also notify the accused of the trial's location. The court must also notify the victim, the defense attorney, the witness, the examination expert, and the translator at least three working days before the trial. Finally, the court also has to inform the procuratorate at least three days before the trial.

Personnel of the Court

↓

President of the Court

↓

Vice Presidents

↓

Chief Judge of the Division
(Criminal, Civil, Economic, and Administrative)

↓

Deputy Judges

↓

Judges

↓

Assistant Judges

Figure 10.3 The Composition of Each Court

Right to Defense Counsel

The accused, apart from having the right to defend himself, has the right to choose to entrust a lawyer, relative, or lay advocate recommended by his work unit to plead on his behalf. The court may also appoint an advocate for the accused at its own discretion. However the defense counsel may only consult the materials of the case, acquaint himself or herself with the circumstances of the case, and interview and correspond with a defendant held in custody. The counsel has no right to participate in the preliminary investigation (McCabe, 1989:123).

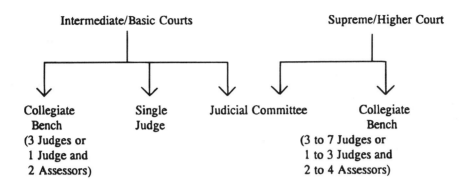

Figure 10.4 Types of Trials in the People's Republic of China

Trial

Criminal cases of both instances are heard in public, unless they involve issues of state secrets, privacy, or juvenile offenders under the age of 18. Occasionally, the criminal court even hears a criminal case in the work unit or college where the defendant is resident. There are several reasons behind this practice. First, as the court exposes and punishes the criminal in the hearing, citizens learn that criminal deeds are dangerous to society and lead to serious consequences. Second, this awareness should increase the citizen's sense of responsibility in obeying the law and fighting crime. Finally the public trial warns potential criminals to give up their intentions and to become law-abiding citizens (Du and Zhang, 1990:103).

In local people's courts, cases of the first instance are tried either by an appointed judge for minor offenses, or before a collegiate bench consisting of an appointed judge and two people's assessors (jurors). The judge of a collegiate bench is appointed by the president of the court or by the chief judge of the division concerned. The two people's assessors may be the defendant's relatives or friends with the permission of the court. This is usually the case when the defendant is disabled, deaf, or mute. In most cases, the two assessors are the citizens elected by the defendant's work unit. Citizens who have reached the age of 23 and are eligible to vote and stand for election may be elected as people's jurors. Article 105 states that assessors have equal status with judges (*Criminal law*, 1984:147). The opinion of the majority prevails, but the minority viewpoint is recorded.

The purpose of the people's assessors is to ensure that the "mass line" is followed, and that the opinion of the people is considered at all court trials. Additionally, the people's assessors serve indirectly as educators. The masses can learn from the assessors in group discussions in work units or neighborhood associations (Rojek, 1985). In other words, this process increases the involvement of the community, bridges the gap between the community and the courts, and has the potential to reduce disparities in sentencing (Allen, 1987a)

There are two possible results of the trial. First, the court may find the accused innocent and acquit him or her immediately. Second, the court may find the accused guilty and sentence him or her at the end of the trial, sending the verdict in writing to the convicted offender and the procuratorate within five working days after the trail.

Penalty

There are five major penalties and three supplementary penalties listed in Criminal Law. These five major penalties are control, criminal detention, fixed-term imprisonment, life imprisonment, and death penalty. The three supplementary penalties are fines, deprivation of political rights, and confiscation of property (*Criminal law*, 1984:17–18). The five major penalties and three additional penalties can be meted out concurrently or independently.

The Chinese judicial system, like those of Nigeria, Ghana, and Sierra Leone, decides on both conviction and sentencing on the same day the trial ends, with the sentence taking immediate effect. This saves time and resources and also prevents any potential interference from outside. Two points need to be elaborated. First, control or surveillance, similar to "probation," ranges from three months to two years. The person sentenced to control can live with his family, continue to work, and enjoy his rights to citizenship; but he must report to the police regularly.

Second, according to the principle of combining punishment with leniency, the court can sentence a defendant to death with a two-year suspension, depending on the circumstances. This means that the person will have a two-year stay of the actual execution of the death sentence. During the two-year period, the person is given a last opportunity to repent and mend his ways by reformation through labor. If he meets the requirements, the death sentence with two-year suspension can be reduced to life imprisonment by the court upon the recommendation of the prison authority. The death penalty or death with two-year suspension is only applied for those persons convicted of the most odious and atrocious offenses, such as murder, rape, counter-revolutionary offenses, and high-level official corruption (Felkenes, 1989:151).

The verdict of capital punishment must be reported to the Supreme People's Court for examination and approval, and becomes legally effective after it is approved. The death sentence must be pronounced or approved by the Supreme People's Court after re-examination by a Higher People's Court.

In 1983, a special statute was passed to stipulate that the Higher People's Court at the provincial level has the authority to approve the death sentence in cases of murder, rape, robbery, and explosion/bombing.

Appeal

Criminal procedure law stipulates the right to one appeal by either the accused or the procurator. When a person has been convicted and sentenced, he or she can appeal to a higher court within 10 working days after the trial, if he or she is dissatisfied with the decision of the court. If the person has been convicted for murder, rape, robbery, or explosion, he or she must appeal within three working days. The person can appeal either to the court of first instance, or go directly up to the court at the next level. By the same principle, the procuratorate at the same level may protest the ordinary criminal judgments or order of a legal supervisory organ of the state by appealing to a court at the next level within 10 working days. Cases involving murder, rape, robbery, or explosion should be protested by the procuratorate within three working days after the trial. If the accused makes appeal, the court can not increase the punishment, but an appeal by the procuratorate can increase punishment (McCabe, 1989:125). The execution of sentences is carried out as originally specified until some appellate body directs otherwise.

Second Instance

The second instance (or appellant instance) is conducted by a higher court, which reviews the verdict of the court of the first instance, when a party concerned appeals or the procuratorate protests against the verdict. Unlike practices in Britain, Nigeria, and the United States, the appellate court reviews both the facts and the laws of the case. A collegiate bench consisting of three to five judges examines the case and comes to a decision. The bench may rebuff the appeal or modify the original judgment. In these two instances, the judgment or order of the higher court is final.

The appellate bench may also withdraw the original judgment and return it to the original court for a retrial. In this case, the accused can appeal again if he disagrees with the new ruling. The court of second instance should notify the appealing party or the protesting procuratorate of its decisions within 10 working days after the review.

Major Principles

Mutual Restraint

In China, the police, the procuratorate, the court, and the corrections are the four major components in the criminal justice system, and are all state organs of law enforcement with separate responsibilities. These agencies not only coordinate but also restrain each other in order to guarantee accurate and effective enforcement of the law (Zhou, 1987). Specifically, the police are responsible for investigating crime and arresting suspects. The arrests must be approved by another branch, the procuratorate, which then decides whether to prosecute, exempt, or waive the case. In turn, the court decides whether to accept the case prosecuted by the procuratorate or return it to the same procuratorate for further investigation, or to request the procuratorate to withdraw the case. The procuratorate on the other hand may disagree with the decision of the court, and may lodge a protest with the next higher court.

Independence

Article 126 of the Constitution states that "the people's court exercises judicial power independently, and is not subject to interference by administrative organs, public organizations or individuals" (the Constitution, 1986:86). That is to say, that the court must try cases based on the facts and according to law, and its performance should not be subject to interference by individuals, governmental offices, or political parties. One measure which guarantees the independence of the judiciary is the appointment system. Unlike practices in some states in the United States, all judges except assistant judges are appointed and dismissed by the Standing Committee of the National People's Congress at the corresponding level. The government and the Communist Party otherwise should not interfere with the administration of justice by the court.

Equality

Everyone is considered equal before the law. The court should treat every citizen equally under applicable law without regard to nationality, race, sex, occupation, social position, religion, education, financial background, or length of residence. Any special privilege is forbidden.

Language

Citizens of all nationalities have the right to use their own spoken and written languages in court procedures. The court should provide interpreters for court proceedings if necessary.

Combining Punishment with Leniency

Article 1 of the Criminal Law states that the criminal law is "formulated in accordance with the policy of combining punishment with leniency in light of actual circumstances." According to this principle, the court takes into account subjective and objective conditions of crime within the range of the law. For instance, different sentences will apply to the primary culprit and the subordinate; to one who actively engages in crime and one who is coerced into a crime; to the first-time offender and the recidivist; to one who refuses to confess and one who surrenders himself to the police. The attitude of the defendant is very important in mitigating the sentence. Adult offenders caught in flagrante delicto, or who involve children in a crime, are punished severely. Finally, crimes against the state are treated very harshly (Felkenes, 1989:146).

Supervision by the Procuratorate

When a case is being tried, the procuratorate is required to attend the trial and to determine whether the court procedures conform to the law. The procurator can make a protest (counter-plea) to the next higher court if he or she believes that the judge has made an error.

Some Factors and Issues
Affecting the Court System

Because the judicial system is a part of the overall social system, it is greatly affected by certain social and political factors. This is especially true of the judicial system in China.

Function of the Law

One essential function of the court system is to administer justice according to law. However, the Marxist view of law has prevailed for some time in China, and regards law as an instrument of class struggle or class oppression. According to this view, laws in a capitalist society aim at protecting the rich and exploiting the poor,

while in China the law protects the ordinary people. This Marxist view fails to take two important points into account. First, laws in the West are used not only to protect or exploit, but also to readjust internal relations within the society, and further to regulate the life of the whole society. In effect, laws in Marxist China are used to achieve the same purpose—exploitation of the proletariat and protection of the life and property of every citizen. Second, if the law in China is nothing but an instrument of class struggle (or class oppression), how can one explain the laws on traffic, sanitation, forestry, and environmental protection?

In recent years, the debate over whether laws should be a function of class or of society has still gone unsettled. However, more and more people hold that the law should be divided into three categories: one related more closely to class structure, another oriented toward social life, and finally, one that combines elements of both. Criminal law falls within the third category, having a class as well as a social orientation. Overall, people throughout the society benefit from the implementation of the laws. Based on this legal ideology, the court keeps a neutral stand in dealing with criminal cases. However, when it deals with crimes against the state, or with "counter-revolutionary" crimes, it shifts to what the party line directs.

The Party Line

In China, the Communist Party is still the ruling party, and it must play some role in the judicial system. The Constitution emphasizes that the court should administer justice independently. In practice, however, the court is required to implement the policies of the party or the "party line." Such a practice is usually initiated and guided by documents or directives from party organizations at various levels. Obviously, conflict between judicial independence and toeing the party line occasionally arises. Up to this point, no sound solutions have materialized.

Further, if a party or government official (or an official's relative or family member) violates the law, can the law be applied equally by the court? In other words, to what extent can the judicial system act independently? These issues remain controversial in China and the Chinese clearly are engaged in a good-faith effort to reform their practices. However, the question remains: to what extent do pressures or interventions by the party vitiate the protection that the legal system purports to provide? (Gelatt, 1982).

Presumption of Innocence

The basic principles set forth in the introductory section of the Criminal Procedure Law do not clearly espouse a presumption of innocence, but do not negate or deny the presumption either (Gelatt, 1982). Basically, the presumption of innocence is a concept missing from the Chinese judicial system. The concept of presumption of innocence was raised during the French bourgeois revolution in opposition to the feudal principle of presumption of guilt. It played a certain progressive role in the struggle against feudal judicial arbitrariness. But in modern China, the concept of presumption of innocence has been regarded as a manifestation of idealism and metaphysics, and has been rejected in favor of a more practical or pragmatic approach, for two reasons. First, China does not wish criminals to escape penalty under a presumption of innocence. Second, China has its own guideline, the principle of "seeking truth from facts," with "facts" here referring to the evidence that both parties concerned can provide in court.

China would also disagree with the notion that the accused should be presumed innocent prior to the trial. In other words, according to the Criminal Procedure Law of PRC, when the court decides to try the case prosecuted by the procurator, the acceptance of the case by the court itself implies that the court agrees that the accused is guilty. This is because the case has gone through a two-stage pretrial investigation, a procuratorial determination, and a preliminary court screening; if the accused were presumed innocent the court would ask the procuratorate to withdraw the case. Also there is the influence of Confucian ideology. Unlike American society, which stresses the rights of the individual, Confucian ideology emphasizes public interest. Therefore, the judicial system is obligated to maximize protection of public interest first, or the innocent majority. Of course, this practice is maintained at the risk of sacrificing the rights of the accused. But the Chinese would reply that the whole is greater than the sum of its parts. In Western society, the dilemma is known as society versus the individual.

In the Anglo-American legal system, the probable cause standard for prosecution and the absence of an extensive pretrial procedure might make the presumption of innocence at trial seem easier to accept (Gelatt, 1982). In brief, the Anglo-American judicial system tends to categorize the accused as either guilty or innocent, while the Chinese judicial system tends to categorize the accused as either guilty or semi-guilty.

A Case Study

During the summers of 1991 and 1992, one of the authors participated in two study tours in the People's Republic of China (PRC) sponsored by the Office of International Criminal Justice at the University of Illinois at Chicago. During the tour, the author was privileged to observe two Chinese criminal trials in addition to local mediation sessions. The trials were conducted by the Chang Ning District People's Court of Shanghai. The following section describes one of the trials and the related legal proceedings. The authors attempt to illustrate some of the Chinese court system via this example.

Charge

The defendant was arrested on March 11, 1992, by police officers of the Public Security Bureau of Shanghai, and charged with four counts of robbery. Under Article 151 of the Criminal Law (Criminal law, 1984:53), " whoever habitually steals or habitually swindles, or steals, swindles or forcibly seizes articles of public or private property of a relatively large amount is to be sentenced to not more than five years of fixed-term imprisonment, criminal detention or supervision." The trial was held on July 1, 1992.

Defendant's Background

The defendant was in his mid-twenties. He had no previous criminal record. He lived in the district where the crimes were committed and where the trial took place. He had a high school education, and was unemployed at the time of the offense and trial.

The Circumstances of the Case

The defendant was accused of waiting outside a public bath house late at night and then robbing young females as they left the premises. The accused allegedly rode a bicycle rapidly past the victims and grabbed their bags, which contained clothing, money, purses, and other items of value. The total value of the items stolen was 900 yuen (about $165 in U.S. currency). In order to help put this figure into perspective, 900 yuen represents four months' average wages in China. Additionally, the defendant reportedly had worn some of the women's undergarments he stole. This became an important issue in the trial, because the defense attempted to convince the collegial panel that the defendant was psychologically disturbed. The defense pleaded that he should not be held fully accountable for his actions, that he should be institutionalized for psychological treatment rather than being sentenced to prison.

The Trial

Jurisdiction

The Chang Ning District Court has jurisdiction over a 44-square-kilometer area with a population of 580,000 citizens. The court adjudicates cases involving criminal, civil, economic, and administrative issues. During 1991, the court heard 3,700 cases, over half of which were criminal cases (1600–1700 cases were civil).

District Court is the lowest level of courts in the Chinese system. Those found guilty have the right of appeal to the Intermediate People's Court.

Physical Setting of the Court

The courtroom itself is not unlike some courtrooms in the U.S. and Europe. The participants were located at the four sides of a rectangle, facing one another. The judge presided over the trial from a central position behind the bench. He was flanked on either side by people's assessors. The defendant stood in a witness box facing the bench. He could view the judge and the assessors as well as the bench. Defense counsels were seated to the right of the bench, equally facing the others. Directly behind the defendant's box were several rows of seats for the public. This is consistent with the Chinese legal premise that trials should serve as a vehicle for public education as well as adjudication.

Components

Judiciary
A judge presided over the trial. Over 70 percent of the judges in China have university degrees. Chinese judges wear gray public service uniforms with red and gold shoulder boards. The judge headed a collegial bench (panel) which included two people's assessors, private citizens selected to assist the judge in reaching a verdict and sentencing. They have no formal legal training, but have authority that almost equals that of the judge.

One of the assessors is elected from the defendant's work unit. The other is selected from the defendant's neighborhood. The verdict is a product of majority rule, which, of course, could result in the judge being outvoted by the assessors.

The judge and people's assessors are active inquisitors in the trial process. Additionally, the judge also may have chosen to be active investigator in the case.

The Procuratorate

The procurator (the prosecutor) is the major figure in filing formal charges against the accused. Often the procurator chooses to play an active role in the investigation of the offense. During trial, the procurator represents the state interest against the defendant, and conducts a direct examination of the accused. The procurator also wears a public service uniform in court.

Defense

The defense was presented by lawyers from the Number Four Law Firm. Lawyers are usually provided for the defense by the court. However, if the defendant and/or the family can afford to hire lawyers of their own, this is permitted. The second option was exercised in the case observed. The two defense attorneys wore civilian clothing.

Summary of the Procedures

1. Court was called to order and the judge proceeded to introduce all of the participants.

2. The defendant was identified.

3. The charges were read.

4. The defendant was advised of his rights under Chinese law and the Constitution.

5. The judge and people's assessors questioned the defendant.

6. The procurator made a statement, questioned the defendant, and verified evidence.

7. The defense entered a statement, and questioned the defendant.

8. The procurator and the defense presented their arguments.

9. No witnesses testified other than the defendant.

10. The defendant was invited to make a statement and he did so.

11. The judge called for a fifteen-minute recess, while he and the people's assessors deliberated.

12. Court was reconvened, a guilty verdict announced, and the defendant was sentenced.

Disposition

The defendant confessed to the offenses and was found guilty by a panel in a unanimous decision. During an interview with the judge following the trial, it was explained that the defense's position was that the defendant was psychologically disturbed or mentally ill, and was therefore not fully responsible for his actions. The collegial panel did not find this argument persuasive.

The Chinese law does not hold a legally insane person culpable of criminal behavior (Criminal law, 1984:14). The test for insanity is based upon the accused being capable of understanding the difference between right and wrong.

The procurator, however, argued that the defendant knew his actions were wrong based on the planning and development of method employed in carrying out the offenses. The defendant planned the offenses and timed them for late night when visibility was poor, and fewer people were on the streets, selected promising victims, and assured that escape could be accomplished easily, therefore the judge and the assessors found the procurator's argument more convincing. The judge added that the defendant apparently did have some minor psychological problems, but not of the sort to make his behavior uncontrollable and certainly not to the level of legal insanity. (The Chinese do not equate medical insanity and legal insanity).

The above description illustrates some important differences between the Chinese legal system and that of the United States. First, the defendant's guilt is established through previous investigations (a two-stage pretrial investigation, a procuratorial determination, and a preliminary court screening). Once this disposition is reached, one is in the position of needing to prove one's own innocence. Second, the purpose of having a trial is to formalize the process, and to allow the defendant and the defense attorney to make statements, offering evidence and mitigating circumstances which would prove innocence.

Sentence

The defendant was sentenced to an eight month "fixed term" in prison. The defense planned to appeal the verdict to the intermediate people's court.

Social Issues

The legal system in China is seen as a major form of social control and an essential element for progress and order in the socialist society. However, informal social controls are believed to be some of the most effective sanctions.

Basic organization of Chinese society is centered on the "work unit" or "the Danwei." The citizens work unit not only provides income, but also assigns housing. Housing police and local neighborhood committees also help to maintain order and settle minor disputes.

When a person is convicted of committing a crime and imprisoned or otherwise sanctioned, the workplace may not accept him

or her back into the community. In this case, the individual must seek a new workplace, and may have to accept a lower pay and less satisfactory housing if a new job is available at all. This situation affects not only the convicted offender, but also his or her family.

Points of Comparison

The following are some preliminary comparisons between the judicial system of China and the United States. Emphasis will be placed on major contrasting points.

First, there are fewer persons involved in the Chinese collegial bench than in a jury in the United States. This may be due to limited resources in the Chinese judicial system.

Second, the Chinese collegial bench is inquisitorial, while the task of the judge and the jury in the United States is to oversee the adversarial process. The judge in China may even have been an investigator for the case.

Third, the people's assessors are active components of the court in which they participate, and enjoy the same rights as judges. In the United States, the jurors are the decision makers, but they do not ask the accused any questions.

Fourth, the court system in China is primarily responsible for the protection of public interest, while the U.S. court system places strong emphasis on the rights of the accused through due process.

Fifth, for certain practical and philosophical reasons, in China there is no presumption of innocence of the accused. In the United States, on the other hand, the adversarial approach is taken; and presumption of innocence is so important that the prosecutor representing the state must prove guilt beyond a reasonable doubt.

Finally, a trial in China is a final stage in the legal process in which the facts are reviewed and a final decision is made. In the United States, on the other hand, the trial is a critical moment in which the guilt or innocence of the accused is decided through adversarial process by judge and jury.

Table 10-1. *Summary of Points of Comparison*

China	U.S.
Public Security Bureau—Usual initial contact with the CJ system, and investigation	Police—same
Defense—provided by state	Same in U.S. if the accused is indigent
Collegial Bench Collegial Bench—inquisitorial	**Jury** Judge presides and referees over adversarial process
Judge—may be active investigator	Judge does not take active role in investigation
People's Assessors—decision makers with authority of judge	Jurors—decision makers, but not directly equivalent to assessors
Procurator—active investigator	Prosecutor—usually less active investigator
Emphasis on protection of public and less on individual	Emphasis on protection of rights of the accused and less toward victim
More flexibility in investigation and interrogation	More restrictive—primarily through 4th, 5th, 6th, 8th, and 14th Amendments to U.S. Constitution
Emphasis on expediency: Quick capture of offender and successful prosecution effective method of crime control	Emphasis more on due process protection of constitutional rights of the accused regardless of slow process and less efficiency
Emphasis on Confession confession = light sentence no confession = more severe sentence	Plea Bargaining—risk innocent pleading guilty for guaranteed lighter sentence
No presumption of innocence at trial	Presumption of innocence until found guilty
Trial—mainly for review of facts, consideration of mitigating factors, and sentencing	Trial—to determine guilt or innocence
Guilty has a right to appeal	Guilty has a right to appeal

Conclusion

This chapter does not seek to judge which system, that of China or that of the United States, is better or worse. Rather it is intended to illustrate and explain the Chinese system with a case study; comparisons are made to enhance understanding of the two systems. China is experiencing rapid changes in many areas, including in its judicial system. It is hoped that this analysis may eventually promote a movement toward a more democratic Chinese judicial system.

Finally, studying another system helps us to appreciate our own with greater sophistication and sensitivity than might be had under rote learning. Comparing crime problems and options for control in countries with different cultures and systems of government adds new perspective to the observation that democratic governments are faced with unusual crime control challenges.

Notes

1. The Common Program was the preliminary constitution for the People's Republic of China, and was passed by the Chinese People's Political Consultative Conference on September 29, 1949.

Discussion and Revision Questions

1. What are formal and informal courts in China?

2. What is the highest legislative body in China?

3. What are the functions of the standing committee of the National People's Congress with regard to criminal justice?

4. At the judicial formal court level, the Chinese judiciary and procedure are to some extent democratic. Discuss.

5. Why are some Chinese criminal court hearings held in the work unit of the defendant, or at the residence of the defendant, or at a college the defendant attends?

6. Compare and contrast the Nigerian High Court and the Higher People's Court of China.

7. Compare and contrast assessors in a criminal court in China and jurors in American criminal courts.

8. What are the five major penalties and three supplementary penalties in the Chinese criminal justice system?

9. Why is it that in the People's Republic of China, as in Nigeria, Ghana, and Sierra Leone, the defendant is sentenced on the same day that he or she is convicted?

10. Name the capital offenses in China.

11. For a capital offense conviction, an appeal must be filed within 3 days in China, within 30 days in Nigeria, and within 6 to 7 months in the state of New York in the United States. What are the merits and demerits of the different appeal deadlines in the three countries?

12. In China the interests of society are held to be superior to individual rights. Discuss this in the light of individual rights in the United States.

13. Give three reasons why China does not recognize the principle of presumption of innocence.

14. Compare and contrast the standard application of the insanity defense in China and the United States.

15. Consider the American adversarial versus the Chinese inquisitorial approach in criminal trials, discussing the merits and demerits of each approach.

16. Write a short paragraph on the following:

a. "Control" as one of the five major penalties in China.

b. The nature of the Chinese death penalty with a two-year suspension.

17. In China, the Appellate Courts review both the facts and the law. Discuss this in the light of Court of Appeal hearings in the United States, Nigeria, and the United Kingdom.

11

The Police System in the People's Republic of China

Zheng Wang

Introduction

The People's Republic of China, with its population of 1.2 billion (a fifth of the world's total population), currently is undergoing many changes toward the development of an open market economy. Under its new "open policy," China desires that its criminal justice system, including its police system, be understood. The police system in China has long been shrouded in secrecy and not been fully revealed to the West, and especially not by people of Chinese origin. This chapter attempts to provide an initial first-hand account of the police system in China. We will describe the historical development of the police force, its overall organizational structure, the types of police forces, dynamic factors influencing and controlling the system, the crime situation which has resulted from Chinese policing, and a comparison between the policing in China and policing in the United States.

In order to better illustrate the system, tables, figures, diagrams, and statistics collected over the past twelve years will be provided.[1]

The police systems in China are usually called the "people's police agencies," or "public security agencies," and policemen are called "public security personnel." Along with the other three major components of the criminal justice system—the procuratorate, the court, and corrections—the police play a major role in maintaining social order in both city and countryside. Therefore, greater understanding of the Chinese police system will be a major step toward understanding China's criminal justice system at large.

Historical Development

The establishment of the public security system can be traced back to the early 1920s, when the Communist Party was an underground movement fighting against the Nationalist government. During the First Revolutionary Civil War (1924–1927), the Special Service Section was set up to lead the workers' union movement (Du and Zhang, 1990:124). In 1938, the Special Service Section was replaced by the Social Affairs Department (SAD) under the direction and jurisdiction of the Politburo (Richelson, 1988:274).

In October 1949, the Ministry of Public Security (MPS) was established under the supervision of the State Council (the central government). The MPS was responsible for countersubversion, counterintelligence, surveillance, protection of economic and military installations, border patrol, management of "labor reform" camps, census registration, routine police administration, and investigation of criminal cases.

Like all the political and economic systems in the People's Republic of China, the current criminal justice system is highly centralized. Its four major components are placed under four different state ministries, with the police system under the supervision of the Ministry of Public Security, the procuratorate under the Supreme People's Procuratorate, the court under the Supreme People's Court, and the corrections division under the Ministry of Justice.

Organizational Structure

On October 15, 1949, the first National Public Security Conference decided on a centralized public security organization, and agencies were to be established at various levels. Security systems were also set up within the military, government agencies, schools, institutes, and factories. These agencies are responsible for the public security within these units, and are auxiliary apparatus of local public security organizations. Overall, the present police system in China still follows the pattern set up forty-four years ago.

The ministries besides Public Security which have their own public security systems are Railway Transportation (MRT), Forestry (MF), Transportation (MT), Air Administration (AD), and Defense (MD). These police forces are responsible for public security within their respective jurisdictions.

Unlike the decentralized police forces in the United States, various security institutions in China follow a "dual supervision system." Each police agency is supervised by higher police agencies which reside under the jurisdiction of the MPS, which is in turn subordinate to the government. All public security agencies are armed forces, and are charged with keeping public order in society.

The Ministry of Public Security, the highest police agency in China, is under the direct leadership of the State Council. Its major functions are to provide policy directions and coordinate criminal investigations that include more than one provincial jurisdiction. Within the Ministry there are 13 bureaus and also several supporting bureaus such as the General Office, the Personnel Administration Department, and the International Cooperation Bureau. In addition, the Ministry runs three police univer-

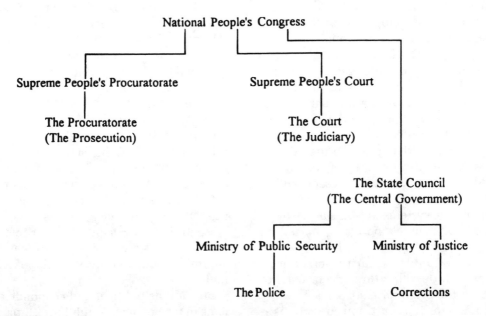

Figure 11–1. Structure of the Criminal Justice System in China

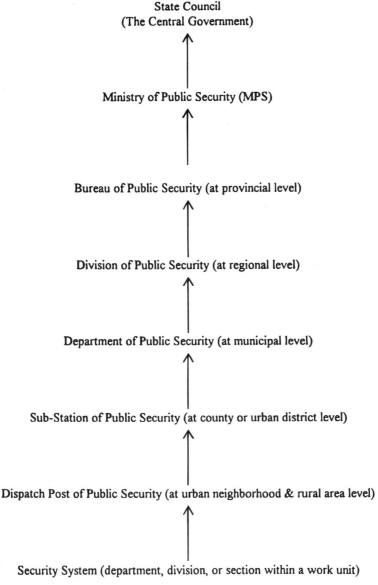

State Council
(The Central Government)

↑

Ministry of Public Security (MPS)

↑

Bureau of Public Security (at provincial level)

↑

Division of Public Security (at regional level)

↑

Department of Public Security (at municipal level)

↑

Sub-Station of Public Security (at county or urban district level)

↑

Dispatch Post of Public Security (at urban neighborhood & rural area level)

↑

Security System (department, division, or section within a work unit)

Figure 11–2. The State Council (Central Government)

sities and three research institutes. Figure 11–4 shows the organization of the MPS.

The major functions of the police bureau at the provincial level are: (1) to handle major or heinous crimes occurring within that province; (2) to conduct forensic/criminalistics analysis of the evidence submitted by the local police stations; and (3) to provide professional supervision for the local police agencies.

At the municipal level, Chinese police departments have greater similarity to Western police departments than is generally the case otherwise.

In urban areas, local police district stations and local neighborhood police stations (dispatch posts) are grassroots agencies and carry the bulk of policing work, conducting criminal investigations, maintaining public order, administering

Ministry of Public Security—Regular Police and Armed Police

Ministry of Railroads—Railway Police

Ministry of Forestry—Forest Police

Ministry of Transportation—Maritime Police

Air Administration—Airport Police

Ministry of Defence—Military Police

Figure 11–3. Vertical Organizational Structure of Chinese Public Security

census registration, managing special trades, controlling criminal activities, and doing routine patrols. We will illustrate with two examples of local police agencies.

Yan An Zhoung Lu Police Sub-Station in Shanghai is considered a medium-sized agency. Its jurisdiction covers an area of 1.7 square kilometers and includes 14,500 households and 50,700 residents. There are 34 police officers and four supervisors in the agency whose average age is 31. They are not usually armed, but carry electric prods when necessary. In 1983, the agency investigated 23 reported criminal incidents, and 22 incidents in 1984. Eighty percent of these cases were solved (Allen, 1987).

The Keiko Road police station in northwest Jianan is an example of the PRC effort to integrate law enforcement within the community. The neighborhood has 11 household registration districts with 6,300 households, 27,000 residents, and some 60 factories and schools. The police station is a two-story, gray stucco building divided into a number of offices, and the staff (as usual) is small in number. The fifteen members include the director, deputy director, two office workers, and eleven policemen, each policeman managing household registration in one district (Johnson, 1983).

Within both large and small public security organizations down to the substation level, division of labor tends to be clear and fixed, as arranged half a century

ago. Each separate responsibility falls within a specific unit, and certain tasks are designated for each unit. Generally speaking, there are twelve units in each public security agency: security for political affairs, criminal investigation, preliminary interrogation, security for economic and cultural affairs, public order, fire-fighting, security guards, reform through labor, reform through education, and armed police.

If we could say that the police district station or sub-station is the first level where there is some degree of specialization, the neighborhood police station is like a general management office for all community affairs (Chang, 1984). It emphasizes "educating the masses" which includes crime prevention efforts, classes on various aspects of the law, and working with juveniles and work groups to develop better lines of communication between the police and the people (Ward, 1985). All the police officers at the neighborhood station level are called census registration police, though in practice there is some division of labor.

Types of Police Forces

According to official data, there are 1.2 million police directed by the Ministry of Public Security, one half of whom are armed. However, it is believed that the ac-

The General Office

The Personnel Administration

The International Cooperation Bureau

The Headquarters of People's Armed Police

Bureau One: Special Investigation (International Crime)

Bureau Two: Traffic Control

Bureau Three: Public Order (Public Safety)

Bureau Four: Preliminary Hearing (Interrogation and Questioning)

Bureau Five: Criminal Investigation (Murder, Armed Robbery, Rape, and National Central Bureau of Interpol)

Bureau Six: Interior Guard (Protection of State Leaders and Foreign VIPs)

Bureau Seven: Residence Registration (Household Administration)

Bureau Eight: Border Control (Border Patrol, Border Check)

Bureau Nine: Education and Training

Bureau Ten: Fire-Fighting and Prevention

Bureau Eleven: Technical Investigation (Surveillance)

Bureau Twelve: Scientific and Technological Development

Bureau Thirteen: Comprehensive Affairs (Budget, Finance, Supply, and General Service)

Public Security University (Beijing)

Police Officers University (Beijing)

Criminal Police College of China (Shenyang)

The First Research Institute (Police Equipment)

The Second Research Institute (Forensic Science and Criminalistics)

The Third Research Institute (Police System and Organization)

Figure 11–4. Organization of the Ministry of Public Security

tual number increased to two million after the Tiananmen Square incident.

There are seven major types of police with different functions within the system: criminal police, public order police, census registration (residence/household registration) police, traffic police, foreign affairs police, fire-fighting police, and armed police. All are under the leadership of the MPS, are housed within one police agency, and are designed to cooperate with each other. The five additional security agencies governed by different ministries work side by side with the regular police force.

The criminal police force is the system's backbone agency. Its major tasks include on-scene response, collecting of evidence, investigation of major crimes (murder, robbery, rape, arson, etc.), conduct of criminalistic laboratory analyses, arresting of criminals, testifying at court, and enforcing sentences imposed by the courts. The sub-

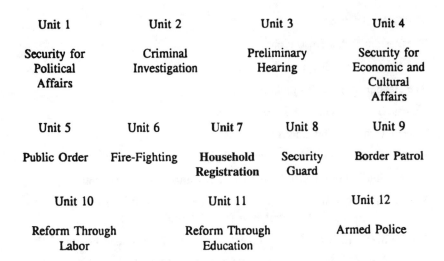

Figure 11–5. Internal Structure of the Police Department

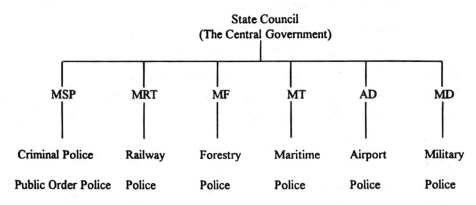

Figure 11–6. Administration of the Chinese Police Force

division within the criminal police force conducting criminalistic analyses are called criminal examiners; the rest are referred to as criminal investigators. The criminal examiners are subdivided further into those specializing in forensic medicine, forensic chemistry, physical evidence, and examination of disputed documents.

Census registration police are responsible for compiling statistics on population growth and movement. Every Chinese must register with a census police officer, and authorization must be obtained from the local census registration police station before anyone can move out of an old residence or into a new one. All births and deaths in the jurisdiction are recorded at the police station. Finally, census registration police are also responsible for supervising probationers and parolees.

Traffic police primarily patrol the highways and maintain an orderly flow of automotive and pedestrian traffic in urban areas. There is a police booth (post) at almost every major street intersection where one or two traffic officers are on duty, and one or two more direct traffic at the center of the street crossing.

Public order police generally oversee special trades, dangerous goods, and public places. Moreover, they concentrate on preventing, controlling, and handling crimes, act on violations of public order, and deal with disastrous accidents. In China, professions whose workers could provide tools for crime are regarded as special trades. A smith's shop, for instance, can produce a key for illegal entry; and a seal or stamp shop can forge seals or stamps for illegal use. Therefore, people working in these professions are required to report to the police if they discover that somebody has made a suspicious request. In terms of dangerous goods, public order police control certain sorts of equipment, and poisonous drugs and medicines. Guns and ammunition are strictly forbidden to individual use. Opium, morphine, and heroin are prohibited save with doctor's permission. Public order police also routinely patrol public places: railway stations, long distance bus stations, parks, shopping centers, free markets, and certain "busy areas"—i.e., prostitution or gambling areas. Finally, public order police keep close working relations with hotels, motels, theaters, and pawn shops in order to detect any criminals or criminal activities.

Foreign affairs police work only at the municipal level, handling crimes and other incidents involving foreigners. Moreover, foreign affairs police examine and approve all applications for going abroad, either for study or for short visits (official and non-official). Finally, foreign affairs police issue passports to those who have obtained approval for going abroad.

The people's armed police force was established in the early fifties, but was abolished in the mid-sixties. In 1983, as a result of the post–Mao Tse-tung disarmament, one million military soldiers were converted into an armed police force, thus reestablishing the armed police. This special police force has its own headquarters within the MPS, and constitutes a special sub-system within the regular police force at various levels. Some regular police tasks have been transferred to the armed police, including border patrol and the guarding of major governmental and party institutions, foreign embassies, key installations (major bridges and tunnels, power and utility centers), airports, and ports. In recent years, anti-terrorist duties have been added to armed police activities. Overall, armed police are housed only in provincial police agencies and in urban districts.

Fire-fighting police and armed police differ from the rest of the police in being not professional but obligatory. Their service resembles that of a soldier in the military and is paid accordingly. In 1988 the armed police started their own military-style ranking system: lieutenant-general, major-general, senior colonel, colonel, lieutenant-colonel, major, captain, first lieutenant, and second lieutenant.

Functions of the Police in the Judicial Process

According to Chinese criminal procedure law, there are several important functions carried out by the police.

The first function is registration of criminal cases. A criminal case is registered when the police department (and court and procuratorate) examine denunciations which inform them that a crime has been committed. The department also registers a criminal case when information is presented by those who surrender themselves to the law, confessing that they have committed a criminal act. A criminal case is formally registered only when the police department believes it necessary to hold the accused criminally responsible for the offense.

The second function is investigation. During this stage, the police agency conducts search and seizure, collects evidence, and handles criminal investigation. Except in emergency situations, police wishing to search must show the suspect a search warrant (*Criminal law*, 1984:125–128). Finally, if they believe that the accused should be held criminally liable, the police draft a request for an arrest. This request, together with all relevant materials, is forwarded to the procuratorate, which can issue a warrant for arrest. The police must obtain an arrest warrant from the procuratorate before carrying out an apprehension or making an arrest (Leng, 1982). Only police agencies may execute arrests.

Persons under suspicion of having committed crimes may also be detained by the police for questioning prior to issue of an arrest warrant. Either in arrest or in detention situations, the family of the detainee or the arrestee should be notified within 24 hours of the time the arrest was made of the reasons for the arrest and the confinement. Interrogation must start within 24 hours after detention or arrest.[3] The detainee or the arrested party must be released without delay if no legitimate grounds for concern are established by the police. When the police department deems it necessary to declare a detainee arrested, the case is submitted to the procuratorate for approval within three days or, in special circumstances, seven days. The procuratorate must either approve the arrest or order a release of the detainee within three days (Article 38–52).

The third function of the police in the judicial process is to conduct preliminary hearings for persons arrested or detained according to law. Such a hearing continues investigatory work and includes examination and interrogation of criminals before they are brought to court for trial (Du and Zhang, 1990:133). According to the law, during the preliminary hearings the police should gather all the facts surrounding the defendant's behavior and the relationships between the defendant and any other criminals in the case. The police must insist on the principle of seeking truth from facts, relying on evidence and investigation, and must refrain from extorting confessions by torture, threat, enticement, or deceit of any other illegal nature (Article 32).

The fourth function is to file a "memorandum of indictment" to the procuratorate for further examination. The procuratorate examines the materials submitted by the police agency. On finding the facts of the crime clear and evidence sufficient to hold the accused responsible for the crime, the procuratorate files an indictment against the accused. The case is then held over for trial by the court. The procuratorate must decide whether or not to prosecute a case within one month to one and a half months (Article 97).

Functions of the Police in the Social Arena

Besides their judicial functions in the legal process, the police in China are also mandated by law to play an important administrative role in crime prevention and social control.

According to the Security Administrative Punishment Act,[4] there are three types of sanctions that the police can implement in dealing with minor crimes or public-order offenses (prostitution, drugs, and gambling) without reference to the procuratorate, the court, and corrections. First, the police agency at the neighborhood level can issue a *warning* to a minor criminal offender. Second, the police agency from urban district level and above can order a *fine* up to 400 yuan ($50) and a *detention* at the police station (up to 15 days). However, a dissatisfied defendant has the right to make an appeal to a police agency at the next level up, and ultimately to a court which is under the supervision of the Ministry of Justice and not the Ministry of Public Security. If the individual wins the appellate case, the police agency as well as the police officer(s) concerned have to apologize to the victim and compensate him or her for any damages.

Reform-through-education[5] is another administrative sanction that police agencies at the urban district level and above can employ in dealing with "anti-societal" behaviors. The police do not need to ask the procuratorate or the court for any approval, but do need to consult with the public security committee[6] in the defendant's neighborhood. The language of this legislation somewhat resembles that of the old vagrancy laws in England and the United States. Both the Security Administrative Punishment Act and the Decision of the State Council Relating to Problems of Reform Through Education require sanctions to be imposed on:

> those who do not engage in productive labor and those who behave like hooligans, . . . those who receive the sanction of expulsion from an organ, organization, enterprise, school . . . and who are without a way of earning a livelihood, . . . those persons who have the capacity to labor, but who for a long period refuse to labor or who destroy discipline, . . . those who do not obey work assignments or arrangements for getting them employment or for transferring them to other employment . . ." (English translation in Cohen, 1968:249–50).

The purpose of this sanction is twofold. First, it brings reeducation and moral reform to an unproductive person. Second, it forces the person to do compulsory labor.

Before an offender is treated, the source of his or her problem with the law must be determined. Generally it is either as a result of ignorance of the law, in which case the offender needs reform through legal education, or the offender is too lazy to work, in which case he or she needs reform through labor.

Commonly a local neighborhood, school, work unit, or family may report to the police that somebody fits the definition of an "unproductive person." If the police and the local neighborhood committee agree after a review of a case, they make recommendations. Next, the case is sent to a district Reform Through Labor Committee that consists of representatives from the police, civil affairs, and labor officials. The committee can decide to send the person to a labor farm for a period of one to three years. The basic programs on the labor farm usually consist of agricultural labor, physical training, skill training, academic education, and political education. It is believed that such administrative sanctions could help an "unproductive person" to learn job skills and learn to labor.

Dynamics of the System

"Following the Mass line" was a slogan that has directed police work from the early 50s to the early 80s. Ideally, this strategy is to call on the police to respect the people's opinion, to experience the people's lives, and accept the people's supervision. However, the police officials are the ones who finally define what the masses want in the field of public security (Bracey, 1989b).

In 1984, a new "Comprehensive Approach" was outlined, containing the following seven major objectives:

(1) to call on society to show concern for the youth and further educate them in lofty ideals, moral codes, discipline, and legality;

(2) to promote mass participation in cultural and sporting activities and enrich young people's lives in their leisure hours;

(3) to clear away all pornographic publications and objects;

(4) to punish severely abettors who lead young people astray;

(5) to accomplish good school education and reduce the number of dropouts;

(6) to make use of retired officials, workers and teachers and encourage them to help and educate delinquents;

(7) to expedite the formulation of a law for protecting the youth (Jiang and Dai, 1990).

In essence, this new program is to organize all possible social forces to educate the young people and to promote a good social order. Since 1984, the police agencies at various levels have asked the members of public security committees to join the police in patrol, and have organized them to do so. Public security committees are similar to neighborhood watch or the Guardian Angels programs in the United States. As of 1991, there were 1.17 million public security committees with 12 million members throughout China (Jiang and Dai, 1990).

Furthermore, the police also assist larger work in setting up civilian security forces (economic police) in big factories, mines, companies, and hotels. These economic police forces are quite similar to private security forces in the United States: they have their own uniforms; they are responsible for security and prevention of offenses such as theft and assault only within the work unit; and they are under direct supervision of the leadership of the work unit. In China, however, the economic police must report to the local police agency on their security work. Essentially, this program emphasizes partnership between the society and the police force to control crime and preserve social order.

Mass education is another strategy used in the Comprehensive Approach. According to Confucianism, human beings are born with the capability of developing a good nature through proper education and training. Moreover, all behavior results from an individual's ideology (values, morals, or viewpoints). The individual's ideology is shaped and influenced by social environment, including education. Deviant behavior also develops gradually over time. Therefore, reinforcing early education, intervention, and rehabilitation will, as they say, "nip crime in the bud."

For this reason, police and local governments in China constantly launch massive campaigns of legal education. Legal education is expected to fulfill two purposes. First, it can shape mass legal thoughts (awareness) about what is right and what is wrong. Second, it warns lawbreakers of the possible consequences of deviant behavior. The legal education takes various forms. The police agency may take to the streets to deliver speeches on laws, may offer legal courses in schools, or may help the court to organize a public trial of a defendant in his or her own work unit.

When mass mobilization and mass education fail in their persuasive functions, punitive measures are necessary to crack down on serious crimes. This is the third important component of the Chinese comprehensive program. The police authorities often relate the sudden increase in crime rates between 1981 and 1983 to an overemphasis on education and persuasion. Punishment and deterrence still have an important role to play in crime prevention. The "Anti-Crime Campaign" of 1983–1984 and the "Anti–Six Evils Campaign" of 1988–1989 directly resulted from this punitive principle. The second campaign focused on six new types of crimes: (1) prostitution; (2) producing, selling, and spreading pornographic objects; (3) kidnapping women and children; (4) planting, gathering, and trafficking in drugs without permission; (5) gambling; and (6) defrauding people of their money by superstition.

Chinese police officers believe that such law enforcement functions must supplement mass mobilization and mass education in order to improve social order.

The "Comprehensive Approach" brought crime under control by 1988 (see Tables 11–1 and 11–2). However, after 1988 the crime rate rose again, due in part to a rapid increase in juvenile offenses. According to official data, the conviction rate in 1989 was 36% above that of 1988. Major Chinese crime statistics from 1981 to 1987 are listed below.

From the late 1980s on, regular patrol emerged as a new direction in police strategy. Contrary to trends in the United States toward community policing, the police in China are switching from "people's policing" to formal patrolling. There are several reasons for this new direction. First, as the economic reform gathers strength, more and more small private businesses are set up in urban areas. Thus, security and protection require immediate attention. Second, more and more young farmers are moving to urban areas for employment. This new transient population tends to be without permanent residence: therefore, the traditional neighborhood police cannot deal effectively with this new social element. Third, the degree of seriousness of crime has escalated: although nonviolent crimes such as theft or larceny have decreased, violent crimes such as robbery, armed robbery, rape, and murder have burgeoned. The police as well as the public are beginning to question the effectiveness of community policing. Finally, as China becomes a more open society, the traditional culture of collectiveness is being challenged (Wang, 1993). This means that the number of people interested in voluntary or low-paying public participation has decreased sharply (Fu, 1991a).

Table 11–1. National Crimes Recorded by Public Security in the People's Republic of China

Crimes	1981	1982	1983*	1984	1985	1986	1987
Homicide	9,567	9,324	----	9,021	10,440	11,510	13,154
Assault	21,499	20,298	----	14,526	15,586	18,364	21,727
Robbery	22,266	16,518	----	7,237	8,801	12,124	18,775
Rape	30,808	35,361	----	44,630	37,712	39,121	37,225
Larceny	743,105	609,481	----	395,319	431,323	425,845	435,235
(Grand)	(16,147)	(15,462)	----	(16,340)	(34,643)	(42,192)	(58,661)
Fraud	18,665	17,707	----	13,479	13,157	14,663	14,693
Counterfeit	1,649	1,763	----	707	491	497	436
Other	41,424	38,024	----	29,414	24,495	25,001	29,630
TOTAL	890,261	748,476	610,478	514,369	542,002	547,115	570,439

Source: Law Yearbook of China

(*) No official crime data available for 1983.

Table 11–2. Rates of Crime in People's Republic of China

Crimes	1981	1982	1983*	1984	1985	1986	1987
Homicide	0.96	0.92	----	0.88	1.00	2.10	2.31
Assault	2.16	2.01	----	1.41	1.50	3.36	3.81
Robbery	2.24	1.63	----	0.71	0.86	2.22	3.29
Rape	3.09	3.50	----	4.33	3.62	7.15	6.53
Larceny	74.72	60.21	----	38.36	41.43	77.83	76.30
Fraud	1.87	1.75	----	1.31	1.26	2.68	2.58
Counterfeit	0.17	0.17	----	0.07	0.05	0.09	0.08
Other	4.16	3.77	----	2.84	2.34	11.57	5.10
TOTAL	89.37	14.02	59.81	49.91	52.06	51.41	54.10
Clearance Rate	73.1%	77.4%	----	76.9%	78.8%	79.2%	81.3%

Source: Law Yearbook of China

(*) No official crime data available for 1983.

Since the late eighties, police patrol of the big cities, such as Beijing, Shanghai, Tianjin, Guanzhong, Shenyang, and Xian, has increased due to social, economic, and cultural changes, and the concomitant public pressure for more police protection, professionalism, and visibility.

The police in China, like those in other countries, tend to be satisfied with the status quo, completely supportive of the government, and somewhat resistant to change (Ward, 1985). The most common complaints and criticisms against Chinese police are corruption, brutality, and too much discretion (Fu, 1991a; Seymour, 1987; Townsend, 1987; and Ma, 1986). Recently, some efforts have been made to improve the situation.

Conclusion

The police system in China is the social product of the country's political and economic systems. Its nature and functions therefore must be analyzed in the Chinese social context.

The Chinese police operate under a highly centralized hierarchy with complex subdivisions. Unlike the police forces in Western societies, the Chinese police play important roles both in legal process and in the social arena; and it is the social (administrative) functions that have enabled police to achieve a unique social control in Chinese society. Police in China and police in the United States use very different approaches, especially in terms of roles, scope of police power, and police discretion in both the legal and the social arenas. However, as political and economic reforms strengthen, the police system in China is facing its new challenges, including control of illegal police power, over-professionalism, and waning public support.

Notes

1. The author would like to express sincere thanks to Professor Robert Davidson of the Justice Studies Program at Northern

Michigan University for his valuable comments and suggestions. Professor Davidson has visited China twice with the Office of International Criminal Justice Delegations.

2. The security system within the military differs from public security in that the military security personnel wear military uniforms, not regular police uniforms. The military also has its own prosecution and court system defendants who commit crimes within military jurisdiction and/or crimes involving military secrets.

3. The difference between "detention" and "arrest" is as follows: detention is the emergency apprehension and confinement of a suspect without an arrest warrant for the purpose of investigating whether there is sufficient evidence to justify arrest. Arrest is apprehension and confinement or continuing confinement of a suspect on the basis of an arrest warrant for the purpose of investigation, and whether there is sufficient evidence to justify prosecution (Leng, 1982).

4. This Act was originally passed in 1957, then republished in 1980, and amended in 1987.

5. Reform-through-education and reform-through-labor are two different types of punishment. The former is an administrative sanction determined by the police agency at the urban district level and above, while the latter is a formal judicial punishment levied by the court.

6. The Public Security Committee and the Mediation Committee are two major components in a Neighborhood Committee. Most members are retired workers, officials, teachers, or housewives. The members of the Public Security Committee patrol the neighborhood and report to the local neighborhood police station when they find a suspicious person in the area (Bracey, 1989b:134–136).

Discussion and Revision Questions

1. What are the duties of the Ministry of Public Security (MPS) in the Chinese Criminal Justice System?

2. What are the four components of the Chinese Criminal Justice System?

3. What are the Divisions of the MPS?

4. Local police district stations and local neighborhood police stations are China's grassroots agencies. Discuss.

5. What are the functions of the following:
   a. Criminal police force
   b. Criminal examiners
   c. Public Order Police
   d. People's Armed Police

6. Which agency issues arrest warrants in China?

7. What are the functions of the police in the judicial process?

8. What are the functions of the police in the social arena?

9. Compare and contrast police services in Great Britain and China.

10. What is meant by "following the Mass Line"?

11. Compare and contrast public security committees in China and the Guardian Angels in the United States.

12. What are the six evils of the Chinese "Anti–Six Evils Campaign"?

13. What is the most influential traditional value system in China?

14. What are the most common complaints against the police in China?

15. Compare and contrast the role of the police in China and the United States.

16. What is the administrative difference between reform-through-education and reform-through-labor?

12

Guided Change in Japan:

The Correctional Association Prison Industrial Cooperative (CAPIC) and Prison Industry

Elmer H. Johnson

Introduction

In 1973 and from 1979 to 1980, the oil producing nations of the Middle East increased the price of oil in several stages and gravely dislocated the world economy. Japan, which depends heavily on oil for its energy, suffered huge increases in the costs of imports, inflation of domestic prices, unemployment (despite a history of labor shortages), and an interruption of remarkable economic growth (Beasley, 1990:249–250).

Under the duress of this financial crisis, the national government of Japan told the Correction Bureau to eliminate the budgetary allocation for purchase of raw materials for prison industries. The prospect of a body blow to prison industries tested the commitment of the national government to continuing industrial operations. As we shall see, this situation turned out to be a "window of opportunity": the Correction Bureau's negotiations culminated in the establishment of the Correctional Association Prison Industrial Cooperative (CAPIC) as an additional participant in the prisons' industrial operation.[1]

A Window of Opportunity for Prison Industries

Penal reform sometimes takes place when demands for changes from outside the correctional agency create a situation favorable for the correctional agency to introduce policies or practices that the executives and personnel of the agency already desire. The reform agenda of the external change-agents provides a "window of opportunity" for the internal change-agents, because the external agenda is susceptible to modification by the correctional agency.

The Correctional Bureau's response to the external demand that it should eliminate the budget item for prison industries showed its vulnerability as a *reactive* institution dependent on developments in society generally and in government specifically. The Correction Bureau found that a crucial element in its budget had been threatened abruptly by a joint decision of the Ministry of Finance and the Ministry of Justice, and had to engage in political bargaining to meet this threat.

Windows of opportunity emerge and are exploited through the society's political

169

process of governmental decision-making. Noting that there is no Japanese word for "opposition," Leiserson (1966:346, 394–395) points out that, from the Japanese perspective, political bargaining within the system (*taisei-gai*) is more likely to effect changes in policy than efforts seeking policy change from outside the system (*taisei-nai*): to have any chance for success, *taisei-nai* must strike some sort of alliance with *taisei-gai*. His terms resemble our earlier distinction between external and internal change-agents: internal-change agents must accommodate to the external change-agenda in order to exploit a window of opportunity.

Before CAPIC was accepted as a solution, negotiations followed the usual budget-making process of the Japanese national government. The following circumstances and special conditions combined within that process to lead to the founding of CAPIC.

Several conditions surrounding this window of opportunity made it possible to preserve industrial prisons and provide for their richer future. The industrial prison was defined, its significance noted, and the conditions for its implementation outlined. It was found that prison labor played an important role in the development of modern Japan and that it has vital connections with private industry through subcontracting. Also, the external parties had a stake in the industrial operations. Furthermore, prison industry played an important role in the stability and purposes of the prison.

These conditions made both external and internal change-agents willing to bargain for the creation and implementation of CAPIC. The external change-agents had superior power in negotiations but also had an interest in preserving prison industries. The internal change-agents were indispensable for implementing any change agenda but depended on the external change-agents for necessary resources.

Factory System and the Prison

In the European putting-out system, the merchant-capitalist or his representative visited the homes of each worker, distributing raw materials, and later collecting the products. The factory system developed during the first industrial revolution (1750–1825) brought workers together in a central shop, and assigned each particular tasks in operating one of a series of specialized machines. Workers sometimes had been assembled in central workshops prior to 1750, but factory labor as a system arose with the development of suitable machinery. The factory system by definition combines the labor of many kinds of workers who tend with appropriate skills a series of productive machines (Taylor-Cooke, 1886:29).

Factory systems require rigorous discipline and regimentation. According to Barnes (1942:107), "It became necessary to issue certain rules defining the hours of labor, the assignment of industrial tasks, the attitude of the employee in his relations with the employer, details of conduct within the factory, and even the matter of orderly entering and leaving." Compared with the putting-out system, the factory system required closer control, supervision, and discipline of labor. A predetermined scheme of production assigned particular tasks to each worker in relation to specialized machines. If any worker came to the factory late or failed to show, he or she would delay the entire process. Failure to perform an assigned task would frustrate the industrial process, and the worker responsible for the failure could be identified easily.

By 1823, the Auburn Prison in New York had exploited the disciplinary potential of the factory system, providing "for the separate confinement of each prisoner in silence in his individual cell at night, and for the work of the prisoners in association during the day" (Lewis, 1922:86). Inmates were forbidden ever to converse with one another in order to prevent ill influences on morale, plotting against the keepers, or escape. Violators were subject to flogging.

The Auburn system enabled the private contractor to transform the prison into a factory at his own expense, to direct the inmate workers, and ultimately to sell their products on the open market. The industrial prison brought orderliness to the prisons, but as Melossi and Pararini (1981:129–130) note, radically changed the form of discipline. Productive work imposes regulations that dictate the form and timing of the interaction of inmate workers; the discipline for work replaces the discipline for purposes of prison custody. To motivate efficient task performance, the prospect of rewards is superior to the threat of punishment. Melossi and Pararini show this principle to have been behind evaluating working ability as a measure of "good conduct," commuting long sentences, and preferring of long-term prisoners for teaching of new work techniques.

Jeremy Bentham (1843:12) set the tone for arguments in favor of the industrial prison when he commented in 1778 on the proposal before the British Parliament to establish "houses of labor":

> The object in view in it, we see, is partly *economical* and partly *moral*: that such a project be drawn from the labor of the convicts as may altogether, or at least in part, compensate the expense of the establishment; and that the morals of the convicts may be improved by a habit of steady and well-directed industry.

Industrial Model in Japan

Industrial prison operations are favored in Japan by the centralized Japanese correctional administration. All correctional activities are carried out on the national level, unlike the American federal, state, and local subdivisions. Centralized administration encourages fiscal efficiency and uniformity in policy and practice, and en-ables use of a national system for recruiting personnel. Quality of personnel is further assured by a long history of in-service training. The official system for classifying adult prisoners supports the needs of industrial operations.

Japanese inmates' engagement in regular industrial labor contributes noticeably to the orderliness in prisons,[2] to the Correction Bureau's rehabilitation goals,[3] and to national revenue.[4] Both "economical" and "moral" purposes are served.

Violence against other inmates is unusual, and aggression against staff and escape attempts are even more rare. As in all custodial prisons, inmates' conduct is constrained by a regimented routine. Workshop assignments make up the greatest number of tightly scheduled daily activities of inmates who breakfast in their cells, begin work at 7:20 A.M., lunch in the workshop, and march back to their congregate cells at 4:30 P.M. for dinner. Silence is not required in the congregate cells, which usually have a half-dozen residents. Individuals whose behavior has caused problems are housed in single-occupancy cells and must assemble paper shopping bags for retail stores. Inmates who are physically unfit for workshop labor assemble paper shopping bags as well, but in congregate cells.

Both threat of punishment and promise of reward motivate task performance. Inmates may not contact one another while at work and must meet a daily work quota. Infractions peculiar to the workshops are violations of safety rules, looking aside while working, leaving the designated place, leaving a machine untended, making shoddy products, damaging products, and manufacturing unauthorized items.[5]

As positive incentives, inmate workers receive modest "remunerations," promotions in the progressive stage system, privileges earned by exceeding the production quota, and satisfactions for exceeding the quota. Not considered the privilege implied by the word "wage," monetary remunerations come in ten grades according to task skill, length of time in prison, and work attitudes.[6] Progressive stages are from the lowest (fourth) at admission to prison to the highest (first), with privileges and chances for parole linked to promotion. If a work quota is exceeded, certain freedoms, such as watching television, are obtained. Competition between workshops in exceeding production quotas expresses the spirit of "Gambare!" ("Persevere!" or "Endure!") that motivates great effort in every facet of Japanese life. According to Duke (1986:122–123) "Gambare is also a major component in developing a strong sense of competition, especially group competition. Regardless of the group's purposes or the ages of the participants, the goals must be pursued through collective effort."

The influence of Japanese culture on work motivation goes beyond the competitive spirit. Previous socialization and the messages of social institutions prepare most inmates to accept the behavioral standards of the industrial prison. The inmates come from a sociocultural system that prefers the interests of the group over those of the individual member. Ozaki (1978:183) summarizes Western culture in the statement: "Do your own thing and go your own way." The Japanese statement, on the other hand, would be: "Find your own group and belong to it. You and the group will rise or sink together. Without belonging you will be lost in the wilderness. Apart from dependence there is no human happiness."

In Western societies relationships tend to be along the horizontal dimension, with work colleagues, persons of similar age, and other peers. In the prison factory, Foucault (1977:238) says, inmates "come together in a strict hierarchical framework with no lateral relation, communication being possible only in the vertical direction." The same pattern has been described for the ordinary life in Japan. There, Nakane (1981:36–37, 44, 68) argues, social ties are vertical rather than horizontal through attachments of *oyabun* (persons of superior rank such as parent, patron, boss) with the *kobun* (persons of subordinate

rank such as child, client, employee). The vertical dimension favors group cohesion in spite of rank differences among members. Officer-inmate contacts draw on the *oyabun-kobun* relationship, with the officer expected to combine the roles of moral educator, lay counselor, and security monitor. "Although some prisoners try to reject their guard, because of the authority that he carries, the majority accept his guidance and advice, at least on an emotional level" (Shikita, 1972:19).

Roots in Japanese History

Japan did not erect a modern prison system until the 1880s, and industrial prisons began even later. Yet prison labor existed in Japan before the eighth century, when Chinese legal principles were followed in specifying penal measures: death by decapitation or strangulation, exile to Hokkaido, beating with a light stick, beating of offenders who lacked a sense of shame with a heavy stick, and penal servitude. Those sentenced to penal servitude were assigned to local confinement stations and, according to local needs and the individual's strength, were ordered to perform a specific kind of labor for 12, 18, 24, 30, or 36 months. They were paid one-tenth of an ordinary worker's wage, and half of the daily income was held until release (Ch'en, 1981:40–43).

The *Ninsoku-Yoseba* (Stockade for Laborers) was established in 1790 on the small island of Ishikawajima at the mouth of the Sumida River. Homeless persons made lime or charcoal balls or paper there, and were paid for their work. In 1820 criminals sentenced to forced labor and exile were admitted (Kyokai, 1943:813; Hiromatsu, 1972:44–49).

On January 3, 1868, a group of feudal lords engaged in a successful coup d'etat in Kyoto terminating the Tokugawa Shogunate that had isolated Japan from the outside world for almost two and a half centuries. The ensuing reform movement known as the Meiji Restoration made great efforts to modernize the socioeconomic infrastructure of Japan. Delegations were sent to Europe and the United States for quick studies of Western social institutions, including laws and prisons. Modern Japan gradually evolved as a combination of lessons from the West and indigenous customs (Beasley, 1972:1–2; Noda, 1976:41–48; Beasley, 1990:22–30, 85–88).

The central prisons of France were a model for Kosuge Prison near Tokyo, and the prison at Miyagi (still existing in modified form) duplicated the Central Prison at Leuven, Belgium. The central prisons in France, at the time of the Meiji Reformation, had initiated a version of the Auburn system in the mid-nineteenth century with its reliance on contracting, although in France and the United States, the industrial prison was under political attack and suffered general decline in the 1880s and later (O'Brien, 1982:23, 152–190).

The Meiji reformers began to establish a modern prison system while laboriously suppressing the 1877 Satsuma Rebellion by imprisoning 27,000 dissident samurai: rice warehouses and stables had to be hastily converted into provisional confinement sites. Rioting, arson, and escapes were frequent until new prisons were constructed (Hiromatsu, 1973:31–32).

Prisoners participated directly in the development of Japan's infrastructure. They reclaimed land, labored in mines, and constructed the Asahikawa-Abashiri highway (1886–1891) in the northern island of Hokkaido while farmed out from Kabato Prison (opened 1881) and Kushiro Prison (opened 1885). Sorachi Prison (opened 1882) provided labor for coal mines. The government began operating the Miike coal mines in Kyushu in 1873 with both free workers and prisoners. Although privatized in 1888, the mines continued to employ prisoners but in declining numbers, until their use was discontinued in 1933 (Yokoyama, 1984:3–4; Hane, 1982:227; Hiromatsu, 1973:35–36).

Factory organization and techniques existed in Japanese prisons at the time of the Meiji Restoration. Sometime during the last two decades of the nineteenth century, Griffiths (n.d.:235–238) reported that Japanese prisons were places of detention, of reformation, and of profitable work. The visitors were surprised to find a couple hundred prisoners making machinery and steam boilers in the first workshop. One warder, carrying only a sword, was in charge of every fifteen men. The prisoners were working on contract orders for private firms, under the supervision of one skilled master and one representative of the firm giving the contract. Another shop contained woodcarvers. There were also papermakers, weavers (who were making fabric for prison clothing), fan-makers, lantern-makers, and workers in baskets, mats, and nets. In one of the shops jinrikishas were being made, in another umbrellas were being elaborately carved, and in another every kind of pottery was being turned out.

The Key Importance of Subcontracting

Small businesses were a powerful force in the nineteenth-century industrial revolution of Japan, and they now account for a larger percentage of total enterprises than in any other industrialized nation (Tadao, 1979:157–158).[7] In the years immediately before and during World War II, manufacturers of military equipment shifted from producing everything themselves to relying on smaller firms through contracts (Nakamura, 1981:15)[8]. Contracting had existed in Japan before the war, but its popularity was stimulated afterward by advantages to "parent" companies such as lower wages, managerial skills in small firms, and willingness to work longer hours (Dore, 1987:172–173).

Primary contractors have direct ties with the parent companies; secondary and tertiary subcontractors are related indirectly to primary contractors. "It is not unusual

to find several 'layers' of hierarchically organized subcontractors in a pyramid-like
pattern, with each performing subcontracting operations for those at a higher
level in the pyramid. Most commonly, the
lower its stratum, the smaller the establishment" (Yoshino, 1968:155).

Parent companies contract with small
firms because, when the economy is de-
pressed, they then have the option of can-
celing the contracts while maintaining the
jobs of regular employees, of postponing
payments to contractors, or of lowering the
rate paid to them (Nakamura, 1981:175).
Kosai and Ogino (1984:72) present a different perspective: "In reality, a great number of Japan's small companies boast a high
level of technology and efficiency and are
valued by their parent company as a vital
link in their organization." The parent
company enters an agreement with such
small firms when only a small order is
needed, and when the small firm is reliable
in delivery and product quality. The advantages for the small firm, Kosai and
Ogino say, are avoiding the costs of sales
promotion, gaining the benefits of stable
work and profits, and being guided otherwise by the parent company.

By acting as secondary or tertiary subcontractors, the adult prisons of Japan are
able to sustain their heavy involvement in
industrial production. Their wide range of
products generate different amounts of annual income (see Table 12–1). Metal work,
tailoring, woodcraft (largely furniture), and
printing contributed 74 percent of the 1990
total income. The table distinguishes projects using equipment supplied by the government from projects using equipment
supplied by private contractors. For the four
major industries, private firms supplied the
equipment for 99.5 percent of project income. For total projects, privately-supplied
equipment accounted for 96.5 percent of the
income. Government-supplied equipment
was prominent in farming and stockraising,
vocational training,[9] papermaking, and
forestry; but only .4 percent of all income
was obtained from those industries.

The staff of each prison, especially its industrial division, plays the primary role in
obtaining subcontracts. All sectors of the staff
have a keen interest in replacing an expiring
subcontract in order to maintain an active inmate labor force. Some headquarters of the
correction region may refer a contractor to an
appropriate prison, or a local company may
approach the prison seeking an arrangement
in its own interest. The prison's correction
fair displaying its goods may awaken a company's interest. Newspaper advertisements
and suggestions by volunteers serving the
prison also spread the word.

Oil Shock and Crisis for Prison Labor

The oil crisis of 1973 occurred after a long
period of economic growth and expanding
government revenue in Japan. The ensuing
financial setback was especially untimely,
because the fiscal budget of 1973 initiated
an unprecedented public investment in social services. Pension benefits for employees almost doubled, insurance coverage of
medical care for dependents increased,
and free medical care was introduced for
the aged (Collick, 1988:214–215). The government debated whether expenditures
should be significantly reduced or whether
they should be retained in order to prime
the economy. Increased taxes were found
to be politically impractical (Woronoff,
1986:241–246). When Finance Minister
Aichi Kiichi died, Prime Minister Kakuei
Tanaka appointed in his place Takeo
Fukuda, a fiscal conservative. The fiscal
year 1974 thus saw, for the first time, a
Prime Minister and Minister of Finance
who both wanted to reverse the growth of
expenditures during the framing of the national budget (Campbell, 1977:259–260).

The national budget undergoes a year-
long process in Japan. In April (the beginning of the fiscal year) the ministries begin
drafting their budget requests for the following fiscal year. Usually the Ministry of
Finance (MOF) expects an increase in bud-

Table 12–1. Income from Prison Industries by Types of Products and State's Versus Contractors' Resources, 1990.

TYPES OF PRODUCTS	TOTAL INCOME (MILLION YEN)	STATE RESOURCES	PRIVATE RESOURCES
		PERCENTAGES	
Metal Work	5,421.9	0.7	99.3
(Assembly)	(3,164.9)	(--)	(100.0)
(Production)	(2,257.0)	(1.6)	(98.4)
Tailoring	3,622.9	--	100.0
Woodcraft	1,990.3	1.3	98.7
Printing	1,364.3	0.2	99.8
Leather Work	997.6	--	100.0
Paper Products	685.8	0.1	99.9
Farm, Stock Raising	413.9	96.5	3.5
Chemical Products	277.3	--	100.0
Paper Bags	159.9	--	100.0
Auto Repair	145.3	0.8	99.2
Ceramics	142.0	5.4	94.6
Vocational Training	124.6	47.0	53.0
Spinning	90.8	--	100.0
Paper Making	72.7	30.7	69.3
Forestry	24.6	100.0	--
Food Processing	22.1	11.3	88.7
Others	1,195.5	--	100.0
TOTALS	16,751.6	3.5	96.5

Source: Ministry of Justice (1991:238–239).

gets, though each ministry is asked to limit requests to no more than a 25 percent gain. The requests reach the MOF by August 31, and then are reviewed by the Budget Bureau of the MOF and discussed with responsible officials of the requesting ministries. In early December the draft budget is ratified, and sometimes modified, in a ministerial conference of the MOF. In the weeks immediately following, the MOF receives appeals and doles out small amounts of supplementary funds. Diet members of the dominant political party also make requests in favor of their political constituencies. The Cabinet ratifies the final version of the budget that is sent to the Diet for passage (Campbell, 1977:9–11). The relative positions of the Diet and MOF in the budget-making process have changed at various times since the end of World War II (Campbell, 1977:9–11), but since 1955 the Diet had modified the MOF draft only three or four times, and all such changes had been minor. The MOF gained influence during the postwar reconstruction and after the oil shock of 1973.

The budget for fiscal year 1974 limited growth of expenditures but did not impose zero growth. In 1975 the government obtained authority from the Diet to issue bonds in addition to its usual "red national bonds" for construction of bridges and similar projects, bonds which would help to bring revenue up to expenditures. Deficit financing rose from 11 percent of expenditures in 1974 to almost 35 percent in 1979 (Woronoff, 1986:241–246).

The drafting of the 1982 budget brought extraordinary fiscal pressures on the ministries from sources external to the government, for the mounting fiscal deficit necessitated zero growth in budgetary allocations. Furthermore, a semi-private entity was introduced into the process. The Provisional Commission on Administrative Reform (RINCHO) was established temporarily in March 1981 to advise on improving public administration.[10] It issued five reports before being dissolved in May 1983. In addressing the opening session of the Commission, Prime Minister Zenko Suzuki instructed its members to assume the additional responsibility of helping to draw up the budget for the 1982 fiscal year in order to eliminate deficit financing (Daiichi, 1988:77–80).

Negotiations Culminating in CAPIC

In July 1982, the MOF requested all ministries to reduce their requests for the 1983 fiscal year by 10 percent of the previous fiscal year's budget. The imposed ceiling enabled the ministries to decide on cuts "during the relatively private and quiet process of request preparation during the summer, rather than in the noisy and highly political hubbub of final budget negotiations" (Campbell, 1985:512).

During negotiations at the ministry level, the MOF and the head of the Accounting Section of the Ministry of Justice noticed an item in the Correction Bureau's budget for four billion yen. The allocation for purchase of raw materials for prison industries amounted to 10 percent of the total budget for the Ministry of Justice. This discovery led to a demand from several parties outside the control of the Correction Bureau that the expenditure for raw materials be eliminated from the Correction Bureau's 1983 budget. Agents of external pressure here included the Prime Minister and the Minister of Finance, who had initiated the framing of a zero growth budget for the fiscal year 1983; RINCHO, which had been pressed unexpectedly into short-term assisting of the MOF in that budget program; and the Ministry of Justice itself, of which the Correction Bureau is a component—although that Ministry also negotiated for preservation of prison industries.

The head of the Correction Bureau Accounting Section told the MOF that eliminating the item would have profoundly adverse consequences for the Correction Bureau and for the government in general. Unless raw materials were available, the Bureau would not comply with Article 24 of the Prison Law: "Prison labor shall be imposed upon inmates, the sanitary condition and general economy of the prison taken into consideration, and also with due attention paid to the term of their penalty and to their health, ability, occupation, and future life, etc . . . " The MOF would have an interest in the continued operation of prison industries, because Article 27 of the Prison Law requires that all proceeds from prison labor "shall be vested in the national treasury" rather than retained by the Correction Bureau.[11] Also, the employment of the majority of inmates in industrial production is a key element in the management of prisoners, the noteworthy tranquillity of prison life, and the official position that inmates are being prepared for return to the free world.

The head of the accounting section had also consulted with officials experienced in prison industrial operations, and was impressed with the possibilities of involving a private organization in the financing of raw materials and expanding the market. In usual practice, the funds for purchase of raw materials would result in the sale of the finished products, but the proceeds of such sales would go into the national treasury without replenishing Correction Bureau funds for further purchase of raw materials. A semi-private organization would not be subject to this practice, but could furnish raw materials as a private contractor, sell the products, and compensate the Correction Bureau for the contribution of inmate labor.

To introduce a semi-private organization into the budgetary process, funds would have to be provided for initial purchase of raw material. The semi-private organization would be able to retain the raw material investment when the Correction Bureau's share of expenses were submitted to the national treasury. By retaining that portion of the proceeds, the semi-private organization would be able to purchase raw materials at least twice during a fiscal year. The consequence would be that two billion yen a year—not four billion yen—would be sufficient to provide raw materials.

MOF agreed to provide a subsidy of two billion yen but insisted that it be spread over the years 1983–1988. Four hundred million yen would be paid each of five years for a total of two billion yen. There would be a shortage of 1.6 billion yen in 1983. MOF agreed to provide additional money for administrative and personnel expenses, and (especially) for paying interest on the 1.6 billion yen debt.

Taking Advantage of an Opportunity

The head of the Accounting Section faced two problems in accomplishing the proposed arrangement: the Correction Bureau had to be persuaded to introduce the plan, and a semi-private organization had to be recruited. The emergence of CAPIC was accomplished in developments that demonstrate how a window of opportunity can be exploited successfully.

The executives and staff of an agency must be receptive to a change agenda proposed from an external source. The Correction Bureau personnel were reluctant to accept multiple use of funds in a fiscal year and concerned about sharing authority with an outside party, but agreed under threat that if they rejected the proposal, the budget item would be eliminated without a subsidy. After the Bureau accepted the change-agenda, its personnel contributed actively and indispensably to CAPIC's success, especially the industrial sections of the Bureau's headquarters and the prisons themselves. Retired prison executives, especially those experienced in prison industries, make up an important sector of CAPIC managers.

Because there was not enough time to create a completely new semi-private organization, the Correction Bureau had recourse to the Japanese Correctional Association (JCA), a society founded in 1888 to improve prison practices and serve prison personnel. The JCA leadership and most of its staff are retired personnel, with the rest of its membership composed of active personnel and retirees. Its headquarters are located on the same grounds as those of the Tokyo Correction Region in Nakano.

The JCA is one of the *gaikaku dantai* (public corporations or extra-departmental groups), incorporated private associations, foundations, or unions initiated by the government bureaucracy. Each is an institutionalized private interest-group which has an affiliated section of government as a client, and is staffed predominantly by retired government officials.[12] In varying degrees, they rely on government funding (George, 1988:124–125). Through CAPIC, JCA received government funds; otherwise, JCA has had the Correction Bureau as a client for a long time.

The directors were reluctant to allow JCA to become the semi-private organization as proposed. Membership dues were sufficient to support the Association's projects, and the large scale of the subsidized industrial activities made the directors doubt that JCA could manage them successfully. After a series of conferences with the Industrial Section in the Correction Bureau's headquarters, JCA agreed to add a special unit to its organization: CAPIC.

The Establishment and Aim of CAPIC

The head office and executive director of CAPIC are located in the JCA headquarters. Divisional CAPIC offices have been established in each headquarters of the Bureau's correction regions, and 68 local branches have been established at each of the prisons with industrial activities. Subsidy payments, including loans to CAPIC, were 1,034 million yen in 1983, 930 million yen in 1984, 767 million yen in 1985, 210 million yen in 1986, and 189 million yen in 1987. Of the total sum of 3,130 million yen, interest charges and administrative costs drew 1,130 million yen.

CAPIC has announced its major goals: "In the first place, it becomes possible to increase the opportunities of prisons receiving orders from outside through the flexible appropriation of funds for raw materials, without being bound by the budget, which serves for securing the stability of the value of work for inmates. Secondly, the introduction of corporate management systems makes it possible to strengthen the production control, time limits of delivery, costs, etc., and also to promote the development and research in new products and high

value-added products" (Japan Correctional Association, n.d.:2).

CAPIC was expected to broaden access to the free market for prison-made goods. As a semi-private organization, it would be more acceptable to the public than a government agency. To increase the volume of sales and to create a more stable market, private enterprises and individual consumers would be assured of a dependable supply and prompt delivery of high-quality products. A catalog of products is issued, and CAPIC participates in a large-scale annual fair displaying prison-made goods. The Correction Bureau has held a national fair in Tokyo for more than 30 years, attracting thousands of individual consumers. Many modest fairs are held at prisons throughout the country each year. Retail stores are located in Tokyo, in Nagoya, and at some prisons.

Economic returns would be enhanced by paying more attention to higher-value products and by introducing more sophisticated technology. The national government contributes to the renovation of workshop equipment and sponsors training of workshop supervisors to help them in their duties and in their improvement of inmate skills. CAPIC pays their secondary expenses for attending courses and seminars. The system's emphasis on prison industries makes regularity of production very important, and CAPIC ultimately hopes to safeguard such regularity by providing 20 percent of prison employment through its own projects.

CAPIC's Place in Prison Industry

CAPIC reports considerable progress in accomplishing its goals, but more progress is necessary. The costs of administration and of transportation of finished goods must be reduced.[13] Changes in markets and customer needs require constant monitoring. The nation-wide operations involve an inventory of some 400 products. For systematic management, plans should be advanced for developing a computerized database.

CAPIC uses three methods to increase sales and stabilize the market. First, CAPIC furnishes raw materials and prison labor, and sells the products. Second, CAPIC obtains orders from customers, provides raw materials, and the prison makes the products. Third, CAPIC purchases raw materials from the contractor and relays them to the prison, and then receives the finished products and sells them to the contractor.

CAPIC has not increased its share of total contracts obtained, but its financial contribution has been enhanced. From 1985 to 1991, CAPIC reports that its share of net revenue rose from 24.8 percent to 32.4 percent; and its share of inmate man-days from 13.2 percent to 23.4 percent. Its sales increased from 4.17 billion yen in 1983 to 15.89 billion yen in 1991, a 387 percent gain. For fiscal years 1989 to 1990, the customers were long-term contractors (46.4 percent), large-scale contractors (8.3 percent), government agencies (8.9 percent), the general public (23.5 percent), and annual fairs (12.9 percent). Gross profits were 3.9 percent of sales in 1983 and 11.2 percent of 1989 sales. However, operating costs also increased at a rate of 374 percent. In the initial years, net income was negative, but it has been positive ever since, reaching 442,784 thousand yen in 1991.

For all prison industries in Japan, metal work and tailoring alone employed 37 percent of all inmate workers in 1988 and made 53.7 percent of the revenue (see Table 12–2). Woodcraft (chiefly furniture), printing, and leather work employed 14 percent and supplied 25.9 percent of the revenue. Those five industries were disproportionately "profitable." Unlike proportions in non-CAPIC revenue, woodcraft and printing brought CAPIC more revenue than metal work and tailoring. The ratios in Table 12–2 indicate that (in addition to woodcraft and printing) CAPIC draws revenue most advantageously from industries contributing relatively less to total revenue: automobile repair and ceramics. CAPIC was especially

helpful in vocational training programs that incidentally generated revenue.

Between 1986 and 1991, the value of CAPIC sales rose an impressive 37 percent (see Table 12–3). In 1986, woodcraft and printing brought the greatest financial return; but tailoring, metal work, and leather work scored greater gains. Woodcraft continued to accrue the most revenue of all industrial categories in spite of a very modest gain proportionately. Printing made a small increase in absolute value of sales but failed to keep pace with other categories.

Other Contributions of CAPIC

CAPIC contributed a total of 347,323 thousand yen to various projects for the personnel and programs of the Correction Bureau in the 1985–1991 period. Among the projects are financial support of overseas study tours for selected Correction Bureau personnel, sponsorship of an athletic marathon, sponsorship of a contest in word-processing, and establishment of a research institute.

While President of JCA, Yoshiho Yasuhara suggested that CAPIC sponsor a new research unit, the Correctional Association Research Institute for Criminology. The Institute is designed to remedy a lack of private research centers in Japan dealing with the fields of corrections and criminology, and has a staff of 14. Governmentally-sponsored variations on the Institute have been developed by the Ministry of Justice and the National Police Agency.

The Institute has five divisions. General Affairs is responsible for administrative support. The Investigation Division negotiates with other research units in planning projects, publishes a journal (*The Bulletin of Correctional Research Institute for Criminology*), reports on the Institute's projects, and prepares teaching materials for personnel training conducted by the Correction Bureau. Three of the five divisions specialize in particular areas of research.

Table 12–2. *Inmate Workers by Kind of Products; Comparing CAPIC and All Prison Industry by Revenue and Kind of Products, 1988*

	ALL INDUSTRY		TOTAL REVENUE FROM INDUSTRIES		CAPIC REVENUE	
	INMATES IN ALL INDUSTRY		TOTAL REVENUE FROM INDUSTRIES		CAPIC REVENUE	
KIND OF PRODUCTS	NUMBER	PCT.	IN MILLION YEN	PCT.	IN MILLION YEN	RATIO*
Metal Work	8,909	20.7	5,389.9	32.6	726.8	.16
Tailoring	7,045	16.4	3,495.8	21.1	761.0	.28
Woodcraft	2,657	6.2	2,012.6	12.2	1,450.0	2.58
Printing	1,776	4.1	1,391.6	8.4	1,054.4	3.13
Leather Work	1,595	3.7	878.1	5.3	207.4	.31
Vocational Training	1,062	2.5	116.4	0.7	94.8	4.39
Farm Forestry, Stock Raising	228	0.5	257.5	1.6	24.1	.10
Ceramics	186	0.4	130.3	0.8	93.7	2.56
Auto Repair	122	0.3	123.0	0.7	116.1	16.83
Paper Work	68	0.2	74.1	0.5	19.8	.36
Others	19,395	45.0	2,666.0	16.1	49.4	.02
TOTAL	43,043	100.0	16,535.3	100.0	4,597.4	.38

Source: CAPIC

* For the ratio, CAPIC revenue was subtracted from total revenue. The ratio is CAPIC revenue divided by non-CAPIC revenue.

The First Research Division examines the causes of crime and delinquency, the methodologies of prediction and trend identification, and crime prevention. In one project, analysis of event-history was examined as a method for follow-up studies. In another project, the eight correctional regions of the Correction Bureau gathered data for an evaluation of treatment methods.

The Second Research Division concentrates on the practical aspects of crime prevention systems such as punitive and protective measures taken against offenders, and rehabilitation-oriented programs. One project studied how prison industries are organized; another followed up prisoners who had completed vocational training.

Table 12–3. CAPIC Sales by Products, 1986–1991 (A)

TYPES OF PRODUCTS	1986		1991		PCT.
	SALES	PCT.	SALES	PCT.	CHANGE
Woodcraft	4,176.7	35.0	5,800.8	35.4	38.9
Printing	2,153.5	18.0	2,270.6	13.9	5.4
Tailoring	2,084.1	17.5	3,272.8	20.0	57.0
Metal Work	1,800.7	15.1	2,695.6	16.5	49.7
Leather Work	704.0	5.9	1,127.8	6.9	60.2
Ceramics	235.4	2.0	328.6	2.0	39.6
Auto Repair	218.1	1.8	241.8	1.5	10.9
Other Products	444.7	3.7	498.2	3.0	12.0
Vocational Training	119.0	1.0	127.1	0.8	6.8
TOTAL	11,936.2	100.0	16,363.3	100.0	37.1

Source: CAPIC

(a) Sales are in million yen.

The Third Research Division considers theories concerning therapeutic responses to offenders, the characteristics of criminals and delinquents, and the development of staff skills for treating offenders. Among the projects are studies of the drawings of family members by female inmates at juvenile training schools, problems encountered in counseling prison inmates suffering from AIDS, and characteristic responses of training school inmates in a sentence comprehension test.

Opposing Outcomes: U.S. and Japan

In nineteenth-century America some three dozen states adopted the industrial prison in the mode of the Auburn system, but opposition appeared soon after the system was created. As the decades passed, the share of inmates employed in industries declined consistently: 90 percent in 1885, 71 percent in 1895, 53 percent in 1932, 10 percent in 1979 (Funke, Wayson, and Miller, 1982:20–21).

Americans have a historical proclivity for joining associations, including political interest groups that mobilize efforts to gain advantages from government in a particular public issue. The American scene is especially congenial to the competition among interest groups. Federalism divides power between the national and state governments, offering several targets for exerting influence. Power is decentralized within two major political parties; politicians of various ideological persuasions are found in both major parties. Party discipline is weakened, and candidates for political office are very susceptible to the demands of interest groups (Keefe et al., 1990:306–311).

The decline in industrial employment of prisoners reflects the growing success of lobbying that persuaded state and national law-makers to restrict prison-made goods. The prosperous contract industries attracted major opposition in the northern states. There were a series of investigations in 11 states during the 1870s and 1880s. Manufacturers in certain industries organized the National Anti-Contract Association in 1886. Reports prepared in 1905 and 1923, Gill (1931:84) declares, set forth "an array of evidence which leaves no doubt that prison industries, by underselling, by dumping, by false labeling, by unfair advertising, by unscientific accounting, by brutal treatment of labor, and by bad management, have been able to take advantage of free industry to the detriment of both labor and capital."

By 1950 the state-use and the public-works-and-ways systems[14] were the dominant forms of inmate employment. The final blow to the industrial prison was struck during the Great Depression with the Hawes-Cooper Act (1929) and the Ashurst-Sumners Acts (1935 and 1940) of the national Congress. These authorized state legislatures to prohibit in their jurisdiction the sale of goods made in prisons of other states, an exception to the U.S. Constitutional reservation of interstate commerce control to the federal government. The state legislatures reacted enthusiastically to the opportunity and also abetted lobbyists by pursuing further sanctions against the sale of goods made in their own prisons (Flynn, 1951:239–241).

In Japan there has been incidental opposition to prisoner-made goods, but resistance is uncommon, especially in times of prosperity and labor shortage. "Japan has experienced neither systematic opposition to prison industries from outsiders, representing business and labor unions, nor legislative action to limit the inmate's employment in order to protect the free market" (Yanigimoto,

1970:216). Primary or secondary contractors would seem the most likely opponents, but they are the primary sources of agreements with prisons. These agreements are general affirmations of prison-made goods, as Japan has consistently lacked an adequate supply of blue-collar workers and skilled manpower.

Japanese political experts usually favor the elitist model of policymaking with a tripartite power group composed of the leaders of the Liberal Democratic Party (LDP), senior bureaucrats, and big businessmen. The LDP has ruled the national Diet almost without interruption since 1954,[15] but the Party depends on interest groups (especially "big business") for campaign funds and on government bureaucracy for expertise and implementation of policy (Fukui, 1977:22–24). "Although organized economic interests, including big business and the agricultural lobby, enjoy an astonishing level of access to policymaking in Japan," Pharr (1990:xi–xii) notes, "when it comes to noneconomic interests, the story is quite different." Interest groups especially concerned about prison issues would be among those noneconomic groups with limited access to policymaking at the national level. They have little incentive to amass the resources of an effective protest group.

CAPIC shows the Correction Bureau's ability to succeed in negotiations when the viability of the industrial prison is threatened. The organization did not emerge from a struggle between political interest groups, but from bargaining between ministries in an unusual but general fiscal crisis. The Correction Bureau was vulnerable to external pressures, but was able to justify its advantageous functions within the structures of government and private industry.

One could say that all of the circumstances of the case were uniquely Japanese: the history of prison labor's contribution to the nation's economy, the contemporary linkage with private industry through subcontracting, the absence of vigorous and organized opposition to prison-made goods, the fundamental position of prison industry in the prison's operations, CAPIC as another example of *gaikaku dantai*, and the Correction Bureau's orientation toward *taisei-gai* bargaining.

Notes

1. This paper is among the products of research financed by a Fulbright award for 1990–1991. Collection of information was especially assisted by Kazuo Kawakani, former Director-General of the Correction Bureau, Keisei Miyamoto, head of CAPIC, and Takehisa Kihara, Director of the Industrial Division, Correction Bureau's headquarters in Tokyo.

2. In 1834 a prison director in France responded to an official inquiry: "I do not know how to concede that work exercises an *essentially reforming* (emphasis in original) effect on them (the inmates). But I do consider work in any large prison to be the surest guarantee of order, peace, and quiet." (Quoted by O'Brien, 1982: 183–184).

3. The Ministry of Justice (1990:35–36) addresses the rehabilitative purpose. "Prison industry is organized so as to serve constructive purposes in the treatment of prisoners. Its objective is not only to provide inmates with vocational knowledge and skills, but also to strengthen their will to work, sense of self-help, and spirit of co-operation through working together in well-regulated circumstances. Thus, prison industry contributes to the correctional aims of resocializing offenders."

4. The budget for adult institutions in 1990 was $1,028,391,361 and the "settled revenue" from prison industries $127,635,408 (130 yen per $1 U.S.).

5. The rules resemble those of a Japanese automobile factory in 1927: "Don't lose your spirit for work. Don't look around while working. Don't think about anything else while working. Talking to someone who is working is prohibited in this factory." (Quoted by Allison, 1975:104).

6. When released from prison in 1990, a male inmate averaged 25,961 yen and a woman inmate 28,449 yen accumulated remuneration. The averages increased consistently with length of sentence: from 1,686 yen for less than three months to 53,923 yen for sentences over three years for males; equivalent range for women was 1,500 to 54,897 yen (Ministry of Justice, 1991:180). In 1990 the exchange rate was 134 yen per U.S. dollar.

7. "In large areas of Tokyo and Osaka back streets rarely visited by outsiders," Van Wolferen (1989:171) comments, "one hears the same incessant clickety-clack of small machines behind hundreds of wooden doors as one did ten or twenty years ago; but the clickety-clack produces entirely different things today."

8. Convinced that small and medium-sized firms would play the key role in post-war economic reconstruction, Yoshisuke Ayukawa purchased a commercial bank in 1952 and organized loans to small companies (Van Wolferen, 1989:388–389).

9. Income accrued from products made incidentally to vocational training courses.

10. Campbell (1985:507–511) relates the effort to deal with the deficit to the more general movement to reduce the size of the national government. He describes RINCHO as a blue-ribbon commission representing "big business" and this direct participation of big business in governmental affairs to be "actually quite a new development." However, RINCHO backed off from rigorous administrative reform in the face of "generally hostile bureaucracy."

11. MOF collects monies from several governmental institutions: primarily postal savings, insurance, national pensions, and welfare pensions (Woronoff, 1986:127).

12. Public corporations pay their own way, provide services, and thus help to keep the Japanese tax rate comparatively low (Johnson, 1978:144–146).

13. By improved administration and accounting methods the prisons were able, by the end of 1992, to stabilize these costs which previously had been increasing.

14. The state-use system produces goods and services exclusively for agencies and political subdivisions of the given state.

Public-works-and-ways includes road construction and repair, reforestation, soil-erosion control and other similar services.

15. At the time of this writing, LDP has lost control of the Diet.

Discussion and Revision Questions

1. What are the advantages and disadvantages of the factory system of corrections prevalent in Japan, China, and Denmark?

2. Why did the factory system of corrections collapse in the United States but survive in major Asian and European countries?

3. Compare and contrast the Japanese congregate cells system and the American Auburn plan.

4. What are the goals of the Correctional Association Prison Industrial Cooperative (CAPIC)?

5. The Japanese Prisons System is self-sustaining. Discuss.

6. What are the reasons why Japanese prisoners accept the behavioral standards of the industrial prisons?

7. How is a stable amount of productivity maintained in Japanese industrial prisons?

8. What is the role of physically unfit inmates in the Japanese industrial prison system?

9. How are Japanese industrial prison products marketed?

10. What are the main unique features of the Japanese prison system?

13

Japanese Version of Community Corrections:

Volunteer Probation Officers and Hostels

Elmer H. Johnson

Introduction

In a VCR orienting the Japanese to the work of the Rehabilitation Bureau, a spokesman says in part:

> Japan is a peaceful and stable society. The system for rehabilitating criminals has played a large role in achieving this . . . We hear about crime and juvenile delinquency in the newspapers and on television every day, but, to protect ourselves and to build a society where we can all live safely, it is not sufficient just to strengthen crime control or to punish criminals. We must work to insure that offenders are reintegrated into society and that crime is prevented . . .
>
> The rehabilitation system is based on the concept of trusting people who unfortunately have committed crimes or have been delinquent so they can reform by developing a greater awareness of themselves and their circumstances. . . . Imprisonment isolates criminals from society, and they often return to crime when they are released. Consequently, the crime rate never decreases. Therefore, the prevention system is very important in assisting offenders when they return to society,

supporting their social rehabilitation and making them productive members of society . . ."

The Rehabilitation Bureau expresses the claims made for community-based corrections in the criminal justice and criminological literature of the West. Similarities in general purposes are suggested, but, unlike in the West, the Rehabilitation Bureau largely relies on private persons and groups for their achievement. Volunteer probation officers (unsalaried private persons) carry out almost all supervision of probationers and parolees. Rehabilitation aid associations operate the halfway houses, serve parolees chiefly, and receive government subsidies meeting only a portion of their operating expenses. This paper concentrates on this major aspect of Rehabilitation Bureau policy.[1]

This chapter will trace precedents in Japanese history for the use of volunteer probation officers (VPOs) and of private groups in aftercare (rehabilitation aid hostels), but also will show what such policies owe to the diffusion of foreign ideas following the modernization of feudal Japan. We will argue that the Japanese concept of "community" can help us understand how the participation of private citizens in community corrections came to be important in Japanese criminal justice. It was a concept formed under the Tokugawa rulers of the rural villages during the Tokugawa Era (1603–1867), the social control system of which brought centuries of unprecedented peace and security. The influence of the Tokugawa system lingers in the behavior and beliefs of contemporary Japanese.

Western nations forced Japan to end centuries of isolation from foreign influences and contributed to the Meiji Restoration, initiated in 1868, at which time Japan made a tardy but hasty effort to develop modern institutions and infrastructure. The social psychology of Japanese community has been affected by modernization, and the motivation and activities of volunteers in criminal justice activities will be assessed in that context. Modern societies believe that things can be changed, that human consciousness can bend destiny to its will. Modernization has contributed to an increasing crime rate, but Japan remains on the whole "a peaceful and stable society."

Modern Japanese society, like other modern societies, believes community correction to be a superior alternative to imprisonment, because it accords with the belief that things can change. The Japanese culture and the structure and operations of Japan's criminal justice system contribute to a remarkably low imprisonment rate, which has dropped from 65 per 100,000 in 1926 to 34 per 100,000 in 1989. The imprisonment rate in the United States, on the other hand, rose from 83 per 100,000 in 1926 to 271 per 100,000 in 1989 (Shikita and Tsuchiya, 1990:371; Ministry of Justice, 1991:24; Flanagan and Maguire, 1991:604).

Japanese criminal justice also authorizes the court, under certain conditions, to suspend a prison sentence after imposing it and to place the offender under "protective supervision" (Penal Code, Articles 25 and 26). Table 13–1 demonstrates that less than

five percent of the courts' dispositions are imprisonment; that almost three percent are suspended imprisonment; and that, of those suspensions, only .39 percent are probationers. More specifically, only a small share of adult convicted offenders receive probation. Judges often are reluctant to require probationary supervision as a condition of suspension, when there are extenuating circumstances (Kouhashi, 1985:4–5). They treat probation as a punitive sanction.

Japan is a paradox among modern societies, because its programs of community corrections are greatly dependent on private citizens, and do not extend the grasp of criminal justice agencies. People have objected to various community strategies in the United States on grounds that they capture a larger proportion of the population in a broader criminal justice network.[2] This criticism has not been borne out in Japan. Before the post-war expansion of community corrections in 1926, only 6.2 Japanese per 100,000 population were placed on probation, and the rate rose to 73.5 in 1950. Thereafter, the rate has dropped to 38.9 in 1970 and to 31.0 in 1988 (Shikita and Tsuchiya, 1990:369–370).

Twin Sources of Community Corrections

Prisons differ in details of procedure, exigencies of daily events, and the philosophies of those administering them, but there are also basic similarities that override variations in time, place, and purpose. "Perhaps this (the set of similarities) is due to a diffusion of ideas, customs, and laws. Perhaps it is a matter of similar social structures arising independently from attempts to solve much the same problems. Most probably it is some combination of both" (Sykes, 1958:xii–xiii).

One can observe both similarities and differences between community corrections in Japan and the practices and poli-

Table 13–1. *Dispositions of Adjudicated Defendants by Courts of First Instance, 1989*

Dispositions	Number	Pct.
Total Defendants	1,306,214	100.00
Imprisonment	61,531	4.71
Fines	1,208,575	92.52
Penal Detention	79	.01
Suspended Imprisonment	35,528	2.72
Simple Suspension	(30,409)	(2.33)
With Probation	(5,119)	(.39)
Acquittals	134	.01
Others[a]	367	.03

Source: Research and Training Institute, Ministry of Justice.

(a) "Others" includes guilty but no penalty, time of legal responsibility was exceeded, and summary sentence was sent by mail but not received by the defendant.

cies of probation, parole, and aftercare in Western societies. In the case of prisons, contemporary practices and policies may be attributed to cultural diffusion from the West and the lingering influence of indigenous traditions. Modern correctional systems emerged later in Japan than in most western societies, especially community corrections. The development of modern Japanese corrections provides a fine example of the mingling of foreign ideas and institutions with indigenous customs and ideology that took place in Japanese society starting with the Meiji Restoration.

Prisoners' post-release difficulties drew the earliest concern. Once, for instance, the emperor granted amnesty to a burglar and gave him some clothes to wear (Satoh, 1989:1). In 1790 the Tokugawa Shogunate opened the *Ninsoku-Yoseba* (Stockade for Laborers) to control homeless wanderers in. After 1820, when it began to house persons sentenced to forced labor, it became a model for other penal facilities. The inmates were paid for their work to give them means for support after release. If those released were farmers, they were given a plot of land. Those from Edo (now Tokyo) were given a shop; otherwise, they were given tools of a trade or granted an allowance (Takigawa, 1972:45, 173–175; Hiromatsu, 1972:44–49, 57).

The Meiji reformers asked Emile Gustave Boissonade to draft a penal code on a French model, and it came into force in 1882. However, a new penal code, developed on a German model, replaced the French version (the "old penal code"), when the Penal Code of 1907 was still in force, although amended in some respects. The Code of 1882 did not provide for government involvement in community corrections, but the Code of 1907 provided strong government commitment to community-based corrections. Early on, the government endeavored to introduce community corrections but lacked sufficient resources. Therefore, "the government requested religious groups, mainly Buddhist organizations, as well as other voluntary organizations, to provide financial assistance and moral support for ex-offenders" (Satoh, 1989:1).

The Napoleonic Code of 1810 had provided for "surveillance"; that is, the supervision and control of released prisoners by the police as an additional punishment. On the other hand, a parole system had emerged from nineteenth-century French patronage societies. These had existed since 1823, and had expanded rapidly in France after 1885; they were private organizations, funded by private donations and partially by state subsidies, which recognized that released prisoners might have problems adjusting. The societies were privately directed but authorized by the government. In the parole system established in 1885, misdemeanants with good conduct could be released from the correctional institution after serving half the sentence and be supervised by a patronage society (O'Brien, 1982:25, 227, 251–254).

In Shizuoka Prefecture, Meisen Kinbara—a philanthropist troubled by a released prisoner who was rejected by his family—pioneered in 1888 the first halfway houses of Japan. In 1907 the government began to help with partial subsidies, and by 1891 two other private halfway houses were opened elsewhere; there were 26 halfway houses by 1900; 61 by 1910; and more than 100 by 1920. Buddhists, Christians, the Salvation Army, and prison personnel were especially active in the movement. The Offenders Rehabilitation Service Law (1934) specified joint responsibility between the government and voluntary organizations for aftercare of prisoners, but World War II stopped its implementation (Udo, 1990:1–2).

Probation of adults emerged in Japan almost as an after-thought, under the authority of the judge to suspend a prison sentence in case of "extenuating circumstances." Article 25 of the Penal Code limits the leniency to persons receiving sentences of three years or less (convicts who have served previous sentences must have satisfied those sentences at least five years previously). Article 25-2 says that the person may be placed under "protec-tive supervision" (probation). Of the total suspended sentences in 1961, only 18.7 percent were with probation and in 1989 probation took up 14.4 percent (Shikita and Tsuchiya, 1990:165).[3]

"Extenuating circumstances" which permit parole include the following: the defendant has no criminal record or a minimal criminal record, or is young enough to change his or her attitudes and lifestyle; the victim excuses the offender; the victim and defendant have agreed to terms of restitution; the offender exhibits readiness for rehabilitation; the offense was accidental, not deliberate. The judges regard probation to be punitive and are reluctant to add probation to the suspension (Kouhashi, 1985:3–5). Supervision is inconvenient for a person with such extenuating circumstances. If probation is required, the individual would be denied another suspension, if a new crime were committed; but suspension without probation would not render a new suspension impossible.

The Japanese Penal Code's provision for suspended sentences was modeled on the Franco-Belgian system (Ancel, 1971:22–26, 36–40). Alarmed by increases in rates of crime and recidivism, nineteenth-century France questioned the usefulness of imprisonment. Conditional suspension of prison sentences emerged in Belgian law in 1888 and in French law in 1891. The prison sentence was pronounced to intimidate the convicted individual, but the casual offender was believed to have the capacity to rehabilitate himself without assistance or probationary supervision. Suspended sentences without probationary supervision were preferred for deserving offenders—as they are today in Japan.

Conditional release from Japanese prisons was first officially specified in the Penal Code of 1881, which authorized police surveillance after three-quarters of a prison sentence had been served. The Penal Code of 1907 reduced the sentence-serving requirement to one-third, but granted parole on a limited scale.

Probation was first formally recognized in 1905 and was incorporated in the Penal Code of 1907, but supervision was lacking. Probation in the full sense was yet to be introduced (Ogawa, 1976:633).

Modern probation and parole were founded after World War II. The Offenders Rehabilitation Law (1949) provides for the organization, principles, and procedures of juvenile law, juvenile parole, and adult parole. The Law for Probationary Supervision of Persons under Suspension of Execution of Sentence (1954) initiated adult probation for convicted offenders, whom the court granted a suspension of prison sentence with supervision. The Law for Aftercare of Discharged Offenders (1950) established criteria for voluntary referrals for post-release assistance and outlined the principles and procedures for rehabilitation aid hostels (halfway houses) operated by private organizations. The Amnesty Law (1947) defined the kinds and variety of pardons. The Voluntary Probation Officer Law (1950) described the qualifications, selection, and duties of VPOs.

When the Japanese system of community corrections was established in 1949 and 1950, it was debated whether the probation and parole services should be professionalized as in many other countries. The decision was to combine professionals and unpaid volunteers. "It is true that the shortage of funds at the time precluded the realization of overall professionalism," the Rehabilitation Bureau recalls (Ministry of Justice, 1990b:13). "But the even greater reason making a determination to maintain volunteers obviously lies in the fact that the trust of the authorities in the potential of volunteer workers was so overwhelming."

Contemporary VPO and Hostel Programs

The Volunteer Probation Officer Law states that the VPO mission will be: "to contribute to the welfare of the individual and the public by helping persons who have committed criminal offenses to improve and be rehabilitated and, at the same time, by leading public opinion for the prevention of offenses and by cleaning up the community, in the spirit of social service." The total number of VPOs for Japan is set at 52,500. They are allocated by the Minister of Justice in "rehabilitation areas" fixed according to population, economic characteristics, crime rates, and other community circumstances.

The Minister of Justice may either delegate the authority to appoint VPOs to the chair of the regional parole board or may appoint them personally. VPOs receive two-year terms, subject to reappointment, according to these criteria: confidence and popularity with the community in character and conduct; enthusiasm and time for the work; financial stability; and being healthy and active. Persons are disqualified if adjudicated as incompetent; as formerly sentenced to prison; or as having organized or been a member of any organization advocating the overthrow of the Constitution of Japan or the Japanese government by force and violence. No salary or allowance is paid, but expenses incurred in the course of performing duties are paid "within the limits of the budget."

There are 50 probation offices responsible for supervising probationers and parolees and for making referrals to rehabilitation aid hostels. These offices provide VPOs with three kinds of training: initial orientation training for recruits (materials for which are prepared by the Investigation and Research Section in the headquarters of the Rehabilitation Bureau); periodic refresher training; and special sessions bringing experienced VPOs together for study of specific topics.

Rehabilitation and hostels are defined by the Law for Aftercare of Discharged Offenders, which requires their certification by the Minister of Justice and delegates their supervision to probation offices. The hostels provide room and board to discharged prisoners, parolees, and probationers referred to them by a probation office. The hostel associations are private organizations, and obtain funds from subsidies by the Rehabilitation Bureau and by private donations; they also may raise support by leasing a part of their land or property to private enterprises, or by other financial means. The 96 hostels have 470 full-time salaried staff plus volunteers. The paid personnel include persons who retired after years of probation or parole service.

The chief of the probation office refers persons to the hostels and sets the official time limit for the stay. For adult parolees, the maximum stay is supposed to be the unserved portion of the prison sentence. A discharged inmate is eligible for a maximum period of six months from date of release. The judge sets the length of probation, ranging from one to five years. Officially, the probationer may stay at the hostel for a full period of probation; but in practice, government funds available for subsidy determine the length of stay. The resident is always responsible for payments beyond that coverage.

Parolees were referred to hostels more often than probationers, and adults more than juveniles. In 1992, of the 13,098 adult parole terminations, 26.5 percent were referred. Others referred were 4.7 percent of the 4,384 juvenile parole terminations; 8.3 percent of the 46,695 juvenile probation terminations; and 2.7 percent of the 5,436 adult probation terminations. In 1992, 69.1 percent of released hostel residents had boarded in the hostel because they lacked relatives on whom to depend for help. Another 13.6 percent had been denied assistance by relatives, and 16 percent of the residents did not want to seek help from relatives. The remainder (1.3 percent) had been referred to the hostels to obtain "training for resocialization" (Ministry of Justice, 1993:126, 162–163).

The rehabilitation aid hostels' receipt of government subsidies is in keeping with the *gaikaku dantai* system—private associations, foundations, or unions incorpo-rated at the initiation of the government bureaucracy. Each of these public corporations or extra-departmental groups has a section of government as a predictable client, is staffed predominately by retired government personnel, and is to some degree reliant on government funds[4] (George, 1988:124–125). Public corporations pay at least a portion of their own way, provide services, and thus contribute to the relatively low tax rate of Japan (Johnson, 1978:144–146).

Tokugawa Controls and the Rural Village

Early Japan was a collection of feudal domains engaged in perennial warfare. Ieyasu, founder of the Tokugawa house, won national hegemony by military victories and in 1603 took the office of *Shogun*, nominally the emperor's military deputy but the *de facto* ruler of Japan (Beasley, 1990:3). To establish political dominance, he used clever military leadership, skillful political treatment of defeated adversaries, and giving fiefs to the *daimyo* (feudal lords) to bind them to him.

The Tokugawa Era (1603–1867) brought centuries of unprecedented peace and security. The *daimyo* who had been early allies (*fudai*) were distinguished from those who had submitted only after Tokugawa military victories (*tozama*). The latter were relegated to distant areas and required to send hostages to Edo (now Tokyo). After pledging loyalty to the Tokugawa regime, the *daimyo* were granted a domain as a fief. To discipline insubordination, the *Shogun* could transfer a lord, or reduce his domain, or confiscate it. By the end of the seventeenth century, bureaucratic administration had been established. The *Shogun* recruited the highest advisors from the *fudai* and sent auditing officials to the domains to check on their wealth, administration, military strength, and size of population (Duus, 1967:88–95).

Formation of a community in Japan was a normal social process that was, unlike in the West, "neither a special privilege nor a legal right to be discussed" (Tonomura, 1992:190). Legal rights such as that of assembly were never demanded from the aristocracy and the Tokugawa state, and the villages seem to have been nothing more than administrative and political arms of the central Tokugawa government. Community solidarity of local people seems to have come from their resistance to the demands of the centralized government.

Although the system of neighborhood associations "was used principally as a political tool, it did nevertheless develop as an autonomous body of neighborhood families for the handling of community problems" (Masland, 1946:355–356). Villagers maintained community solidarity because the feudal system of social control accorded autonomy to the villagers as long as the Tokugawas' political purposes were served, and because of technological factors associated with rice agriculture.

The Tokugawa system of rule was designed to maintain law and order, to enforce official programs of frugality and morality, to collect taxes, and to suppress anti-Tokugawa activities. Only one castle town was permitted in each domain; all other strongholds were dismantled. The *samurai* were forced to live in a castle town and serve as salaried bureaucrats or to surrender their aristocratic status. "While the physical distance of the *samurai* from the farming land enhanced their bureaucratic character, it also restricted them from direct intervention in village affairs. With minimal involvement of the urban bureaucrats, the primary producers paid taxes and kept the local peace and order" (Tonomura, 1992:169).

The agricultural village had a central role in creating peace and order. With the *samurai* bureaucrats unable to interfere directly in village affairs, authority was delegated to villages to collect taxes, to maintain law and order, and to regulate the daily life of local persons (Sato, 1990:50–51). The village's headman was appointed by the government from among the local people, and represented them in contacts with the government. He also was held responsible for the village in satisfying the tax assessment (calculated in units of rice), in overseeing the registration of members of households, and in disseminating the rulers' orders. Local officials were able to oversee conduct of residents because of the information provided by household registration: name, sex, occupation, birth, marriage, divorce, death, and movements of household members (Tonomura, 1992:172–174). Especially in feudal times, the rural hamlet exerted heavy social pressure for conformity with local community norms. Ostracism by vote had great force because of cultural emphasis on harmony among residents, and because agricultural production demanded the neighbors' cooperation (Smith, 1961:522–525; Steiner, 1965: 210–212). Rice growing was a group endeavor, and the entire village worked so closely at it that cooperation was second nature. Tasks were not specialized: everyone took turns at all chores. The work was repetitive from year to year. Perseverance was demanded more than innovation, and operations could be conducted through a consensus without strong individual leadership (Hayashi, 1988:87–92).

In 1597 Hideyoshi Toyotomi ordered that the peasants be organized into five-householder groups (the *gonin-gumi*). (The idea of organizing Japan in small community groups was borrowed from China.) The head of each group was obligated to make certain that the peasants lived frugal lives, worked hard, and paid taxes (Braibanti, 1948:140). In the Tokugawa era, this system for controlling the peasantry was again borrowed from the Chinese (Dore, 1958:255). The Tokugawa regime went deeper than Toyotomi in copying the Chinese village-oriented social organization. In ancient Japan, the *gonin-gumi* system had either imposed criminal liability on the offender's relatives (*enza*) or an unrelated person serving in the same office (*renza*). Later the responsibility had been extended to the offender's neighbors (Ishii, 1980:51, 58, 89).[5]

In the 1620s and 1630s, the Tokugawa regime acted to forbid contacts with Europeans because contacts were thought to encourage Japanese dissidents, and because Christianity was believed to corrupt Japanese values. Foreign trade was limited to a Dutch trading port and a few Chinese junks. Christianity was savagely persecuted (Beasley, 1990:22). Foreign intervention, however, eventually did succeed in challenging the isolation, and precipitated Japan's entry into the modern age.

Twin Sources of the Meiji Restoration

Commodore Matthew C. Perry entered Edo Bay in February 1854 with his Black Fleet of eight American warships. In the following years, foreign powers forced treaties on the Tokugawa government specifying the principle of extra-territoriality; that is, foreign nationals in Japan would be subject to the laws of their own countries, not to the laws of Japan. The principle had earlier resulted in the loss of China's independence and its domination by Western imperialism. To avoid China's fate, the leaders of Japan set out to create the military force and infrastructure of a modern nation. The term "Meiji Restoration" refers to a coup d'etat carried out in Kyoto on January 3, 1868, with a group of feudal lords taking control of the Imperial Court, terminating the Tokugawa Shogunate, and proclaiming the Emperor's direct responsibility for government. Their series of reforms established the institutional structure of a new Japan. The process of institutional change was carefully controlled. Delegations were sent to Europe and the United States for quick studies of western social institu-

tions (Noda, 1976; Beasley, 1990:22–30, 85–88, 142).

The feudal system of the Tokugawa state had been in decline, and something like the Meiji Restoration may have come without the intervention of foreign nations (Craig, 1961:85–86). Also, the Japanese differed from other Asian nations in their reaction to foreign pressure because of factors internal to Japan. Entering the modern age well after the industrial revolution in Europe, Japan confronted the foreign threat with a common language and with a set of values consolidated through two centuries of isolation from the external world.

Studies of Western institutions guided the development of Japan's modern political and economic systems. The timing was exceptionally appropriate for the examination of Western institutions, because "all of the great powers at that time were engaged in organization-building on a major scale" (Westney, 1987:11). State structures of France were being refashioned into patterns appropriate to the Third Republic; the unified German Empire was emerging; Great Britain was striving for stability at home and within the Empire; and the United States was rebuilding its administrative structure after the Civil War.

The lessons learned from the West were accommodated to Japanese values and social patterns. The ultimate outcome illustrates the principle that mass transfer of foreign ideas encounters resistance: people are slow to change their familiar ways, and new ideas must be accomodated to existing institutions and values.

Community in Twentieth-Century Japan

Massive and sweeping changes since the Meiji Restoration have affected community solidarity and modified the nature of relationships among the local residents. In his study of potters in Kyushu, Moeran (1984:174–175) describes the effects of such change on rural residents: "They still share their lives; they still participate in communal events. Everyone turns out to help when it comes to building a new house." Nevertheless, traditional solidarity grounded in the unity of all households has been weakened by materialism and erosion of the authority of traditional leadership. The appreciation of the classic pottery by outsiders has given potting households greater income than non-potting households and introduced social stratification. Recognition of the skills of master potters has undermined the traditional gerontocracy.

With the termination of the Tokugawa state, its system for controlling rural villagers was weakened, and new conditions altered the nature of community ties. After the Meiji Restoration, the new regime officially abolished the *gonin-gumi* with the intention of substituting reverence to the Emperor for loyalty to the immediate neighborhood (Braibanti, 1948:1). Nevertheless, the groups survived, and neighborhood gatherings for weddings, funerals, festivals, harvesting, and care of the sick still exist.

For wartime mobilization of civilians, the Home Ministry of the national government in 1940 ordered the prefectures (equivalent to the American states) to enlist neighborhood associations. The rural *buraku-kai* were based on the traditional communal units. In urban areas, the *chonaikai* (district or block associations) were composed of 400 to 600 households. Legislation in 1943 authorized local governments to enlist the aid of the unit heads and to control the property and expenditures of neighborhood associations. Although the neighborhood associations were based on mutual cooperation and were examples of local self-government, their wartime functions recalled the services of feudal villages for the Tokugawa dictatorship (Masland, 1946:356–357; Shihgetoh, 1943:984–985).

Because the *chonaikai* were identified with wartime service to the military dicta-

torship, the allied occupation authorities ordered them disbanded. Also, post-war developments magnified the effects of migration and technological change on the social solidarity of local community groups. In rural areas, the need for neighbors' cooperation had been reduced by mechanization of agriculture. Electric cooking and heating eased the demand for communal forests. Other types of roofing replaced thatched roofs and ended the need for neighbors' assistance in rethatching (Steiner, 1965:224).

Social changes and the orders of the allied occupation have failed to eliminate the *chonaikai*, but the groups' nature has been modified. The *chonaikai* is unquestionably the neighborhood's most important and visible organization. In some senses it acts as "a semi-official local government, providing services to residents both at local initiative and at the behest of the municipal authorities" (Bestor, 1985: 126–127).

The *chonaikai* hovers between a group for communal fellowship and a semi-official component of formal government. It is multifunctional in contrast to the specialized functions of government agencies. Households, not individuals, are members; membership is taken for granted rather than being a conscious or clearly compulsory act (Nakamura, 1968:191–192, 201–207).

Voluntary associations emerged only with the end of World War II, because previously "all groups were subordinated to the emperor system" and then were in practice "more or less dependent on government." Because political parties and labor unions had failed to deal with pollution and other post-war local issues, "the citizens felt that they had no organization that could support them and so they started a voluntary organization to tackle the problem" (Ishida, 1983:16–17). In contrast to the earlier *chonaikai* that served government, the post-war version in urban fringe areas have opposed local governments by voicing demands of citizens who believe their rights have been violated in a given problematic situation (Aoyagi, 1983:105).

Groups especially interested in criminal justice issues, however, have little incentive to amass resources for organized political activities. "Although organized economic interests, including big business and the agricultural lobby, enjoy an astonishing level of access to policy-making in Japan, when it comes to non-economic interests the story is quite different," (Pharr, 1990:xi–xii). The management of criminals ranks among non-economic issues, especially in a nation with a crime rate as low as Japan's.

VPOs and Community Participation

The Tokugawa system of controlling villagers lingers in the attitudes of many contemporary Japanese. Plath (1964:141–142) notes "there is no doubt that the Japanese have tended to be more accepting than Americans of government surveillance and control of organizations." The difference is not universal, however. Plath also notes that some Japanese find active membership in community groups to be exciting, and some Americans "volunteered" for participation in PTAs and charities. However, Plath continues: "Americans tend to underline the voluntary aspects of association membership. Japanese are more aware of its compulsory facets of the moral pressure of the *waku*." The social control system (the *waku*) presses them to give priority to group interests over narrow self-interests and to seek participation in community groups as a duty.

In an interview, a Yokohama VPO told this writer that such a sense of duty had motivated his accepting the service:

My father owns a Japanese restaurant, a Western restaurant, a Chinese restaurant, and an Italian restaurant. I manage the family business. Twenty-two years ago the prefectural government sent me

to see youth programs in the Soviet Union, England, Germany, Switzerland, and Italy. The government decided to build a youth hostel. The officials said to me: "You spent the government's money to go abroad; now you should do volunteer probation work." My family expected me to do something without pay. I had no reason to say "no." So I said: "Okay! I will do that."

VPOs are drawn heavily from members of the middle classes who are likely to be active in other volunteer organizations and often leaders in the *chonaikai* (Anagata, 1990:4). "It was markedly apparent that Japanese small entrepreneurs over fifty years old in Arakawa ward (a section of Tokyo) as elsewhere who had some leisure time were apt to devote it to some form of voluntary community activities, such service is a recognized and compelling way to gain prestige within Japanese society" (Wagatsuma and DeVos, 1984:29).

Other long-term VPOs observed by this writer in Sendai also expressed the duty theme, but added more personal explanations for accepting the responsibilities: need to be active during retirement, the satisfactions derived from working with other persons, and the persuasion of a friend who was a VPO. The older Japanese are particularly public-service oriented. Frager and Rohlen (1976:266–268) believe that such "spiritual improvement will bring general social betterment." They continue: "The impression given to the cynical outsider is at best one of saccharine naivete, yet many of the country's great men participate in and frequently lead such efforts with a degree of personal devotion and energy that is amazing."

The competence and dedication of the older and experienced VPOs impressed this writer when he witnessed their discussions during a training session. Nevertheless, the VPO program has its problems. The volunteers in community corrections tend to be middle class and older, whereas their clients are drawn predominately from less affluent younger adults. The long-term trend has been away from occupational groups particularly apt to share life-perspectives and hold the ready cooperation of their clients. From 1958 to 1990, the VPO occupations have shifted toward the unemployed, including retired persons and housewives, from 13 percent to 25.7 percent. Other major occupational categories have slipped in representation: fishing and farming, religious figures, government and company employees, and sales personnel. Women VPOs have consistently increased their presence from 7 percent in 1953 to 21.1 percent in 1990. The average age of VPOs was 53.2 years in 1953 and rose consistently to 61.7 years at the end of 1990. Meanwhile, the median length of service increased from 6.93 years in 1953 to 11.61 years in 1990 (Anagata, 1990:18–19).

Assessing the Volunteer System

"Without about 48,000 volunteer probation officers who are actively engaged in the offenders rehabilitation service across the country," declares former Director-General Kunpei Satoh (1989:17) of the Rehabilitation Bureau, "we have only 1,000 probation officers in 50 probation offices, to take care of about 100,000 persons placed under probation or parole."

As community leaders, volunteers are expected to be more familiar with the local scene than full-time professional probation officers (PPOs) who are more likely to be transferred to other communities. When PPOs are also volunteers in other social service programs, they have the knowledge of and accessibility to refer probationers and parolees, when the services are needed. Although representatives of government, the *hogoshi* (PPOs) are more likely to obtain client rapport and less likely to attract the neighbors' attention as private citizens. Not bound strictly by regulations and working hours, they are more flexible in service delivery

than rule-bound PPOs. Responsibilities of PPOs end with termination of supervision, while personal ties of VPOs and clients can continue (Anagata, 1990:5; Hashimoto, 1983:185–186; Wagatsuma and DeVos, 1984:37). A leading official told this writer: "Volunteer involvement in the probation service has been well accepted in our country and instrumental over the past years, in particular, in terms of its aid-oriented service."

Article 20, The Offenders Rehabilitation Law, which specifies the relationship between the VPO and the PPO, states: "The volunteer probation officer provided for in the Volunteer Probation Office Law shall assist the professional probation officer and make up for inadequacies of the latter's work, and engage in the work coming within the scope of the specific function of RPB (Regional Parole Board) or the Probation Office . . . " Instead of assisting the PPO, however, the VPO performs the treatment function. Anagata (1990:9) contends: "We are short of professional probation officers, and there is little prospect of a rapid increase of professional probation officers because of the presence of the VPO system." Since 1974 the probation offices in Tokyo and Osaka have found difficult cases require a level of supervision beyond the grasp of VPOs. In direct supervision units, several PPOs assume supervisory responsibilities for selected cases. Five PPOs in Tokyo supervise an average of 20 cases, compared with 150 or so cases managed by a PPO who works through VPOs. The offenders in direct supervision have general characteristics such as mental disorders not requiring hospitalization, gross environmental handicaps such as grave parent-child conflicts or mental disorders of parents, or foreigners unable to adjust to Japanese society.

As lay persons, VPOs tend to treat clients from particular personal experiences rather than on basis of principles. The PPO may not be properly informed on the client's actual situation. "When two probationers show the same progress,"

Hashimoto (1983:86) notes, "one may be discharged from probation based on the favorable reports of a lenient VPO, where the other may remain under the further supervision of a strict VPO." Competent VPOs are especially difficult to recruit for high delinquency areas. The progressive effects of urban conditions on community solidarity make for difficult cases. Some volunteers are hopelessly out of touch with the clients' changing needs. VPOs may neglect supervisory duties because of their own business and family obligations (Wagatsuma and DeVos, 1983:37).

Recognizing that extended use of community corrections requires more emphasis on professionalism, the Rehabilitation Bureau plans to strengthen training of junior PPOs. It is hoped that promoting professionalism in rising PPOs will advance the quality of community corrections while preserving the advantages of the VPO services.

Shortage of funds, the Rehabilitation Bureau notes (Ministry of Justice, 1990a:19–20), compromises the administration of rehabilitation aid hostels. Those running profit-making businesses have an advantage but are exceptional. In fiscal year 1989, the halfway houses took in an average income of 26,790,069 yen from the following sources: reimbursement and subsidy from probation offices and family courts (49.6 percent); workshop income (20.6 percent); donations (9.6 percent); property dividends (5.8 percent); residents' board and room payments when they stay past subsidy (6.9 percent); local government subsidy (1.3 percent); membership fees (1.5 percent); and miscellaneous sources (4.7 percent).

The financial difficulties stem from the insufficiency of government subsidy payments which, in turn, may be traced to a combination of too few residents and short average stays. The number of hostels dropped from 150 to 98 in 1988, and the total authorized capacity from 3,921 to 2,400. In spite of these declines, the use of available bedspace dropped from 74 per-

cent in 1958 to 58 percent in 1988 (Udo, 1990:9). In 1992 the residents stayed in hostels for a median of 28 days (Ministry of Justice, 1993:167).

Conclusion

"The rehabilitation system is based on the concept of trusting people who unfortunately have committed crimes," the Rehabilitation Bureau announced in a public statement. By not trusting criminals, the Bureau implies, the prison isolates them from the curative powers of normal community relationships.

The idea of trust has particular implications for urbanites who inhabit a social world that is more complex and variable than social worlds of more direct and stable character. As Luhmann (1979:5–6, 20, 68–69) comments, the urban scene tends to lose its taken-for-granted familiarity, because daily experience can only envisage it in a fragmentary way. In personal trust, confidence is placed in other persons with whom one is in relatively intimate social interaction. System trust entails placing confidence in a long chain of events, without full knowledge or direct experience of the interactions that are supposed to deliver benefits. Trust in either persons or systems will figure in any motive for offering or refusing benefits. However, Luhmann notes, trust operates within the constraints of social relationships that normatively channel its expression.

From arrest to conviction by trial, decision makers extend forgiveness to many of the defendants who are believed to be worthy of trust. This is one reason why Japan has one of the lowest imprisonment rates among developed societies. Even after a prison sentence has been pronounced, the court may return the offender to the free community with or without probation. The judges' trust in granting suspensions is underscored by their reluctance to require even probationary supervision.

Japanese society has surpassed Western societies in retaining both personal and system trust in spite of massive socioeconomic changes in the last century. Rural relationships generated trust among villagers, partly in defense against Tokugawa authoritarianism. Villagers were held accountable for the crimes of their family members and non-relatives. These traditions linger in community associations of more recent decades, but community ties have also been constructed in opposition to government, when residents believe their interests are not being respected. Management of convicted offenders is not among major public issues in Japan—no surprise, given its low crime rate.

By enlisting the services of VPOs and rehabilitation aid associations, the government has shown its tendency to avoid major investment in social services when feasible, and its faith in the willingness and capacity of private citizens to deliver needed services to the community. Although there are fragmentary linkages with events in earlier Japan, modern community corrections were initiated for the most part immediately after World War II, when there were heavy demands on the public purse.

This writer—a "cynical outsider," as Frager and Rohlen (1976:266–268) would put it—is indeed tempted to describe the enthusiasm of many VPOs and hostel workers as "saccharine naivete" falling far short of the performance of professional probation and parole officers. It may well be that future developments in the social psychology of the Japanese will justify "cynicism." At this moment in the history of Japanese community corrections, however, Japanese private supervision and aftercare programs deserve a more favorable assessment than their American counterparts. The Japanese government's trust in private persons' ability to deliver programs of community correction is proper reciprocity for the Japanese people's personal and system trust which suppresses any upsurge in their country's imprisonment rate.

Notes

1. Research for this paper was conducted in Japan under a Fulbright grant and the sponsorship of the Rehabilitation Bureau and Correction Bureau of the Japanese Ministry of Justice. Study of the operations of the Rehabilitation Bureau would have been impossible without the firm support of successive Directors-General: Keiji Kurita, Kunpei Satoh, Tsuneo Furuhata, and Hiroyasu Sugihara. A number of staff members provided extraordinary assistance and insights, especially Masaru Matumoto, Director of the Supervision Department of the Bureau.

2. For example, Blomberg (1987:219) says: "The tendency of diversion and other community programs to widen the control net produces results that are increasing rather than reducing the number of individuals coming into contact with the formal criminal justice system."

3. Data for 1989 were supplied by the Research and Training Institute, Ministry of Justice.

4. In 1959 the Social Education Act was amended to allow the government to subsidize "social education groups" (Ishida, 1983:16).

5. Spitzer (1983:317–318) argues that the *gonin-gumi* strategy is an example of the weaknesses of central government: "The fact that local elites had to be kept in place and manipulated under Tokugawa law, rather than totally destroyed, is one indication of the political and ideological weaknesses characteristic of certain types of precapitalist states."

Discussion and Revision Questions

1. What are the duties of volunteer probation officers?

2. Why do the Japanese extol community corrections as a superior alternative to imprisonment?

3. Compare and contrast imprisonment rates in Japan and the United States. Discuss.

4. Compare and contrast the role of patronage societies in corrections in Japan and Brazil.

5. To what extent did the European correctional system (Belgian and French penal laws) play a part in the Japanese penal code?

6. Why did nineteenth-century France question the usefulness of imprisonment?

7. Describe in detail community corrections in Japan under volunteer probation officers.

8. Why did the Tokugawa Shogunate forbid Japanese from having contact with Europeans from the seventeenth through the nineteenth centuries (1603–1867)?

9. What is the "principle of extraterritoriality"?

10. On what principle is the Japanese rehabilitation system based?

11. As in Nigeria, Ghana, Sierra Leone, and China, Japanese villagers are held accountable for the crimes of their village members. Is it possible to hold a community responsible for the crime or crimes of its members in the United States?

12. Why is the management of convicts not a major public issue in Japan?

Glossary

Actus reus: A wrongful deed which renders the actor criminally liable if combined with *mens rea*, a guilty intention.

Addendum: A thing added or to be added.

Advocate: A person who pleads or speaks in favor of another person in a matter or case.

Alkhali Court: This is the lowest Muslim Court in Northern Nigeria, where cases involving Muslims are tried. The judge is versed in Islamic Law.

Allotment: Share, portion, something set apart for a purpose.

APC: All People's Congress. This was a political party that ruled Sierra Leone from 1968 through April 29, 1992 when it was overthrown in a coup d'etat by the present (1995) military regime.

Appellant: The person who challenges the correctness of a court order or judgment by seeking a review and relief in a higher court having appellate jurisdiction, or the person in whose behalf this is done.

Appellate Court: A court which has the primary function of reviewing the judgments of lower courts in a country or state. It may not act as a trial court or court of first instance.

Arcane: Secret; hidden; intended only for the initiated.

Assessor: An expert in customary law who helped colonial court judges in interpreting the law of the land. In China, a lay member of the court as a juror, but (unlike a juror in the United States) having equal power with the court judge in adjudication of a case. An advisory assistant.

Bona fide: In good faith; legally valid; genuine; sincere.

Buraku-Kai: Rural traditional communities in Japan.

Certiorari: A writ issued from an appellate court for the purpose of obtaining from a lower court the record of its proceedings in a particular case.

Chonai-Kai: In Japanese, district or block associations of 400 to 600 households.

Criminal Code: Written substantive criminal law specifying acts that are crimes and punishments for violations.

Cultural Genocide: A program of action deliberately designed to destroy the values, standards, beliefs, and norms of a whole country, race, or ethnic group by replacing the indigenous cultural values with alien values, through alien based education. The result is total disorganization of the indigenous society.

Customary Court: A court where rules and regulations (laws) emanating from the immemorial customs and traditions of the people are enforced by a chief, or an elder, or a council of elders. Such courts are found throughout sub-Saharan Africa.

Daimyo (Daimio): During the Japanese feudal era, a hereditary Japanese nobleman.

Danwei: A Chinese work unit which assigns income and housing to its members.

Day Leave: A type of leave granted to a Danish prisoner for the purpose of employment or job training outside of the prison. It can be granted if such employment or job training is not available in the prison institution.

De Novo: Anew; from the beginning.

Denunciation: An act of public condemnation or accusation.

Disparate Treatment Case: A case involving a charge against an employer for basing a decision not to hire or promote a person on unjustifiable or discriminatory grounds.

Double Jeopardy: The danger of being tried, and perhaps convicted and punished, twice for the same offense.

DPP: Director of Public Prosecution. This is an individual who heads the prosecution department of the Ministry of Justice in such countries as England, Nigeria, Kenya, Ghana, and Sierra Leone. He or she decides whether an accused in a felonious offense should be indicted or not. The DPP is a civil service position, but is not elected like a prosecutor in the U.S.

Due Process of Law: The due course of legal proceedings according to the rules and forms which have been established for the protection of private rights. These are rights guaranteed by the Fifth, Sixth, and Fourteenth Amendments of the U. S. Constitution.

Duress: Unlawful threats of harm or other pressure used to force someone to act against his or her will. Duress may also mean illegal imprisonment, or legal imprisonment for an illegal purpose.

Enza: (Japanese) relatives; opposite of renza.

Exclusionary Rule: In law of evidence, this is the principle applicable in both State and Federal Courts in the United States, that evidence illegally obtained may not properly be received at the trial.

Ex Parte: One sided; on, or in the interest of, one side only.

Felony Murder Rule or Felony Murder Doctrine: At common law, one who, without intent, killed another in an intent to commit another felony was guilty of murder. While some states in the United States still follow the common law rule, today the law of Felony Murder varies substantially throughout the country.

Fief: An inheritable piece of land in the feudal period held from an overlord in return for service. The right to possess such land.

Fudai: (Japanese) Allies of the Tokugawa regime (Shogunate).

Gaikaku: (Japanese) a public corporation.

Gaikaku Dantai: (Japanese) public corporations or extra-departmental groups.

Gemeinschaft: A German concept invented by Ferdinand Tonnis (1855–1936) referring to a small community characterized by personalized, face-to-face relationships such as those found in the family, rural villages, and very small towns where everyone knows everyone else. Interpersonal relationships are informal.

Gesellschaft: Ferdinand Tonnis' concept for societies, usually urban, where interpersonal relationships are formal and contractual.

Gonin-gumi: (Japanese) Household groups, usually five households together.

Grand Khadi: The judge of an Alkhali court in Northern Nigeria (see Alkhali above).

Habeas Corpus: (Latin: You have the body.) The name given to a variety of writs having for their object to bring a party before a court or judge. The primary function of the writ is to release a person from unlawful imprisonment, or to determine whether a person in the custody of legal authorities is being lawfully detained.

Hogoshi: (Japanese) representatives of the government.

Importunate: Urgent or persistent in demanding or asking for something.

Interlocutory: Provisional; temporary; not final.

Interlocutory Appeal: An appeal which does not resolve the controversy, but which is essential for a later adjudication of the case on its merits.

Interlocutory Decree: A preliminary or provisional order. It is a decree made during a lawsuit to ascertain a matter of law or fact in preparation for a final decree.

Interlocutory Judgment: A judgment of the court which does not determine all the issues relating to all the parties, but instead leaves something further to be adjudicated at a later proceeding.

Mutatis Mutandis: The necessary changes having been made. With the necessary changes in detail to be made in compliance with one major change.

Naira: The name given to Nigeria's money in 1973, a change from the country's original "pound" medium of exchange. In 1985, one Naira (N1.00) was equal to $1.80. In March 1995, the official rate was $1.00 = N80.00.

Opprobrium: Shame; or anything that brings shame or disgrace.

Ordinary Imprisonment: An imprisonment from one month to life in Denmark.

Organic Solidarity: Emile Durkheim's term for an urban society where interpersonal relationships are contractual and formalized. Cities exemplify Durkheim's organic solidarity type of collectivity.

Lenient Imprisonment: In Denmark, imprisonment for not more than 18 days.

Maliki Law: The source of Islamic Law in Africa.

Mandamus: (Latin: We command.) A writ or order issued by courts to a public official or corporation, commanding the performance of some public duty required by statute.

Mechanical Solidarity: Emile Durkheim's concept describing a community with personalized, face-to-face interaction such as is found in more traditional societies. There is mutual obligation among the members of the community, and peace and harmony prevail.

Jinrikisha: A small, two-wheeled carriage with a hood, pulled by one or two men in Japan or in other Far Eastern societies.

Jurisdiction: Authority by which courts and judicial officers hear and determine cases. The geographical delimitation of a given court's power to hear and determine cases.

Justice of the Peace: A judicial officer of lesser rank who has jurisdiction over minor criminal and civil cases. A person who judges less serious cases in a local court of law; a magistrate.

Kabun: (Japanese) persons of subordinate rank; opposite of oyabun.

Lay Advocate: One versed in the customary law of his land who pleads or speaks on behalf of another in Chinese Courts or African Customary Courts.

Ostracize: To exclude somebody from a community, group, or society as a form of punishment for crime or a breach of norms. The group refuses to meet or talk to the individual.

Oyabun: (Japanese) persons of superior rank; opposite of kabun.

Parrot's Perch: A type of punishment in which an offender is tied up and suspended on a cross-bar by the knees, and then abused; commonly practiced in Brazilian prisons.

Penal Code: A body of law dealing with the punishments for various crimes or offenses.

PPO: Professional Probation Officers; to be contrasted with volunteer probation officers (VPO) in Japanese corrections.

Prefecture: The office, authority, territory, or residence of a prefect or administrative official.

Preposterous: Ridiculous; so contrary to nature, reason, or common sense as to be laughable; absurd.

Presumption of Innocence: An important principle of criminal law in the United States holding that the state (government) has the burden of proving every element of a crime beyond a reasonable doubt, and that the accused has no burden to prove his or her innocence.

Prima Facie: (Latin: On its face.) Describing a fact convincing on first examination, without any further proof of validity.

Prima Facie Case: A case in which the plaintiff has presented sufficient evidence to entitle him to a decision by the judge or jury; a case which compels a favorable decision when no contrary or rebutting evidence is presented.

Procurator: In China, a person who manages the prosecution division (Procuratorate) of the Chinese Criminal Justice System. He or she resembles the DPP in England or Nigeria (though he or she has more power), represents the government in all criminal matters, and is not an elected official. (In general terms, a procurator is one employed to manage the affairs of another, an agent.)

Procuratorate: The office and powers of a procurator.

Prohibition: An act or law making something or behavior illegal; especially, the prohibition of the manufacture, sale, or transportation of intoxicating liquors except for medicinal purposes by the 18th Amendment to the United States Constitution (1920). (This prohibition amendment was later repealed by the 21st Amendment in 1933.)

Raison d'etre: Reason for being; justification for existence.

Renza: (Japanese) unrelated persons; opposite of enza.

Samurai: The aristocrats of the pre-Tokugawa era who became the bureaucrats of the Tokugawa regime in Japan.

Self-Incrimination: Any action or admission made by a person, either before trial or at trial, that implicates him/her in the commission of a crime.

Sharia Court: In Northern Nigeria and Middle Eastern nations, a court where only Islamic laws are applied.

Sharia Law: Synonymous with Maliki Law or Islamic Law.

Shogun: Any of the feudal military governors of Japan who made up a quasi dynasty, exercised absolute power, and relegated the emperors to a titular head of state.

Shogunate: The powers, territories, and reign of a Shogun.

Taisei-nai: (Japanese) outside the system.

Taisei-gai: (Japanese) within the system.

Tozama: Those samurai who submitted to the Tokugawa regime in Japan only after the Tokugawa gained control over Japanese affairs.

Ultra Vires: Beyond granted powers. Conduct that exceeds the powers given to an office holder such as a prime minister, president, or CEO of a corporation.

VPO: Volunteer Probation Officer (used in Japanese corrections).

Waku: (Japanese) the social control system in which group interest is superior to self-interest.

Bibliography

Achebe, Chinua. 1959. *Things fall apart.* New York: McDowell Obolensky.

Adewoye, Omoniyi. 1977. *The judicial system in southern Nigeria, 1854–1954: Law and justice in a dependency.* Atlantic Highlands, NJ: Humanities Press.

Adler, F. 1983. *Nations not obsessed with crime.* Littleton, CO: Fred B. Rothman.

Aguda, Akinola T. 1974. *The law of evidence in Nigeria.* London: Sweet and Maxwell.

_____. 1980. *The law and practice relating to evidence in Nigeria.* London: Sweet and Maxwell.

Ai, Xue. 1989. New "People's Mediation Committee's Organic Rules" promulgated in China. *Outlook Weekly* 42:10.

Alemika, E., and O. Kayode. 1981. Some attributes of recidivism: A study of the inmates of a Nigerian prison. *International Journal of Comparative and Applied Criminal Justice* 5 (2):187–195.

Alemika, Etannibi E. O. 1983. The smoke screen: Rhetoric and reality of penal incarceration in Nigeria. *International Journal of Comparative and Applied Criminal Justice* 1:137–149.

Allen, G. Frederick. 1987a. Reforming criminals in China: Implications for corrections in the West. *International Journal of Comparative and Applied Criminal Justice* 11 (1):77–86.

_____. 1987b. Where are we going in criminal justice? Some insights from the Chinese criminal justice system. *International Journal of Offender Therapy and Comparative Criminology* 31:101–109.

Allison, Gary D. 1975. *Japanese urbanism: Industry and politics in Kariya, 1872–1972.* Berkeley: University of California Press.

Allott, A. N. 1963. *The future of law in Nigeria.* London: Sweet and Maxwell.

Americas Watch. 1989. *Prison conditions in Brazil.* New York: Human Rights Watch.

Amin, S. 1974. *Modern migrations in West Africa.* London: Oxford University Press.

Anagata, Shizuo. 1990. "Some aspects of volunteer probation officer (hogoshi) system in Japan." Paper delivered at the United Nations Asia and Far East Institute for the Prevention of Crime and the Treatment of Offenders (UNAFEI), Tokyo.

Ancel, Marc. 1971. *Suspended sentence.* London: Heinemann Educational Books.

Annual statistical digest. 1970. Sierra Leone Government, Freetown: Central Statistics Office.

_____. 1971. Sierra Leone Government, Freetown: Central Statistics Office.

_____. 1984. Sierra Leone Government, Freetown: Central Statistics Office.

_____. 1989. Sierra Leone Government, Freetown: Central Statistics Office.

_____. 1990. Sierra Leone Government, Freetown: Central Statistics Office.

Anthony, R. 1992. An investigation of the requirement for the Metropolitan Police Service to include the words "sexual orientation" in its statement of equal opportunities policy. Master's dissertation: University of Exeter, England.

Aoyagi, Kiyotaka. 1983. Viable traditions in urban Japan: Matsuri and chonaikai. In *Town-talk: The dynamics of urban anthropology,* edited by Haus Ansari and Peter J. M. Haus, 96–107. Leiden, Denmark: E. J. Brill.

Archer, D., and R. Gartner. 1984. *Violence and crime in cross-national perspective.* New Haven, CT: Yale University Press.

Arikpo, Okoi. 1967. *The development of modern Nigeria.* Baltimore: Penguin Books, Inc.

Arthur, J. 1991. Development and crime in Africa: A test of modernization theory. *Journal of Criminal Justice* 19:499–513.

Association of Chief Police Officers (ACPO). 1990. *Statement of common purpose and values.* London: Scotland Yard.

Austern, David. 1987. *The crime victim's handbook.* Harrisonburg, VA: R. R. Donnelley and Sons Company.

Awe, B. 1968. "History of the prison system in Nigeria." In *The Prison System in Nigeria,* edited by T. O. Elias, 28–36. Lagos, Nigeria: Faculty of Law, University of Lagos.

Balkin, J. 1988. Why policemen do not like police women. *Journal of Police Science and Administration* 16:29–38.

Bandura, A. 1977. *Social learning theory.* Englewood, NJ.: Prentice-Hall.

Barnes, Harry Elmer. 1942. *Social institutions in an era of world upheaval.* New York: Prentice-Hall.

Bayley, D. 1992. A Fresh Perspectives Paper: *The best defence.* Washington, D.C.: Police Executive Research Forum.

Beasley, William G. 1972. *The Meiji Restoration.* Stanford, CA: Stanford University Press.

_____. 1990. *The rise of modern Japan.* Tokyo: Charles E. Tuttle.

Bentham, Jeremy. 1843. "A view of the Hard-Labor Bill." In *Works of Jeremy Bentham,* Vol. 4, edited in 1962 by John Bowring. New York: Russell Sage Foundation.

Benyon, J. 1987. Interpretations of civil disorder. In *The roots of urban unrest,* edited by Benyon and Solomos. London: Pergamon Press.

Bestor, Theodore C. 1985. Tradition and Japanese social organization: Institutional development in a Tokyo neighborhood. *Ethnology* 24:121–135.

Bevins, A. 1992. Labour MP says police are sexist. *Independent,* 18 July.

Birch, R. 1990. *Operational policing review.* Surbiton: Sierra Leone Joint Consultative Committee.

Black, Henry Campbell. 1979. *Black's law dictionary,* 5th Edition. St. Paul: West Publishing Company.

Blomberg, Thomas G. 1987. "Criminal justice reform and social control: Are we becoming a minimum security society?" In *Transcarceration: Essays in the sociology of social control,* edited by John Lowman, Robert J. Menzies, and T. S. Polys, 218–226. Alderholt, England: Gower.

Bossard, A. 1990. *Transnational crime and criminal law.* Chicago: The Office of International Criminal Justice (OICJ).

Bracey, Dorothy H. 1989a. "Corrections in the People's Republic of China." In *Social control in the People's Republic of China,* edited by Ronald Troyer, John Clark, and Dean Rojek, 159–168. New York: Praeger Publishers.

Bracey, Dorothy H. 1989b. "Policing the People's Republic." In *Social Control in the People's Republic of China,* edited by Ronald Troyer, John Clark, and Dean Rojek, 130–140. New York: Praeger Publishers.

Brady, James P. 1982. *Justice and politics in People's China: Legal order or continuing revolution?* New York: Academic Press.

Braibanti, Ralph J. D. 1948. Neighborhood associations in Japan and their democratic potentialities. *Far Eastern Quarterly.* 7 (2):136–164.

Brecher, E.M., and the editors of *Consumer Reports.* 1972. *Licit and illicit drugs.* Boston: Little, Brown.

Brett, Sir Lionel, and Ian McLean. 1963. *The criminal law and procedure of Lagos, eastern Nigeria and western Nigeria.* London: Sweet and Maxwell.

Brewer, John D., Adrian Guelke, Ian Hume, Edward Moxon-Browne, and Rick Wilford. 1988. *The police, public order and the state policing in Great Britain, Northern Ireland, the Irish Republic, the USA, Israel, South Africa, and China.* New York: St. Martin's Press.

_____. 1973. "Evolution of crime in the Ivory Coast." In *Urban and rural crime and its control in West Africa,* edited by Young Brillion, 112–124. Montreal: University of Montreal Center for International Criminology.

Brillion, Y. 1974. "Crime prevention and sentencing in the Ivory Coast." Paper presented at the 4th West African conference on comparative criminology, April 25–27, Abidjan, Ivory Coast.

Brook, L. 1992. Exit Collor, enter confidence. *Newsweek,* October 12:48.

Brooke, J. 1992a. Brazil's police enforce a law: Death. *New York Times,* November 4:A22.

_____. 1992b. Looting Brazil. *New York Times,* November 8:31–33, 42, 45, 70.

Brown, L., and M. Wycoff. 1986. Policing Houston: Reducing fear and improving service. *Crime and Delinquency,* January.

Brown, M. 1988. *Working the street: Police discretion and dilemmas of reform.* New York: Russell Sage Foundation.

Brownson, Anna. 1994. *Judicial staff directory, 1995.* Mt. Vernon, VA: Staff Directories Ltd.

Bureau of Justice Statistics (BJS). 1991. *Sourcebook of criminal justice statistics.* Washington, D.C.: U.S. Department of Justice.

BJS. 1992a. *Criminal victimization in the United States, 1991.* Washington, D.C.: U.S. Department of Justice.

BJS. 1992b. *Census of State and Federal correctional facilities, 1990.* Washington, D.C.: U.S. Department of Justice.

BJS. 1993. *Census of State and local law enforcement agencies, 1992.* Washington, D.C.: Department of Justice.

BJS. 1994a. *Prisoners in 1993.* Washington, D.C.: U.S. Department of Justice.

BJS. 1994b. *Comparing Federal and State prison inmates, 1991.* Washington, D.C.: U.S. Department of Justice.

BJS. 1994c. *Pretrial release of felony defendants, 1992.* Washington, D.C.: Department of Justice.

BJS. 1994d. *Capital punishment, 1993.* Washington, D.C.: U.S. Department of Justice.

BJS. 1994e. *Criminal victimization in the United States, 1992.* Washington, D.C.: Department of Justice.

Burns, Alan. 1929. *History of Nigeria.* London: George Allen & Unwin Limited.

Butler, R. F. and M. Garsia, eds. 1966. *Archbold pleading, evidence and practice in criminal cases,* 36th ed. London: Sweet and Maxwell.

Caldwell, J. C. 1969. *African rural-urban migration.* Canberra: Australia National University.

Campbell, John Creighton. 1977. *Contemporary Japanese budget politics.* Berkeley: University of California Press.

_____. 1985. Governmental responses to budget scarcity: Japan. *Policy Studies Journal* 13:506–516.

Carter, D., A. Sapp, and D. Stephens. 1989. *The state of police education.* Washington, D.C.: Police Executive Research Forum.

Centre for Police Studies (CPS). 1989. *The effect of the Sex Discrimination Act on the Scottish police service.* University of Strathclyde, UK: Centre for Police Studies.

Ch'en, Paul Heng-Chao. 1981. *The formation of the early Meiji legal order.* Oxford: University Press.

Chang, D. H., ed. 1976. *Criminology: A cross-cultural perspective,* vol. 1. Durham, NC: Carolina Academic Press.

Chang, David W. 1984. Government and crime control in China: Its relevance to U.S. Criminal Justice. *International Journal of Comparative and Applied Criminal Justice* 2:94–111.

Chapin, Bradley. 1983. *Criminal justice in colonial America, 1606–1660.* Athens, GA: University of Georgia Press.

Chen, Dahao. 1993. Inmates' human rights in China. *Outlook Weekly* 9:8.

Chen, Phillip M. 1973. *Law and justice: The legal system in China—2400 B.C. to 1960 A.D.* New York: Dunellen Publishing Company.

Chevigny, P. 1990. Police use deadly force as social control: Jamaica, Argentina and Brazil. *Criminal Law Forum* 1:3.

Children and Young Persons Act. 1945. Cap. 44 of the Law of Sierra Leone. Freetown: Government Printer.

Clark, John P. 1989. "Conflict management outside the courtrooms of China." In *Social control in the People's Republic of China,* edited by Ronald Troyer, John Clark, and Dean Rojek. New York: Praeger Publishers.

Clifford, W. 1963. The evaluation of methods for the prevention and treatment of juvenile delinquents in Africa south of the Sahara. *International Review of Criminal Policy (UN)* 21:11–17.

_____. 1964. The African view of crime. *British Journal of Criminology* 4:477–486.

_____. 1973. *Development and crime.* Chichester, England: Rose.

_____. 1974. *Introduction to African criminology.* Nairobi: Oxford University Press.

Clifford, William. 1977. White collar and corporate crime: The modern challenges to Commonwealth criminal justice Systems. *Commonwealth Law Bulletin* 3(4):679–689.

Clinard, Marshall B., and Daniel J. Abbott. 1973. *Crime in developing countries: A comparative perspective.* New York: John Wiley and Sons.

Coffee, S., J. Brown, and S. Savage. 1992. Policewomen's career aspirations: Some reflections on the role and capabilities of women in policing in Britain. *Police Studies* 15:13–19.

Cohen, Jerome A. 1968. *The Criminal Process in the People's Republic of China: 1949–1963.* Cambridge: Harvard University Press.

Cole, George F. 1986. *The American system of criminal justice.* Monterey, CA: Brooks/Cole Publishing.

_____, ed. 1989. *Major criminal justice systems: A comparative survey.* Beverly Hills, CA: Sage Publications.

_____. 1981. "The United States of America." In *Major criminal justice systems,* edited by George F. Cole, Stanislaw, J. Fankowski, and Marc G. Gertz, 3–27. Beverly Hills, CA: Sage.

Collick, Martin. 1988. "Social policy: Pressures and responses." In *Dynamics and immobilist politics in Japan,* edited by J. A. A. Stockwin, 205–236. Honolulu: University of Hawaii Press.

Constitution of the Federal Republic of Nigeria. 1963. Sec. III, 2 and Sec. I, 1. Lagos: Government Printing Press.

The Constitution of the People's Republic of China. 1986. Beijing: Foreign Languages Press.

Constitution of Sierra Leone. 1961. Order-in-Council, Public Notice No. 78.

Government of Sierra Leone. Freetown: Government Printer.

_____. 1971. Act No. 6. Government of Sierra Leone. Freetown: Government Printer.

_____. 1978. Act No. 12. Government of Sierra Leone. Freetown: Government Printer.

_____. 1991. Act No. 6. Government of Sierra Leone. Freetown: Government Printer.

Council on Europe. 1989. *Prison information bulletin* 13 and 14:16.

Court of resolution law, Cap. 28. Law of Northern Nigeria, 1963. Revision Section 3, 1. Lagos: Government Printing Press.

Courts Act, No. 31. 1965. Government of Sierra Leone. Freetown: Government Printer.

Coyle, Andrew. 1977. Prisons in Africa. *West Africa*, November 1–7.

Craig, Albert M. 1961. *Chosu in the Meiji Restoration.* Cambridge: Harvard University Press.

Criminal law and the criminal procedure law of China. 1984. Beijing: Foreign Language Press.

Criminal Procedure Act, No. 32. 1965. Government of Sierra Leone. Freetown: Government Printer.

Criminal procedures ordinance. 1960. Lagos, Nigeria: Government Printing Press.

Crosby, P. 1990. *Leading.* London: McGraw-Hill.

Cross, Sir Geoffrey, and G. D. G. Hall. 1964. *The English legal system.* London: Butterworths.

Cullop, Floyd G. 1984. *The Constitution of the United States: An introduction.* New York: Penguin Books.

Customary courts edict, no. 2. 1966. Lagos, Nigeria: Government Printing Press.

Daiichi, Ito. 1988. "Policy implications of administrative reform." In *Dynamics and immobilist politics in Japan*, edited by J. A. A. Stockwin et al., 77–105. Honolulu: University of Hawaii Press.

David, Rene, and John E. C. Brierly. 1989. *Major legal systems in the world today.* New York: The Free Press.

Day, F. D. 1964. *Criminal law and society.* Springfield, IL: C.C. Thomas.

Dike, Kenneth O. 1959. *Trade and politics in the Niger Delta, 1830–1891.* Oxford: Oxford University Press.

Dore, Ronald P. 1958. *City life in Japan: A study of a Tokyo ward.* Berkeley: University of California Press.

Dore, Ronald. 1987. *Taking Japan seriously: A Confucian perspective on leading economic issues.* London: Athlone Press.

Drug Enforcement Administration (DEA). 1985. *Drugs of abuse.* Washington, D.C.: U.S. Department of Justice.

Du, Xichuan, and Zhang, Linyuan. 1990. *China legal system: A general survey.* Beijing: New World Press.

Duke, Benjamin. 1986. *The Japanese school: Lessons for industrial America.* New York: Praeger.

Durkheim, Emile. 1964. *The division of labor in society.* New York: Free Press.

Duus, Peter. 1967. *Feudalism in Japan.* New York: Alfred A. Knopf.

Ebbe, Obi N. I. 1977. The seriousness of selected criminal offenses: A cross-cultural inquiry. Master's thesis, Western Michigan University, Kalamazoo.

_____. 1982. *Crime in Nigeria: An analysis of characteristics of offenders incarcerated in Nigerian prisons.* Ann Arbor: University Microfilms International.

_____. 1985a. The correlates of female criminality in Nigeria. *International Journal of Comparative and Applied Criminal Justice* 7:171–192.

_____. 1985b. Power and criminal law: Criminalizing conduct norms in a colonial regime. *International Journal of Comparative and Applied Criminal Justice* 9 (2):113–122.

_____. 1988. Juvenile justice system in southern Nigeria. *International Journal of Comparative and Applied Criminal Justice* 12 (2):191–204.

_____. 1989. Crime and delinquency in metropolitan Lagos: A study of crime and delinquency area theory. *Social Forces* 67:751–765.

Edgeworth, Linda, et al. 1991. *Sierra Leone: A pre-election assessment report.* Washington, D.C.: International Foundation for Electoral Systems.

Edwards, Terry. 1995. University of Louisville, Justice Administration. Phone conversation with author, April 7.

Elias, Oluwale Taslim. 1954. *The groundwork of Nigerian law.* London: Routledge & Kegan Paul, Ltd.

_____. 1963. *The Nigerian legal system.* London: Routledge & Kegan Paul, Ltd.

_____. 1967. *The British Commonwealth: The development of its law and Constitution—Nigeria*, Vol. 4. London: Steven & Sons, Limited.

_____. 1972a. *The Nigerian magistrate and the offender.* Benin City: Ethiope Publishing Company.

_____, ed. 1972b. *Law and social change in Nigeria.* Lagos, Nigeria: Evans Brothers Ltd.

Encyclopedia of new China. 1987. Beijing: Foreign Language Press.

Fairchild, E. 1993. *Comparative criminal justice systems.* Belmont, CA: Wadsworth Publishing Company.

Fairmanner, S. 1992. Equal opportunities in two countries. Master's dissertation, University of Exeter, England.

Fang, Y. 1988. "Public Security Organization." In *Analyzing informal mechanisms of crime control: A cross-cultural perspective,* edited by Mark

Findlay and Ugljesa Zvekic. Rome: United Nations Research Institute for Social Development (UNRISD).

Federal Bureau of Investigation (FBI). 1994. *Uniform crime reports for the United States—1993.* Washington, D.C.: U.S. Department of Justice.

Felkenes, George T. 1989. "Courts, sentencing, and the death penalty in the PRC." In *Social control in the People's Republic of China,* edited by Ronald Troyer, John Clark, and Dean Rojek, 141–158. New York: Praeger Publishers.

Flanagan, Timothy J., and Kathleen Maguire. 1991. *Sourcebook of criminal justice statistics—1990.* Washington, D.C.: Bureau of Justice Statistics, U.S. Department of Justice.

Flynn, Frank T. 1951. Employment and Labor. In *Contemporary corrections,* edited by Paul W. Tappan, 238–253. New York: McGraw-Hill.

Foucault, Michael. 1977. *Discipline and punish: The Birth of the Prison.* Translated by Alan Sheridan. New York: Pantheon Books.

Fox, Vernon B., and Jeanne B. Stinchcomb. 1994. *Introduction to corrections.* Englewood Cliffs, NJ: Prentice Hall.

Frager, Robert, and Thomas P. Rohlen. 1976. "The future of a tradition: Japanese spirit in the 1980s." In *Japan: The paradox of progress,* edited by Lewis Austin, 255–278. New Haven, CT: Yale University Press.

Fu, Hualing. 1991b. Police accountability: The case of the People's Republic of China. *Police Studies* 14:40–49.

Fukui, Haruhiro. 1977. "Studies in policymaking: A review of the literature." In *Policymaking in contemporary Japan,* edited by T. J. Pempel, 22–59. Ithaca, NY: Cornell University Press.

Funke, Gail S., Billy L. Wayson, and Neal Miller. 1982. *Assets and liabilities of correctional industries.* Lexington, MA: Lexington Books.

Fyfe, Christopher, and Eldred Jones. 1968. *Freetown: A Symposium*. Freetown: Sierra Leone University Press.

Gallagher, G. P. 1992. *Risk management behind the blue curtain: A primer on law enforcement liability*. Arlington, VA: Public Risk Management Association.

Gates, D. F., and D. K. Shah. 1992. *Chief: My life in the LAPD*. New York: Bantam Books.

Geary, R. 1985. *Policing industrial disputes 1893–1985*. London: Methuen.

Gelatt, Timothy A. 1982. The People's Republic of China and the presumption of innocence. *The Journal of Criminal Law & Criminology* 73:259–316.

Geller, William A. 1992. *Deadly Force: What We Know, A Practitioner's Desk Reference on Police Involved Shooting*. Washington, D. C.: Police Executive Research Forum.

George, Aurell A. 1988. "Japanese interest group behaviour: An institutional approach." In *Dynamic and immobilist politics in Japan*, edited by J. A. A. Stockwin et al., 106–137. Honolulu: University of Hawaii Press.

Gifford, Lord. 1986. *Independent enquiry into the disturbances at Broadwater Farm Estate—Tottenham*. London: Broadwater Farm Enquiry.

Gill, Howard B. 1931. The prison labor problem. *Annals of the American Academy of Political and Social Science* 157:83–101.

Glensor, R. 1990. Community oriented policing—Plus. *Report for the Reno Police Department*, August.

Goldstein, H. 1977. *Policing a free society*. New York: Ballinger.

——————. 1990. *Problem oriented policing*. New York: McGraw-Hill.

Gong, Jian-guo. 1989. Interpretation of the constitution and statutes of the People's Republic of China. *Criminal Justice Review* 14:166–175.

Gottfredson, Stephen D., and Sean McConville. 1987. *America's correctional crisis: Prison populations and public policy*. Westport, CT: Greenwood Press.

Grassi, A. 1989. "Combating organized crime: The Maxi trials in Sicily." In *Transnational crime: Investigative responses*, edited by Harold Smith, 37–46. Chicago: OICJ.

Greve, V., O. Ingstrup, S. V. G. Jensen, and M. Spencer. 1984. "The Danish System of Criminal Justice: An Outline." Paper delivered at the Fourth Colloquy on the Use of computers in the administration of justice and Computers in correctional administration and links with ciminal justice, sponsored by the Council of Europe, Copenhagen.

Griffiths, Arthur. n.d. *Oriental prisons: Prisons and crime in India, the Andman Islands, Burmah, China, Japan, Egypt, Turkey*. London: Grolier Society.

Gutteridge, H. C. 1949. *Comparative law: An introduction to the comparative methods of legal study and research*, 2nd ed. Cambridge: Cambridge University Press.

Hagan, F. E. 1987. *Introduction to criminology*. Chicago: Nelson-Hall.

Halford, A. 1987. Until the twelfth of never. *Police Review* 18:2013–2019.

Hane, Mikiso. 1982. *Peasants, rebels, and outcastes*. NY: Pantheon Books.

Harrell-Bond, B., and Ulrica Rijinsdrop. 1974. *Family law in Sierra Leone: A research report*. Leuiden: Sierra Leone. Africa Studicentrum.

Harris, J., and M. Todaro. 1970. Migration, unemployment and development: A two sector analysis. *American Economic Review* 3:126–142.

Hashimoto, Noboru. 1983. "Japan's use of volunteers in community-based treatment." In *Proceedings of 12th Annual Congress of Correction*, 183–189. College Park, MD: American Correctional Association.

Hayashi, Shuji. 1988. *Culture and Management in Japan*. Translated by Frank Baldwin. Tokyo: University of Tokyo Press.

Hazou, Winnie. 1990. *The social and legal status of women: A global perspective*. New York: Praeger Publications.

Heikers, D. 1993. Fernando Collor De Mello. *U.S. News and World Report* 114 (January 11):12.

Henderson, Dwight. 1985. *Congress, courts, and criminals: The development of federal criminal law, 1801–1829*. Westport, CT: Greenwood Press.

Hiromatsu, Yashiro. 1972. *History of penal theory and practice of penalties* (in Japanese). Tokyo: Sobunsha.

_____. 1973. History of penal institutions in Japan. *Law in Japan* 6:1–48.

Hirst, M. 1990. *The ACPO statement of common purpose and values—New Scotland Yard*. London: HMSO.

Hoffman, Mark S., ed. 1991. Info Please. New York: The World Almanac.

Holdaway, S. 1990. Recruiting a multi racial police force. London: HMSO.

Home Office. 1982. *Report of a study group: Recruitment into the police service of members of ethnic minorities*. London: HMSO.

Home Office. 1989a. *Equal opportunities policies for the police service*. Home Office Circular 87/89. London: HMSO.

Home Office. 1989b. *Review of police consultancy arrangements*. Home Office Circular 62/1989. London: Home Office.

Hornum. F. 1986. "The criminal justice system of Denmark." In *International criminal justice system*, edited by Dorothy H. Bracey and Charles R. Fenwic, 2–14. Omaha, NE: The Academy of Criminal Justice Sciences.

Hubbard, Sally. 1992. "The Halford Case . . . " *The Independent*, July 26, 38.

Humpheries, D., and D. Greenberg. 1981. "The dialectics of crime control." In *Crime and capitalism*, edited by David Greenberg, 205–254. Palo Alto, CA: Mayfield.

Igbinovia, P. 1984. A comparative and analytical appraisal of crime and criminality in Nigeria. *International Journal of Offender Therapy and Comparative Criminology* 3:11–19.

The important documents of the First Plenary Session of The People's Political Consultative Conference. 1949. Beijing: Foreign Languages Press.

Inciardi, James A. 1984. *Criminal justice*. New York: Academic Press.

Ingraham, Barton L. 1987. *The structure of criminal procedure laws and practice of France, the Soviet Union, China, and the United States*. New York: Greenwood Press.

Ishida, Takeshi. 1983. *Japanese political culture: Change and continuity*. New Brunswick, NJ: Transaction Books.

Ishii, Ryosuke. 1980. *A history of political institutions in Japan*. Tokyo: University of Tokyo Press.

Jackson, R. M. 1953. *The machinery of justice in England*. Cambridge: University Press.

Japanese Correctional Association. n.d. *A guide to CAPIC*. Tokyo: Correctional Association Prison Industry Cooperative.

Jasanoff, Sheila. 1989. *Science on the witness stand. Issues in Science and Technology*, 80–87. New York: Russell Sage Foundation.

Jepsen, J. 1991. "Denmark." In *Imprisonment today and tomorrow: International perspective on prisoners' rights and prison conditions*, edited by Dirk van Zyl Smit and Freider Dunkel, 99–160. Boston: Kluwer Law and Taxation.

Jiang, Bo, and Yisheng Dai. 1990. Mobilize all possible social forces to strengthen public security—a must for crime prevention. *Police Studies: The International Review Of Police Development*. 2:1–9.

Johnson, Chalmers. 1978. *Japan's public policy companies*. Washington, D.C.:

American Enterprises Institute for Public Policy Research.

Johnson, Elmer H. 1983. Neighborhood and the police: The People's Republic of China. *International Journal of Comparative and Applied Criminal Justice* 7:209–215.

Jones, Kenneth, Louis Shainberg and Curtin Byer. 1979. *Drugs and alcohol.* New York: Harper and Row.

Jones, S. 1987. *Policewomen and equality.* London: MacMillan.

Jones, T., J. Young, and B. MacClean. 1982. *Islington Crime Survey: Crime, Victimization, and Policing in Inner-City London.* Brookfield, VT: Gower.

Juran, J. M. 1989. *Juran on leadership for quality.* London: Free Press.

Kaplan, Irving, et al. 1976. *Area handbook of Sierra Leone.* Washington, D.C.: U.S. Government Press.

Karibi-Whyte, A. G. 1964. Some recent amendments to the criminal code (Nigeria). *Nigerian Law Journal* 10:156–164.

Kasumu, A. B. 1978. *The Supreme Court of Nigeria.* London: Heinemann.

Kayode, O. and E. Alemika. 1984. An examination of some socioeconomic characteristics of inmates of a Nigerian prison. *International Journal of Comparative and Applied Criminal Justice* 8 (1): 85–91.

Keay, E. A., and S. S. Richardson. 1966. *The nature of customary courts in Nigeria.* London: Sweet & Maxwell.

Keefe, William J., William H. Flanigan, Morris S. Ogul, Henry J. Abraham, Charles O. Jones, and John W. Spanier. 1990. *American democracy: Institutions, politics, and policies,* 3rd ed. New York: Harper and Row.

Kercher, L. C. 1981. *The Kenya penal system.* Washington, D.C.: University Press of America.

Kinsey, R., J. Lea, and J. Young. 1986. *Losing the fight against crime.* London: Basil Blackwell.

Kiralfy, A. K. R. 1967. *The English legal system.* London: Sweet and Maxwell.

Kolasa, Blair, and Bernadine Meyer. 1987. *The American legal system,* 2nd ed. Englewood Cliffs, NJ: Prentice-Hall.

Korn, Richard, and Lloyd McCorkle. 1959. *The Highfields Story: An Experimental Treatment Project for Youthful Offenders.* New York: Holt.

Kosai, Yutaka, and Yoshitaro Ogino. 1984. *The contemporary Japanese economy.* Translated by Ralph Thompson. London: Macmillan.

Kouhashi, Hiroshi. 1985. "Courts' selection of offenders to be placed under probationary supervision." Paper delivered at UNAFEI, Tokyo.

Kowalski, B. J. 1993. Death-penalty debate. *World Press Review* 40(4):28.

Krase, Jerome, and Edward Sagarin. 1980. "Formal and informal social control in cross-cultural perspective." In *Crime and Deviance: A Comparative Perspective,* edited by Graeme R. Newman. Beverly Hills, CA: Sage Publications.

Kube, E. 1989. "Technological research and international crime." In *Transnational Crime: Investigative responses,* edited by Harold Smith, 125–132. Chicago: OICJ.

Kurian, G. T. 1989. *World encyclopedia of police forces and penal systems.* New York: Oxford University Press.

Kyokai, Keimu. 1943. *Manuscript for history of Japanese prison administration in modern age* (in Japanese). 2 vols. Tokyo: Keimu Kyokai.

Langworthy, Robert H., and Lawrence Travis, III. 1994. *Policing in America: A balance of forces.* New York: Macmillan Publishing Company.

Law of northern Nigeria. 1963. Lagos: Government Printing Press.

Law yearbook of China. 1992. Beijing: China's Law Press.

Legum, Colin, ed. 1961. *Africa: A handbook.* London: Anthony Blood.

Leiserson, Michael. 1966. "Political opposition and political development in Japan." In *Regimes and oppositions*, edited by Robert Dahl, 341–398. New Haven, CT: Yale University Press.

Leng, Shao-Chuan. 1982. Criminal justice in post-Mao China: Some preliminary observations. *The Journal of Criminal Law and Criminology* 73:204–237.

Lewis, Orlando F. 1922. *The development of American prisons and prison customs, 1776–1845.* Montclair, NJ: Patterson Smith.

Lindquist, John H. 1988. *Misdemeanor crime: Trivial criminal pursuit.* Newbury Park, CA: Sage.

Local Courts Act, No. 20. 1963. Government of Sierra Leone. Freetown: Government Printer.

Lock, J. 1987. How long must she wait. *Police Review* 95:1810–1811.

Lombardo, Lucien X. 1989. *Guards imprisoned: Correctional officers at work.* Cincinnati, OH: Anderson Publishing Company.

Lubman, Stanley B. 1983. Emerging functions of formal legal institutions in China's modernization. *China Law Reporter* 4:196–266.

Lugard, Frederick. 1913. *Sir Frederick Lugard: Political memorandum.* Ibadan, Nigeria: National Archives Library, University of Ibadan.

Luhmann, Niklas. 1979. *Trust and power.* New York: John Wiley.

Luiz, A. F. 1993. Penal philosophy: A perspective from Brazil. *American Jails* 6:70–71.

Luthra, M. 1986. Increasing the black in the blue line: Some key questions on recruitment of black officers and equal opportunities in the Police. London: HMSO.

Ma, Stephen K. 1986. Reform corruption: A discussion on China's recent development. *Pacific Affairs* 58 (4):129–136.

Manning, P. K. 1989. "The occupational culture of the police." In *The encyclopedia of police science,* edited by L. Hoover, et al. Dallas: Garland Press.

Mao, Tse-tung. 1966. *Four essays on philosophy.* Peking: Foreign Language Press.

Marcussen, E. 1981. *Social welfare in Denmark,* 4th rev. ed. Copenhagen: Det Danske Selska.

Marenin, O. 1989. "Ghana." In *World encyclopedia of police forces and penal systems,* edited by G. T. Kurian, 146–151. New York: Oxford University Press.

Martin, J. M., and A. T. Romano. 1992. *Multinational crime: Terrorism, espionage, drug and arms trafficking.* Beverly Hills, CA: Sage Publications.

Martin, S. E. 1979. Policemen and policewomen: occupational role dilemmas and choices of female officers. *Journal of Police Science and Administration* 7:314–323.

Martin, Steve J., and Sheldon Ekland-Olson. 1985. *Texas prisons: The walls came tumbling down.* Austin: Texas Monthly Press.

Masland, John W. 1946. Neighborhood associations in Japan. *Far Eastern Survey* 15 (23): 355–358.

Maurice, J. F. 1981. *Politics in Denmark.* London: St. Martin's Press.

McCabe, Edward J. 1989. "Structural elements of contemporary criminal justice in the People's Republic of China." In *Social control in the People's Republic of China,* edited by Ronald J. Troyer et al., 115–129. New York: Praeger Publishers.

McCabe, Sarah. 1988. *The Police, Public Order, and Civil Liberties: Legacies of the Miners' Strike.* New York: Routledge and Paul.

McKenzie, I. K., and Gallagher, G. P. 1989. *Behind the uniform: Policing in Britain and America.* New York: St. Martins Press.

Melossi, Dario, and Massimo Pavarini. 1981. *The prison and the factory: Origins of the penitentiary system*. Translated by Glynis Cousin. London: Macmillan.

Metcalf, Dac. 1990. *Report into the Trafalgar Square Riots of 30 March 1990*. London: Metropolitan Police.

Michael, Jerome, and Mortimer Adler. 1971. *Crime, law and social science*. Montclair, NJ: Patterson Smith.

Ministry of Justice. 1990a. *Community-based treatment of offenders in Japan*. Tokyo: Rehabilitation Bureau.

Ministry of Justice. 1990b. *Correctional institutions in Japan*. Tokyo: Correction Bureau.

Ministry of Justice. 1991. *Annual report of statistics on corrections for 1990*, Vol. 1. Tokyo: Correction Bureau.

Ministry of Justice. 1993. *Annual Report of Statistics on rehabilitation for 1992*. Tokyo: Rehabilitation Institute.

Moeran, Brian. 1984. *Last innocence: Folk craft patterns of Onta Japan*. Berkeley: University of California Press.

Munro, Donald J. 1977. *The Concept of Man in Contemporary China*. Ann Arbor: University of Michigan Press.

Munyard, T. 1988. Homophobia at work and how to manage it. *Personnel Management*, June, 48.

Nagel, Stuart S. 1972. "The rights of the accused: Overview, effects, causes." In *The rights of the accused,* edited by S. Nagel. Beverly Hills, CA: Sage.

Nakamura, Hachiro. 1968. "A re-examination of Chonaikai (Urban Ward Association)." In *Readings in urban sociology,* edited by R. E. Pahl, 190–207. Oxford: Pergamon Press.

Nakamura, Takafusa. 1981. *The postwar Japanese economy*. Tokyo: University of Tokyo Press.

Nakane, Chie. 1981. *Japanese society*. Tokyo: Charles E. Tuttle.

National Institute of Justice (NIJ). 1993. *Videotaping interrogations and confessions*. Washington, D.C.: Department of Justice.

NIJ. 1995. *NIJ research plan: 1995–1996*. Washington, D.C.: U.S. Department of Justice.

Newcombe, Tod. 1993. High-tech tools for war on crime. *Governing*, August, 20–21.

Nigerian Contitution Order-in-Council. 1960. Lagos, Nigeria: Government Printing Press.

Nigerian Law Reform Commission. 1983. *Report and draft bills for the reform of prisons in Nigeria*. Lagos: N.L.R.C.

Niven, C. R. 1957. *A short history of Nigeria*. London: Longmans, Green & Co., Ltd.

Noda, Tosiyuki. 1976. *Introduction to Japanese law*. Translated by Anthony H. Angelo. Tokyo: University of Tokyo Press.

Northern region law report, 94. 1960. Lagos: Nigerian Law Reform Commission.

Nwabueze, Boniface B. 1963. *The machinery of justice in Nigeria*. London: Butterworths.

O'Brien, Patricia. 1982. *The promise of punishment: Prisons in nineteenth-century France*. Princeton, NJ: Princeton University Press.

Obilade, A. O. 1969. Reform of customary law court systems in Nigeria under the military government. *Nigerian Law Journal* 3:29–36.

———. 1979. *The Nigerian legal system*. London: Sweet and Maxwell.

Odekunle, F. 1978. Capitalist economy and the crime problem in Nigeria. *Contemporary Crises* 2:83–96.

Ogawa, Taro. 1976. "Japan." In *Criminology: A cross-cultural perspective,* Vol. 2, edited by Dae Chang, 586–656. Durham, NC: Carolina Academic Press.

Okonkwo, Cyprain O., and Michael Naish. 1964. *Criminal law in Nigeria (exclud-*

ing the North). London: Sweet and Maxwell.

Oloyede, E. O. 1972. "The Present Scope of the Nigerian Criminal Law." In *Law and Social Change in Nigeria*, edited by Taslim O. Elias. Lagos, Nigeria: Evans Brothers, Ltd.

Opolot, J. 1976. *Criminal justice and Nation building in Africa.* Washington, D.C.: University Press of America.

_____. 1979. Organized crime in Africa. *International Journal of Comparative and Applied Criminal Justice* 4:177–183.

_____. 1980. Analysis of crime in Africa by the mass media in the 1960s and 1970s. *International Journal of Comparative and Applied Criminal Justice* 4:43–48.

_____. 1981. *Crime in the new states of Africa.* Washington, D.C.: American University Press.

Ostrom, E., R. Parks, and G. Whitaker. 1978. *Patterns of metropolitan policing.* Cambridge, MA: Ballinger.

Owomero, B. 1987. Crime rates and development in Africa: Empirical analysis of data from Nigeria, Kenya and Tanzania. *Indian Journal of Criminology* 2:107–120.

Ozaki, Robert S. 1978. *The Japanese: A cultural portrait.* Tokyo: Charles E. Tuttles.

Palmer, John W. 1973. *Constitutional rights of prisoners.* Cincinnati, OH: Anderson.

Perkins, Rollin M. and Ronald N. Boyce. 1984. *Criminal Law and Procedure.* Mineota, NY: The FoundationPress.

Pettigrew, T. F. 1989. "Police and ethnic minorities." Paper read at a conference on Police Organizations and Minority Groups. Noordwijk, Netherlands, January.

Pharr, Susan J. 1990. *Losing face: Status politics in Japan.* Berkeley: University of California Press.

Pinheiro, P. S. 1992. "The legacy of authoritarianism in democratic Brazil."

Paper presented at the Fifth University Seminar on Human Rights, Columbia University, New York.

Plath, David W. 1964. *The after hours: Modern Japan and search for enjoyment.* Berkeley: University of California Press.

Police Act, No. 7. 1964. Government of Sierra Leone. Freetown: Government Printer.

Questions and answers on the professional work of the Procuratorate. 1986. Beijing: Law Publishing House.

Raphey, D.M. 1979. "Racial discrimination in urban police departments." Cited in Winship, P.J. 1982. Towards a Multiracial Police Service. 19th Senior Command Course, Police Staff College: Bramshill, Hants.

Reid, Sue Titus. 1992. *Crime and criminology.* New York: Holt, Rinehart and Winston.

_____. 1994. *Crime and criminology.* Orlando, FL: Harcourt Brace and Co.

Reiner, R. 1992. Fin de siecle: The police face the millenium. *Political Quarterly* 63 (1):37–49.

Reiss, A. 1992. "Police organization in the twentieth century." In *Modern policing*, edited by M. Tonry and N. Morris. Chicago: University of Chicago Press.

Ren, Jianxin. 1993. "Stop smuggling illegal immigrants into foreign countries." *People's Daily,* Aug. 7.

Richelson, Jeffrey T. 1988. *Foreign intelligence organization.* Cambridge, MA: Ballinger Press Company.

Roberts-Wray, Sir Kenneth. 1959. The need for study of native law. *Journal of African Law* 1:82.

Rodriquez, M. 1989. "Strategy and reality." In *International Drug Trafficking*, edited by Dennis Rowe, 135–152. Chicago: OICJ.

Rogers, J. 1989. Theories of crime and development: An historical analysis.

Journal of Development Studies 25:314–328.

Rojek, Dean G. 1985. The criminal process in the People's Republic of China. *Justice Quarterly* 2:117–125.

Samaha, Joel. 1993. *Criminal law,* 4th ed. Minneapolis: West Publishing.

Santos Rodrigues, J. J. 1993. "The new beat of black Brazil sets the pace for self-affirmation." *New York Times,* April 1.

Satchell, M. 1988. "The just war that never ends." *U.S. News & World Report,* December 19.

Sato, Tsuneo. 1990. "Tokugawa villages and agriculture." In *Tokugawa Japan: The social and economic antecedents of modern Japan,* edited by Chie Nakane and Shinzaburo Oishi, 37–80. Tokyo: University of Tokyo Press.

Satoh, Kunpei. 1989. "Rehabilitation services in Japan: Present situation and problems." Paper delivered at UNAFEI, Tokyo.

Scarman, L. J. 1981. *The Brixton disorders: 10–12 April 1981.* (Cmnd, 8427). London: HMSO.

Schafer, S. 1976. *Introduction to criminology.* Reston, VA: Reston Publishing Co.

Sellin, Thorsten. 1938. *Culture, conflict and crime.* New York: Social Science Research.

Serrill, M. S. 1977. Profile Denmark. *Corrections Magazine* 3:23–29, 34–43.

Sessions, William E. 1992. Image technology: Enhancing investigative capability. *Vital Speeches of the Day* (unpublished essay collection), 624–626.

Seymour, James D. 1987. Cadres accountability and law. *Australia Journal of Chinese Affairs* 3:95–107.

Sheley, Joseph F. 1995. *Criminology: A contemporary handbook,* 2nd ed. Belmont, CA: Wadsworth Publishing Company.

Shelley, L. 1982. *Crime and modernization.* Carbondale: Southern Illinois University Press.

Shihgetoh, Hozumi. 1943. The Tonari-Gumi of Japan. *Contemporary Japan* 12:984–990.

Shikita, Minoru. 1972. The rehabilitative programmes in the adult prison of Japan. *International Review of Criminal Policy* 30:11–19.

Shikita, Minoru, and Shinichi Tsuchiya. 1990. *Crime and criminal policy in Japan from 1926 to 1988.* Tokyo: Japan Criminal Policy Society.

Shivji, I. G. 1982. "Semi-proletarian labor and the use of penal sanctions in the labor law of colonial Tanganyika." In *Crime, Justice and Underdevelopment,* edited by Colin Sumner, 40–60. London: Heinemann.

Si, Wen. 1989. The forging system of people's mediation. *Outlook Weekly* 42:9.

Siegel, Larry J. 1989. *Criminology.* St. Paul: West Publishing.

——————. 1992. *Criminology: Theories, patterns, and typologies,* 4th edition. St. Paul: West Publishing.

Skitt, B. 1991. "The implementation of equal opportunities in the police service." Unpublished papers, The Police Staff College, Bramshill, Hampshire, England.

Skolnick, J., and D. Bayley. 1986. *The new blue line: Police innovations in six American cities.* New York: Free Press.

Skolnick, Jerome H., and James Fyfe. 1993. *Above the law: Police and the excessive use of force.* New York: Macmillan.

Smith, D. J. 1982. *Police and people in London: A survey of Londoners.* Report No. 618. London: Policy Studies Institute.

Smith, J. 1988. *Psychology, homosexuality and homophobia.* New York: Haworth Press.

Smith, J. C., and B. Hogan. 1978. *Criminal law.* London: Butterworths.

Smith, Robert J. 1961. The Japanese rural community: Norms, sanctions, and ostracism. *American Anthropologist.* 63:522–533.

Sparrow, M., M. Moore, and D. Kennedy. 1990. *Beyond 911: A new era for policing*. Basic Books: New York.

Spitzer, Steven. 1983. "The rationalization of crime control in capitalist society." In *Social control and the state: Historical and comparative studies*, edited by Stanley Cohen and Andrew Scull, 321–333. Oxford: Martin Robertson.

Steiner, Kurt. 1965. *Local government in Japan*. Stanford, CA: Stanford University Press.

Stephens, Gene. 1990. High-Tech Crime: Fighting the threat to civil liberties. *Futurist*, July/August, 20–25.

Stewart, J. K. 1989. "International research and the federal role." In *Transnational crime: Investigative responses*, edited by Harold Smith. Chicago: OICJ.

Stucky, G. 1986. *Procedures in the criminal justice system*. Columbus, OH: Charles E. Merrill.

Sumner, C., ed. 1982. *Crime, justice and underdevelopment*. London: Heineman.

Sykes, Gresham M. 1958. *The society of captives: A study of a maximum security prison*. Princeton, NJ: Princeton University Press.

Tadao, Kiyonari. 1979. "Small businesses." In *Politics and economics in contemporary Japan*, edited by Murakani Hyoe and Johannes Hirschmeier, 157–182. Tokyo: Japan Culture Institute.

Takigawa, Seijiro. 1972. *A history of prison administration in Japan* (in Japanese). Tokyo: Seikeibou.

Talarico, S.M. 1987. Social control in the People's Republic of China. *Criminal Justice Review* 15:137–139.

Tamuno, T. 1970. *The police in modern Nigeria*. Ibadan, Nigeria: Ibadan University Press.

Taylor-Cooke, R. Whately. 1886. *Introduction to a history of the factory system*. London: Bentley and Son.

Taylor, O. P. 1975. "The position of women under Sierra Leone customary law." In *African indigenous law*, edited by T. O. Elias, S. N. Nwabara, and C. O. Akpamgbo. Nigeria: University of Nsukka.

Taylor, S., N. Ainsworth, and P. Gallan. 1990. *The Metropolitan Police seminars on recruiting and retention of black and Asian officers: Analysis of data from Seminar, July 1990*. London: Metropolitan Police.

Terrill, Richard T. 1984. *World criminal justice systems*. Cincinnati, OH: Anderson Publishing Company.

——————. 1987. *World criminal justice systems: A survey*. Cincinnati, OH: Anderson Publishing Company.

Thames Valley Police. 1990. "Making quality contact." London: Report of Thames Valley Police.

The criminal law and the criminal procedure law of China. 1984. Beijing: Foreign Languages Press.

The criminal procedure law of the People's Republic of China. 1982. *The Journal of Criminal Law and Criminology* 1:171–203.

Thomas, Charles. 1987. *Corrections in America: Problems of the past and the present*. Newbury Park, CA: Sage.

Thompson, Bankole. 1991. Child abuse in Sierra Leone: Normative disparities. *International Journal of Law and The Family* 5:13–23.

——————. 1992. Constitutionalism in Sierra Leone: Prospects–The Proposal 1991 Multi-Party Constitution. *Commonwealth Law Bulletin* 18:338–346.

Todaro, M. 1969. A model of labor migration and urban unemployment in less developed countries. *American Economic Review* 16:138–148.

——————— and J. Stilkind. 1981. *City bias and rural neglect: The dilemma of urban development*. New York: Population Council.

Tonomura, Hitomi. 1992. *Community and commerce in late medieval Japan: The corporate villages of Tokuchin-ho.* Stanford, CA: Stanford University Press.

Townsend, Deborah E. 1987. The concept of law in post-Mao China: A Case study of economic crime. *Stanford Journal of International Law* 23:78–92.

Treason and State Offences Act, No. 10. 1963. Government of Sierra Leone. Freetown: Government Printer.

Udo, Goro. 1990. "Rehabilitation aid hostels in Japan." Paper delivered at UNAFEI, Tokyo.

Umbreit, M. 1980. Danish use of prisons and community alternatives. Federal Probation 44 (2):24–28.

Van Wolferen, Karel. 1989. *The enigma of Japanese power.* London: Macmillan.

Vito, Gennaro, and Ronald Holmes. 1994. *Criminology: Theory, research and policy.* Belmont, CA: Wadsworth.

Wagatsuma, Hiroshi, and George A. DeVos. 1984. *Heritage of endurance: Family patterns and delinquency formation in urban Japan.* Berkeley: University of California Press.

Walsh, William F. 1932. *A history of Anglo-American law,* 2nd ed. Indianapolis: Bobbs-Merrill.

Wang, Zheng. 1993. Some new crime trends in China: Their impact on the United States. *Police Studies: The International Review of Police Development* 17:12–23.

Ward, Richard H. 1985. The Police in China. *Justice Quarterly* 2:111–115.

Weschler, J. 1993. *The human rights watch global report.* New York: Human Rights Watch.

West Africa annual. 1971. Lagos, Nigeria: John West Publications.

West, Nancy. 1992. "New Hampshire Police defend use of high-tech snooping to find marijuana growers." *New Hampshire News.* 11 October.

Westney, D. Eleanor. 1987. *Imitation and innovation: The transfer of Western organizational patterns in Meiji Japan.* Cambridge: Harvard University Press.

Weston, Paul B., and Kenneth M. Wells. 1987. *The Administration of justice,* 5th ed. Englewood Cliffs, NJ: Prentice-Hall.

Whittacker, B. 1979. *The police in society.* London: Methuen.

Woronoff, Jon. 1986. *Politics the Japanese way.* Tokyo: Lotus Press.

Xu, Qingzhang. 1992. "Enterprise crime and public order." In *Enterprise crime: Asian and globe perspectives,* edited by Ann Lodl. Chicago: The University of Illinois at Chicago Press.

Yanigimoto, Masaharu. 1970. Some features of the Japanese prison system. *British Journal of Criminology* 10:209–244.

Yett, C. E. 1989. "Employment law for peace officers and other government employees." Unpublished paper, Austin, TX: Attorney General's Office.

Yokoyama, Minoru. 1982. "How have prisons been used in Japan?" Unpublished paper delivered at the World Congress of the International Sociological Association, Mexico City in 1982.

Yoshino, Michael Y. 1968. *Japan's managerial system: Tradition and innovation.* Cambridge: The MIT Press.

Zhang, Min, and Shan Changzong. 1990. Inside China's court system. *Beijing Review* 45:15–20.

Zhang, Xiufu. 1993. "Illegal financial institutions are not protected by law." *People's Daily,* July 22.

Zhou, J. 1987. An introduction to the present legal system of the People's Republic of China. *North Carolina Criminal Justice Today* 5:8–15.

Index